T0354305

# THE KING IS COMING

## THE TESTIMONY OF CHRIST THROUGH THE OLD AND NEW TESTAMENTS

### BOOK 2 OF A TWO-PART SERIES

## LOUISE A. FUGATE

WESTBOW
PRESS®
A DIVISION OF THOMAS NELSON
& ZONDERVAN

WestBow Press books may be ordered through booksellers or by contacting:

WestBow Press
A Division of Thomas Nelson & Zondervan
1663 Liberty Drive
Bloomington, IN 47403
www.westbowpress.com
1 (866) 928-1240

ISBN: 978-1-5127-3462-1 (sc)
ISBN: 978-1-5127-3463-8 (hc)
ISBN: 978-1-5127-3461-4 (e)

Library of Congress Control Number: 2016904410

Print information available on the last page.

WestBow Press rev. date: 4/7/2016

# Copyrights

# ACKNOWLEDGMENTS

I thank the Lord for giving me the opportunity and the ability to write this two-part series, which has made His Word more alive to me than ever. I pray that those who read it will be drawn closer to Him by reading His Word and that they will remember that He will always be faithful to keep His promises.

Along the way, while researching and writing this series, I have had tremendous support from the men and women at Westbow Press who have shown much patience with me over this six-year journey. Thank you all so much!

I would like to express my gratitude to the following men of faith for sharing their God-given artistic gifts to be used in this series.

To Spencer Williams for the use of his paintings for the front covers of both *A Shadow of Good Things to Come* and *The King Is Coming*. Both Spencer and his wife, RhuNella, are genuinely gracious and have extended their hands of fellowship to me. Spencer's paintings can be found online at "Spencer Williams Gallery": **www.jesuspaintings.com**

To Chris Evans for drawing the illustration, *The Stone the Builders Rejected*, displayed in the interior of this book. I appreciate the friendship of both Chris, and his wife, Vicky, who have always received me with Christ's love and encouragement.

To Joe Olivio for the use of his illustrations throughout book 1, A *Shadow of Good Things to Come*. As a lover of Jesus, he was so happy to share. Joe's illustrations in his book, *The Tabernacle Tour,* can be purchased at http://www.greatpassionplay.org/store/c1/Storefront.html#.VmhWVM_SnIU **joeolivio@gmail.com**, P.O. Box 482, Powell, TN 37849, (865-951-3474).

To Savannah Bollinger for her editing services. Her attention to detail was, without question, a saving grace for me. I also thank her parents Rick and Mercedes Bollinger, for sharing their daughter's time with me.

I am also thankful to my husband and family members, for their patience, love, and belief in me that I would finish this task. Your support has been amazing! I love you.

To my "Southbank" friends, God bless you for being so sweet and for checking on my progress on a regular basis.

There have been those along the way, who have spurred on my faith, and those who have prayed for me in my deepest times of darkness, holding me up, so I could continue to run my race: Roy and Pam Holloway, Pastor Tim Harrison, and Elke Drescher. Others, who are included in this list and have gone on to heaven to be with Jesus, are:

My parents, Raymond (stepfather) and Irene June Brown
My dad, Harold A. Miller, for always loving me
My adopted grandparents Harry and Huldah Markwart
My God mother Lillian Grant
My spiritual mentors Bill and Jean Brown
Intercessor Wes Martin

# CONTENTS

# PREFACE

In studying about the history of the Jews as it pertains to their relationship with God, we find a parallel between them and the rest of humanity. That parallel is sin and the need for a Savior. That is why Jesus came and died on the cross. Knowing how doubtful and full of unbelief we all are, God gave us blueprints and prophecies to show us His plan of salvation through His Son, Jesus. It was a plan which was implemented through the Jewish nation, and then He left His footprints to show us He had been here. Both history and science document what He has done, but He is not through yet.

While the world is wreathing in sin, disaster, and terrorism, we all wonder how this will end. We have hope! God is still in control. God's prophecies are still being fulfilled, and they show us that His plan has not yet reached completion. Right now, our Savior is calling us to come to Him to receive forgiveness, restoration, and a promise of eternal life, but the Scriptures tell us a day is coming when He will return as King to be our Judge. The King Is Coming!

# INTRODUCTION

In Book 1 of this series, *A Shadow of Good Things to Come*, we learned how sin caused man to be separated from God and how God has pursued the heart of man ever since.

To implement His prophetic plan of salvation for humanity, God chose a small group of Hebrew people, who would later become known as the Israelites, and He made an everlasting covenant with them. Even though they struggled with rebellion and unbelief, God was faithful to His promises to them and and always saved a remnant of faith-filled people, who would become the human ancestors of His Son Jesus Christ, the Messiah, the Savior of the world.

Eventually, God selected a righteous king for them who was a man after God's own heart. During his reign, King David brought the Ark of the Covenant to Jerusalem and restored the Mosaic Law and the sacrificial system, which brought God's blessings of peace between God and their nation. God gave David this promise: "And thine house and thy kingdom shall be established for ever before thee: thy throne shall be established for ever" (2 Samuel 7:16).

As time went on, King David expressed his desire to build a permanent temple for God to replace the portable Tabernacle that had been built by Moses, and God denied his request. God had other plans, and those plans would come through his son Solomon. God told King David:

"I will set up *thy seed* after thee, which shall proceed out of thy bowels, and I will establish his kingdom. He *shall build a house for my name*, and I will stablish the throne of *his kingdom for ever*" (2 Samuel 7:12–13; emphasis added).

This is where we begin—King David is on his deathbed, and his son Solomon is next in line to be the third king of the Israelites.

# CHAPTER 1

## KING SOLOMON

### Solomon Becomes King of Israel

Information about King Solomon is found in: Second Samuel; 1 Kings 1–12; 1 Chronicles 3-5, 22; Ecclesiastes 1.

The period of time is about 970 BC, and King David is now old and on his deathbed. Adonijah, the son of one of David's wives, knew the king's condition and devised a deceptive plan to exalt himself as the new king. He told, Joab (David's military commander); Abiathar, the priest, and his mother what he was getting ready to do. They gave him their support, but there were some who remained loyal to King David: "Za´-dok the priest ... Be-nai´-ah the son of Je-hoi´-a-da (leader of the Aaronites), Nathan the prophet, Shim´-e-i and Re´-i, and the mighty men which belonged to David" (1 Kings 1:8).

When Nathan heard what was happening, he went and told Solomon's mother, Bathsheba, about Adonijah's deceptive plan to become king over Israel. He told her to go warn King David. When she did, she reminded him that he had sworn to her that her son Solomon would sit upon his throne, not Adonijah. As soon as she finished talking with the king, Nathan came and confirmed what she had told him about Adonijah. David then asked for Zadok and Benaiah to be brought to him, and he told them what to do to ensure that Solomon would become king:

> Take with you the servants of your lord, and cause Solomon my son to ride upon mine own mule, and bring him down to Gi´-hon: And let Za´-dok the priest and Nathan the prophet anoint him there king over Israel:

and blow ye with the trumpet, and say, God save King Solomon. Then ye shall come up after him, that he may come and sit upon my throne; for he shall be king in my stead: and I have appointed him to be ruler over Israel and over Judah. (1 Kings 1:33–35)

When Adonijah heard the report that David had given his throne to Solomon, he was afraid and hung on to the horns of the altar saying, "Let King Solomon swear unto me today that he will not slay his servant with the sword" (1 Kings 1:51).

When Solomon heard this, he said, "If he will show himself a worthy man, there shall not a hair of him fall to the earth: but if wickedness shall be found in him, he shall die" (1 Kings 1:52).

## David Makes Preparations for the Lord's House

Earlier, King David had planned to build a house for the Lord, but God had said he would not be the one to build it—his son Solomon would do it. So David began to make preparations for this great event. He gathered iron, brass, and cedar for his son Solomon to use. He told Solomon:

> My son, as for me, it was in my mind to build a house unto the name of the LORD my God: But the word of the LORD came to me, saying, Thou hast shed blood abundantly, and hast made great wars: thou shalt not build a house unto my name, because thou hast shed much blood upon the earth in my sight.
>
> Behold, a son shall be born to thee, who shall be a man of rest; and I will give him rest from all his enemies round about: for his name shall be Solomon, and I will give peace and quietness unto Israel in his days. He shall build a house for my name; and he shall be my son, and I will be his father; and *I will establish the throne of his kingdom over Israel for ever.* (1 Chronicles 22:7–10; emphasis added)

Is it any wonder that Satan had influenced Adonijah to deceitfully try to take the throne? Satan did not want David's family line to continue through Solomon. He knew it had been prophesied that Jesus would be called the "Son of David" through Solomon's lineage. David told Solomon:

> Now set your heart and your soul to seek the LORD your God; arise therefore, and build ye the sanctuary of the LORD God, to bring the ark of the covenant of the LORD, and the holy vessels of God, into the house that is to be built to the name of the LORD. (1 Chronicles 22:19)

Before David died, he selected the Levite priests to serve in the new house of the Lord, dividing them and establishing their duties. He also chose musicians, prophets, and doorkeepers to serve. He set up army divisions, rulers over each tribe, and overseers for the king. He did this in obedience to the Law that God had handed down to Moses. Then King David gathered all his leaders and captains and told them what the Lord had done.

> The LORD God of Israel chose me before all the house of my father to be king over Israel for ever: for he hath chosen Judah to be the ruler; and of the house of Judah, the house of my father; and among the sons of my father he liked me to make me king over all Israel:
>
> And of all my sons, (for the LORD hath given me many sons,) he hath chosen Solomon my son to sit upon the throne of the kingdom of the LORD over Israel. And he said unto me, Solomon thy son, he shall build my house and my courts: for I have chosen him to be my son, and I will be his father. ... I will establish his kingdom for ever, if he be constant to do my commandments and my judgments, as at this day. ... know thou the God of thy father, and serve him with a perfect heart and with a willing mind: for the LORD searcheth all hearts, and

understandeth all the imaginations of the thoughts: if
thou seek him, he will be found of thee; but if thou
forsake him, he will cast thee off for ever. (1 Chronicles
28:4–9)

Then David gave Solomon the pattern for the temple and all the
buildings connected to it, which was given to David by the Spirit of the
Lord. He supplied Solomon with gold and silver to make everything that
would be used for service in the holy place and the most holy place. Then
he encouraged him to trust in the Lord.

> Be strong and of good courage, and do it: fear not, nor
> be dismayed: for the LORD God, even my God, will be
> with thee; he will not fail thee, nor forsake thee, until thou
> hast finished all the work for the service of the house of
> the LORD. (1 Chronicles 28:20)

David spoke to the congregation about all the things he had prepared
and contributed to the new temple of God. Then the leaders, from their
hearts, willingly gave their gold, silver, brass, iron, and precious stones.
King David gave thanks to God and blessed them all, and then He prayed:

> O LORD God of Abraham, Isaac, and of Israel, our
> fathers, keep this for ever in the imagination of the
> thoughts of the heart of thy people, and prepare their
> heart unto thee: And give unto Solomon my son a perfect
> heart, to keep thy commandments, thy testimonies, and
> thy statutes, and to do all these things, and to build the
> palace, for the which I have made provision. (1 Chronicles
> 29:18–19)

David made Solomon king in his place, and before David died, he
told Solomon:

> I go the way of all the earth: be thou strong therefore, and
> show thyself a man; And keep the charge of the LORD

thy God, to walk in his ways, to keep his statutes, and his commandments, and his judgments, and his testimonies, as it is written in the law of Moses, that thou mayest prosper in all that thou doest, and whithersoever thou turnest thyself: That the LORD may continue his word which he spake concerning me, saying, If thy children take heed to their way, to walk before me in truth with all their heart and with all their soul, there shall not fail thee (said he) a man on the throne of Israel. (1 Kings 2:2–4)

After reigning as king for forty years, David died, and Solomon cleaned house, just as his father had told him to do. Adonijah was struck down and killed; Solomon ordered the death of Joab for shedding the blood of Abner and Amasa behind King David's back; Zadok became priest in Abiathar's place; and Benaiah became commander over the army in Joab's place. Three years down the road, King Solomon gave orders to kill Shimei for all the wrong doings he had committed against King David and for going to Gath without telling King Solomon.

## The Lord Promises Wisdom and Wealth to King Solomon

King Solomon married the daughter of the king of Egypt, and she went to live with him in Jerusalem. Solomon obeyed the Lord, and he also offered sacrifices in the high places "because there was no house built unto the name of the LORD, until those days" (1 Kings 3:2).

When King Solomon went to Gibeon to offer his one thousand burnt offerings on the altar, the Lord spoke to him one night in a dream:

Ask what I shall give thee. And Solomon said…Give therefore thy servant an understanding heart to judge thy people that I may discern between good and bad: for who is able to judge this thy so great a people? And the speech pleased the LORD, that Solomon had asked this thing. (1 Kings 3:5–10)

The Lord gave Solomon much more than he asked for:

> Because thou hast asked this thing, and hast not asked for thyself long life; neither hast asked riches for thyself, nor hast asked the life of thine enemies; but hast asked for thyself understanding to discern judgment; Behold, I have done according to thy words: lo, I have given thee a wise and understanding heart; so that there was none like thee before thee, neither after thee shall any arise like unto thee. And I have also given thee that which thou hast not asked, both riches, and honor: so that there shall not be any among the kings like unto thee all thy days. (1 Kings 3:11–13)

He also gave Solomon a *conditional promise*:

> And *if thou wilt walk in my ways*, to keep my statutes and my commandments, as thy father David did walk, then *I will lengthen thy days*. And Solomon awoke; and, behold, it was a dream. And he came to Jerusalem, and stood before the ark of the covenant of the LORD, and offered up burnt offerings, and offered peace offerings, and made a feast to all his servants. (1 Kings 3:14–15; emphasis added)

King Solomon reigned over a very large kingdom— "from the river unto the land of the Philis´-tines, and unto the border of Egypt" (1 Kings 4:21), and he became very wealthy. He had eleven chief officials to help him rule over Israel and twelve district governors to supply him with daily provisions, and Judah and Israel lived in peace and prosperity and grew in great numbers. These were the gifts God gave to Solomon:

> Wisdom and understanding ... largeness of heart ... Solomon's wisdom excelled the wisdom of all the children of the east country, and all the wisdom of Egypt. ... He was wiser than all men; ... and his fame was in all nations round about. And he spake three thousand proverbs: and his songs were a thousand and five. (1 Kings 4:29–32)

Most of Proverbs has been attributed to King Solomon, and he is also thought to have been the author of the Song of Solomon.

## King Solomon Builds a Temple for the Lord

Solomon sent a message to King Hiram of Tyre, who had loved King David, telling him of his plan to build the house of the Lord: "I purpose to build a house unto the name of the LORD my God, as the LORD spake unto David my father, saying, Thy son, whom I will set upon thy throne in thy room, he shall build a house unto my name" (1 Kings 5:5).

> I build a house to the name of the LORD my God, to dedicate it to him, and to burn before him sweet incense, and for the continual showbread, and for the burnt offerings morning and evening, on the sabbaths, and on the new moons, and on the solemn feasts of the LORD our God. This is an ordinance for ever to Israel. (2 Chronicles 2:4)

He told King Hiram to send him craftsmen who could work in gold, silver, brass, and iron, and those who could work with purple, crimson, and blue materials. He also asked for logged cedar, fir, and algum trees to be used in the Lord's house. Solomon agreed to send wheat, barley, wine, and pure oil to King Hiram's servants in exchange for what he had asked for. Hiram, pleased about the trade of goods, agreed to cut and float the cedar and fir trees on rafts by sea to King Solomon.

When Solomon had ruled over Israel for four years, he began building the Lord's temple—480 years after the Lord had delivered the Israelites out of Egypt. The construction of God's new house would be of wood and stone. The furnishings for the temple were crafted of burnished bronze, and the furnishings within the Lord's temple were of pure gold. No tools were used on the temple site as it was being constructed.

In seven years, the work was completed, and "Solomon brought in the things which David his father had dedicated; even the silver, and the gold, and the vessels, did he put among the treasures of the house of the

LORD" (1 Kings 7:51). The description of the temple and its furnishings are found in 1 Kings 6 and 2 Chronicles 3 and 4. Solomon built "the house of the LORD at Jerusalem in mount Mo-ri´-ah, where the LORD appeared unto David his father, in the place that David had prepared in the threshing floor of Or´-nan the Jeb´-u-site" (2 Chronicles 3:1).

That the temple "stood within the area now called 'haramesh-Sherif' at the E side of the 'Old City' of Jerusalem is undisputed. The precise location within the vast enclosure is less certain. The highest part of the rock (now covered by the building known as 'The Dome of the Rock') may have been the site of the innermost sanctuary or of the Altar of Burnt-Offering outside (2 Ch. 3:1). This rock was presumably part of the threshing-floor of Araunah, bought by David for a sum given as 50 silver shekels (2 Sa. 24:24) or 600 gold shekels (1Ch. 21:25)."[1]

## Solomon Brings Up the Ark of the Covenant

All the elders of Israel came, and the priests took up the ark. And they brought up the ark of the LORD, and the tabernacle of the congregation, and all the holy vessels that were in the tabernacle, even those did the priests and the Levites bring up. And King Solomon, and all the congregation of Israel, that were assembled unto him, were with him before the ark, sacrificing sheep and oxen, that could not be told nor numbered for multitude. And the priests brought in the ark of the covenant of the LORD unto his place, into the oracle of the house, to the most holy place, even under the wings of the cher´-u-bim. (1 Kings 8:3–6)

There was nothing in the ark save the two tables of stone, which Moses put there at Hor´-eb, when the LORD made a covenant with the children of Israel, when they came out of the land of Egypt. And it came to pass, when the priests were come out of the holy place, that the cloud filled the house of the LORD, So that the priests could not stand to minister because of the cloud: for the

glory of the LORD had filled the house of the LORD.
(1 Kings 8:9–11)

Before the Altar of the Lord in front of all Israel, King Solomon prayed a prayer of supplication regarding the Lord's covenant with Israel.

That thine eyes may be open unto the supplication of thy servant, and unto the supplication of thy people Israel, to hearken unto them in all that they call for unto thee. For thou didst separate them from among all the people of the earth, to be thine inheritance, as thou spakest by the hand of Moses thy servant, when thou broughtest our fathers out of Egypt, O LORD GOD. (1 Kings 8:52–53)

Then Solomon blessed the people of Israel:

Blessed be the LORD, that hath given rest unto his people Israel, according to all that he promised: there hath not failed one word of all his good promise, which he promised by the hand of Moses his servant. The LORD our God be with us, as he was with our fathers: let him not leave us, nor forsake us: That he may incline our hearts unto him, to walk in all his ways, and to keep his commandments, and his statutes, and his judgments, which he commanded our fathers. And let these my words, wherewith I have made supplication before the LORD, be nigh unto the LORD our God day and night, that he maintain the cause of his servant and the cause of his people Israel at all times, as the matter shall require: That all the people of the earth may know that the LORD is God, and that there is none else. (1 Kings 8:56–60)

King Solomon offered twenty-two thousand cattle and one hundred twenty thousand sheep and goats as fellowship offerings to dedicate the Lord's new temple. He also consecrated the temple courtyard with burnt and meat offerings and the fat of the fellowship offerings. The celebration lasted for fourteen days.

## God's Covenant Continues with Solomon

The Lord appeared to Solomon again with a *conditional* blessing:

> I have heard thy prayer and thy supplication that thou hast made before me: I have hallowed this house, which thou hast built, to put my name there for ever; and mine eyes and mine heart shall be there perpetually. And *if thou wilt walk before me, as David thy father walked, in integrity of heart, and in uprightness, to do according to all that I have commanded thee, and wilt keep my statutes and my judgments:* Then I *will establish the throne of thy kingdom upon Israel for ever,* as I promised to David thy father, saying, There shall not fail thee a man upon the throne of Israel.
>
> But *if ye shall at all turn from following me,* ye or your children, and will not keep my commandments and my statutes which I have set before you, but go and serve other gods, and worship them: *Then will I cut off Israel out of the land* which I have given them; and this house, which I have hallowed for my name, will I cast out of my sight; and Israel shall be a proverb and a byword among all people." (1 Kings 9:3–7; emphasis added)

## Solomon's Wealth and Wisdom

God had made Solomon wise in his heart, and everyone wanted to sit with Solomon and hear this wisdom. He received income from merchants, Arabian kings, and governors. When people came to see him, they brought him items made of silver and gold; and clothes, armor, spices, horses, and mules. King Hiram's ships brought Solomon gold, almugwood, and precious stones. Solomon also received 1,400 chariots and twelve thousand horses from Egypt. He became wealthier than any other king.

King Solomon's fame, success, and wisdom were heard about throughout the lands. The Queen of Sheba came to test his wisdom and brought a large caravan of supplies with her for him—spices, gold, and precious stones. There was not anything she asked Solomon that he could not answer for her, and she was impressed with him. Everything she had ever heard about him was true.

She told him, "Blessed be the LORD thy God, which delighted in thee, to set thee on the throne of Israel: because the LORD loved Israel for ever, therefore made he thee king, to do judgment and justice (1 Kings 10:9).

## The Sins of King Solomon

The ancestors of Jesus were not perfect, and that included King Solomon. His weakness was in loving pagan women, which turned his heart away from God.

> King Solomon loved many strange women, together with the daughter of Pharaoh, women of the Mo´-abites, Am´-mon-ites, E´-dom-ites, Zi-do´-ni-ans, and Hit´-tites; Of the nations concerning which the LORD said unto the children of Israel, Ye shall not go in to them, neither shall they come in unto you: for surely they will turn away your heart after their gods: Solomon clave unto these in love. (1 Kings 11:1–2)

He took these women and made seven hundred wives, princesses, and three hundred concubines. As the years went by and Solomon became old, he apparently failed to remember to thank God for what He had done for him. His great wisdom became foolish, as he became wise in his own eyes. He "changed the truth of God into a lie and worshiped and served the creature more than the Creator, who is blessed for ever" (Romans 1:25).

King Solomon began to worship the pagan gods of his wives—the Sidonian goddess, Ashtoreth, the Ammonite god, Molek, and the Moabite god, Chemosh. The Lord was angry with Solomon for not keeping His covenant and commands, and He told him what He was going to do:

> Forasmuch as this is done of thee, and thou hast not kept my covenant and my statutes, which I have commanded thee, I will surely rend the kingdom from thee, and will give it to thy servant. ... in thy days I will not do it for David thy father's sake: but I will rend it out of the hand of thy son. Howbeit I will not rend away all the kingdom; but will give one tribe to thy son for David my servant's sake, and for Jerusalem's sake which I have chosen. (1 Kings 11:11–13)

## God's Prophecy of the Divided Kingdom

Before Solomon died, the Lord stirred up three enemies against him—Hadadezer an Edomite, and Rezon who ruled in Aram. These two men had fled from previous battles against his father, David, and his men. They had heard that King David had died and began opposing King Solomon throughout his reign. The third enemy was Jeroboam I, one of Solomon's officials. One day as Jeroboam I, dressed in new clothing, was leaving Jerusalem, a prophet by the name of Ahijah met him on a country road.

> Ahijah caught the new garment that was on him, and rent it in twelve pieces: And he said to Jer-o-bo´-am, Take these ten pieces ... I will rend the kingdom out of the hand of Solomon, and will give ten tribes to thee: (But he shall have one tribe for my servant David's sake, and for Jerusalem's sake, the city which I have chosen out of all the tribes of Israel. (1 Kings 11:30–32)

The Lord also gave Jeroboam I a *conditional* promise:

11

> And it shall be, *if thou wilt hearken unto all that I command thee, and wilt walk in my ways, and do that is right in my sight*, to keep my statutes and my commandments, as David my servant did; that I will *be with thee, and build thee a sure house*, as I built for David, and will give Israel unto thee. And I will for this afflict the seed of David, but not for ever. (1 Kings 11:38–39; emphasis added)

Then Solomon wanted to kill Jeroboam, so Jeroboam ran away into Egypt until Solomon died after serving as king for forty years. After his death, King Solomon was buried in Jerusalem.

# In Conclusion

God had selected Solomon to sit upon David's throne and to build His new permanent house, and God had promised David, "I will establish the throne of his kingdom over Israel for ever" (1 Chronicles 22:10.) As in the past, when God had a plan, Satan tried to foil it. This time, he influenced Adonijah to deceptively try to take the king's position; however, God's prophecies did come to pass, and Solomon became king.

When God asked King Solomon what he would want God to give him, his answer might come as a surprise— "an understanding heart to judge thy people, that I may discern between good and bad" (1 Kings 3:9). Not only did God give him what he asked for, but He also gave him riches and honor. King Solomon became wiser than any man, and he became very wealthy.

King Solomon completed God's house in seven years, and he brought the ark of the Lord's covenant out from the tent that David had prepared for it and placed it in the new temple. Once again, the glory of the Lord filled the house of God. After Solomon's prayer of supplication to the Lord, the Lord promised to establish His throne upon Israel and His everlasting covenant through him; however, these promises were conditional. King Solomon and his descendants must obey God's commands and not turn away from Him, or God would "cut off Israel out of the land he had given them" (1 Kings 9:7). Even knowing what God had told him, Solomon eventually followed his pagan wives into their idol worship, forsaking God.

God promised to take the ten tribes of Israel out of Solomon's son's hands and give them to Jeroboam I. Jeroboam will become the king of the ten tribes of Israel, but what kind of king will he be? What will happen to the other two tribes?

## Deeper Insights:

1.  Besides Solomon's writings of the Song of Solomon in the Bible, the Book of Ecclesiastes contains some of King Solomon's words, penned by an unknown author in about 940 BC. He referred to Solomon as the "Preacher, the son of David, king in Jerusalem" (Ecclesiastes 1:1).

    Read the following Scriptures from Ecclesiastes to get an idea about the great wisdom God gave to Solomon: 1:16–18; 2:10–11; 3:11–15; 5:15; 6:7–9; 7:1; 8:11; 10:20; 11:5; 12:13–14.

2.  There are two psalms that are attributed to King Solomon. Read Psalm 72, which appears to have been written by King David for Solomon, and Psalm 127, which was also written for King Solomon by an unknown author.

3.  After Solomon had built God's house and brought the ark to the temple, what did he do? Read 1 Kings 8:22–66.

    God spoke with Solomon again. What did He promise King Solomon? Read 1 Kings 9:4–7.

4.  God had blessed King Solomon more than any other king, yet he failed to meet the condition the Lord had given him.

    What did King Solomon do that started the beginning of his failure to meet God's condition? Read 1 Kings 3:1.

    What were the sins of King Solomon? Read 1 Kings 11:1–8.

    What had God told the Israelites in Exodus 34:11–17?

What did God tell Solomon He would do because of his disobedience? Read 1 Kings 11:9–13.

5. What does God tell Christians even today in the New Testament? Read 2 Corinthians 6:14–18 and 1 Corinthians 5:9–13.

# CHAPTER 2

## THE KINGS OF THE DIVIDED KINGDOM

### God Divides the Kingdom

After King Solomon's death, his son, Rehoboam, went to Shechem to be appointed king of all Israel. Jeroboam I, the rebellious official of Solomon, who had fled to Egypt to get away from King Solomon, came back with the people of Israel and spoke to King Rehoboam. He asked that he not be as oppressive over them as his father Solomon had been at the last, and then they would serve him. King Rehoboam consulted with the young men he had grown up with, and they told him to be even harder than his father had been. The Bible says that the king did not listen to Jeroboam and the people of Israel, but listened, instead, to the young men, because this was the Lord's doing to fulfill the prophecy that Ahijah had spoken to Jeroboam, "I will take the kingdom out of his son's hand, and will give it unto thee, even ten tribes" (1 Kings 11:35).

When Israel realized that King Rehoboam would not listen to them, they became indignant and said:

> What portion have we in David? neither have we inheritance in the son of Jesse: to your tents, O Israel: now see to thine own house, David. So Israel departed unto their tents. But as for the children of Israel which dwelt in the cities of Judah, Re-ho-bo´-am reigned over them. ... So Israel rebelled against the house of David. (1 Kings 12:16–19)

The people pulled away from King Rehoboam, causing a division in the kingdom. Israel became the Northern Kingdom with ten tribes under King Jeroboam I, and Judah became the Southern Kingdom with one tribe—Judah, which followed after the house of David, under King Rehoboam. The tribe of Benjamin also remained with Judah. King Rehoboam gathered men from the tribes of Judah and Benjamin to prepare for war to try to regain the ten tribes who had left the kingdom; however, God had a different plan. The Lord spoke to King Rehoboam through a man of God by the name of Shemaiah, "Ye shall not go up, nor fight against your brethren the children of Israel: return every man to his house; for this thing is from me" (1 Kings 12:24). With that, they listened to the Lord and returned to their homes.

## Rehoboam, the First King of Judah, the Southern Kingdom

Information about King Rehoboam can be found in 1 Kings 11–12, 14; 2 Chronicles 11

During Rehoboam's reign, he built many cities of defense in the land of Judah: Bethlehem, Etam, Tekoa, Bethzur, Shoco, Adullam, Gath, Mareshah, Ziph, Adoraim, Lachish, Azekah, Zorah, Aijalon, and Hebron. He was a good king until he turned his back on the Lord, building places to practice idolatry: "high places, and images, and groves, on every high hill, and under every green tree. And there were also sodomites in the land: and they did according to all the abominations of the nations which the LORD cast out before the children of Israel" (1 Kings 14:23–24).

Then Shishak, the king of Egypt, along with "the Lu´-bim, the Suk´-ki-im, and the E-thio´-pi-ans" (2 Chronicles 12:3) came and captured all the cities of defense in Judah, and came also to Jerusalem to do the same. The prophet Shemaiah came and spoke to the leaders of Judah: "Thus saith the LORD, Ye have forsaken me, and therefore have I also left you in the hand of Shi´-shak" (2 Chronicles 12:5).

With that word from the Lord, the leaders and the king became humble before Him. When the Lord saw that they had become humble, he told the prophet he would not allow them to be destroyed by Shishak;

but they would, instead, become his servants for a period of time. Shishak attacked Jerusalem and stole treasures from the king and from the temple, including the gold shields Solomon had made. King Rehoboam tried to replace the shields by making new ones out of brass, which almost cost him his life with the Lord; but once again, he humbled himself before the Lord and was spared. After his death, his son Abijam succeeded him as king, practicing the same sins that his father had practiced, and he did not have a heart for God. Even so, the Lord would not forget Judah, the line of King David.

## Jeroboam I, the First King of the Northern Kingdom

Information about King Jeroboam I can be found in 1 Kings 11–15; 2 Chronicles 11, 13; Amos 7

King Jeroboam I lived and ruled over his kingdom from Shechem, in Mount Ephraim. He was worried that if the people were allowed to go to the temple in Jerusalem to make their sacrifices, they might join up with King Rehoboam in Judah. So he built two golden calves for the people to worship, giving them the excuse that it would be too hard for them to go up to Jerusalem. He put one of the idols in Bethel and one in Dan, and the people in Israel worshiped the calves. When he did these things, the Levites, and the other people who loved God, left and went to Judah, which made Judah even stronger.

After that, King Jeroboam took priestly things into his own hands and established a feast similar to the feasts that God had set up with Moses. He ordained priests, and he made sacrifices on the altar he had made, which he had no right to do, because he was disobeying the Law God had given Moses regarding these matters. The Lord sent a prophet from Judah to the altar where King Jeroboam was making sacrifices. The man of God prophesied to the altar about its future:

> O altar, altar, thus saith the LORD; Behold, a child shall
> be born unto the house of David, Jo-si´-ah by name; and
> upon thee shall he offer the priests of the high places that
> burn incense upon thee, and men's bones shall be burnt

upon thee. And he gave a sign the same day, saying, This
is the sign which the LORD hath spoken; Behold, the
altar shall be rent and the ashes that are upon it shall be
poured out. (1 Kings 13:2–3)

When King Jeroboam stretched out his hand to the altar and
commanded them to sieze the man of God, his hand shriveled up, and
the altar split in two. After the king told the man of God to pray for him,
his hand was restored. Jeroboam wanted to give him a reward, but the man
of God refused him, because the Lord had told him, "Eat no bread, nor
drink water, nor turn again by the same way that thou camest" (1 Kings
13:9). Unfortunately, the man of God did not return the way he had come.
He stopped to eat bread and drink water at another man's house— a man
who had deceived him by causing him to believe he was a prophet as well.
Due to the prophet's disobedience to the Lord, a lion killed on his way
home. When the false prophet found out what had happened, he buried
the man of God in his own grave. He told his sons that when he died, they
were to bury him there beside the bones of the man of God, because the
words he had spoken to the altar would come to pass.

After King Jeroboam had heard the prophet, he still did not change.
He continued to appoint and consecrate himself and ordinary people to be
priests for the high places of worship. When Jeroboam's son Abijah became
ill, he sent his wife to the prophet Ahijah to find out what was going to
happen to his son. The Lord had already told Ahijah that Jeroboam's wife
was coming. When she arrived, he gave her a prophetic message for the
king from the Lord, because the king had entered into idolatry:

> I will bring evil upon the house of Jer-o-bo´-am, and will
> cut off from Jer-o-bo´-am him that pisseth against the
> wall, and him that is shut up and left in Israel, and will
> take away the remnant of the house of Jer-o-bo´-am, as a
> man taketh away dung, till it be all gone.

> Him that dieth of Jer-o-bo´-am in the city shall the dogs
> eat; and him that dieth in the field shall the fowls of
> the air eat: for the LORD hath spoken it. Arise thou

therefore, get thee to thine own house: and when thy feet enter into the city, the child shall die. And all Israel shall mourn for him, and bury him: for he only of Jer-o-bo'-am shall come to the grave, because in him there is found some good thing toward the LORD God of Israel in the house of Jer-o-bo'-am. Moreover the LORD shall raise him up a king over Israel, who shall cut off the house of Jer-o-bo'-am that day. (1 Kings 14:10–14)

Ahijah also prophesied that the Lord would exile Israel from their land because they were worshiping pagan gods: "For the LORD shall smite Israel, as a reed is shaken in the water, and he shall root up Israel out of this good land, which he gave to their fathers, and shall scatter them beyond the river" (1 Kings 14:15).

## Abijam and Jeroboam I Go to War

When Abijam, son of King Rehoboam, was reigning as king of Judah, he climbed up on Mount Zemaraim and began to yell to King Jeroboam I of Israel: "Ought ye not to know that the LORD God of Israel gave the kingdom over Israel to David for ever, even to him and to his sons by a *covenant of salt?*" (2 Chronicles 13:5; emphasis added)

In Leviticus 2, Moses had told the Israelites to always season their meat offerings with the "*salt of the covenant.*" Salt was also used as a preservative to ensure that certain foods would last. God used salt symbolically to emphasize His everlasting covenant with the Israelites: "It is *a covenant of salt for ever* before the LORD unto thee and to thy seed with thee" (Numbers 18:19; emphasis added).

King Abijam continued to point out that Israel had forsaken the Lord and had left the Mosaic Law regarding the priests.

Have ye not cast out the priests of the LORD, the sons of Aaron, and the Levites, and have made you priests after the manner of the nations of other lands? so that whosoever cometh to consecrate himself with a young bullock and seven rams, the same may be a priest of them that are no gods. But as for us, the LORD is our God, and we have not forsaken him; and the priests, which minister unto the LORD, are the sons of Aaron, and the Levites wait upon their business. (2 Chronicles 13:9–10)

After that, Jeroboam and his men ambushed Judah, before and behind, but the army of Judah "cried unto the Lord, and the priests sounded with the trumpets. Then the men of Judah gave a shout: and as the men of Judah shouted, it came to pass, that God smote Jer-o-bó-am and all Israel" (2 Chronicles 13:14–15). Judah's army slaughtered five hundred thousand Israelite men. King Abijam didn't stop there—he pursued King Jeroboam and captured his cities of Bethel, Jeshanah, and Ephraim, and eventually, the Lord killed Jeroboam.

King Abijam did not have a perfect heart toward the Lord, committing the same sins that his father, King Rehoboam, had done. Even so, before Abijam's death, the Lord gave him a righteous son named Asa to succeed him "for David's sake...to set up a lamp in Jerusalem...to establish Jerusalem: Because David did that which was right in the eyes of the LORD, and turned not aside from any thing that he commanded him all the days of his life, save only in the matter of U-ri´-ah the Hit´-tite" (1 Kings 15:4–5).

## Kings Who Rule the Divided Kingdom

After King Solomon, Israel and Judah each had twenty kings reign over them during the time of the divided kingdom. The following list contains names and dates of those forty kings. The dates and names were taken from the New Bible Dictionary.[1] The Bible refers to each king as "one who did right in the eyes of the LORD," or, "one who did evil in the eyes of the LORD." Some of Judah's kings were considered to be **good kings,** and are indicated by **bold** print—there were no good kings in Israel. Judah's kings, which have an asterisk (*) after them, are listed in the genealogy of Jesus Christ in Matthew 1:6–11.

| Israel's Kings—Samaria | Year BC | Judah's Kings—Jerusalem | Year BC |
| --- | --- | --- | --- |
| Jeroboam I, son of Nebat | 931/30-910/9 | Rehoboam, son of Solomon * | 931/30-913 |
| Nadab, son of Jeroboam | 910/9-909/8 | Abijam(h), son of Rehoboam* | 913-911/10 |
| Baasha, son of Ahijah | 909/8-886/85 | Asa, son of Abijam * | 911/10-870/69 |
| Elah, son of Baasha | 886/85-885/84 | Jehoshaphat, son of Asa * | 870/69-848 |
| Zimri, servant of Elah | 885/84 | Jehoram, son of Jehoshaphat * | 848-841 |
| Tibni, son of Ginath | 885/84-880 | Ahaziah, son of Jehoram | 841 |
| Omri, commander of the army | 880-874/73 | Athaliah, mother of Ahaziah | 841-835 |
| Ahab, son of Omri | 874/73-853 | Jehoash, son of Ahaziah | 835-796 |
| Ahaziah, son of Ahab | 853-852 | Amaziah, son of Joash | 796-767 |
| Joram, son of Ahab | 852-841 | Azariah, son of Amaziah * | 767-740/39 |
| Jehu, son of Jehoshaphat | 841-814/13 | Jotham, son of Uzziah * | 740/39-732/31 |
| Jehoahaz, son of Jehu | 814/13-798 | Ahaz, son of Jotham | 732/31-716/15 |
| Jehoash, son of Jehoahaz | 798-782/81 | Hezekiah, son of Ahaz * | 716/15-687/86 |
| Jeroboam II, son of Jehoash | 782/81-753 | Manasseh, son of Hezekiah | 687/86-643/42 |
| Zachariah, son of Jeroboam II | 753-752 | Amon, son of Hezekiah | 643/42-641/40 |
| Shallum, son of Jabesh | 752 | Josiah, son of Amon | 640/39-609 |
| Menahem, son of Gadi | 752-742/41 | Jehoahaz, son of Josiah | 609 |
| Pekahiah, son of Menahem | 742/41-740/39 | Jehoiakim, son of Josiah | 609-597 |
| Pekah, son of Remaliah | 740/39-732/31 | Jehoiachin, son of Jehoiakim | 597 |
| Hoshea, son of Elah | 732/31-723/22 | Zedekiah, son of Josiah | 597-587 |

# Evil Kings

King Jeroboam I had set an evil precedence for all the succeeding kings in the Northern kingdom of Israel and many of the kings in the Southern Kingdom of Judah. These kings did not follow the ways of King David. The kings and the people would eventually reach a stage of moral and spiritual depravity because they would not give up idol worship and pagan lifestyles. All the kings of Israel were referred to as those who "did evil in the eyes of the LORD." They fell heavily into worshiping the gods of the nations the Lord had driven out when they had first entered their Promised Land. Instead of worshiping their Creator, Who had promised such great blessings to them, they worshiped the creature Satan that had caused Adam and Eve to fall in the Garden of Eden. The kings of Israel rejected the Lord, and they reigned with all kinds of evil and violence.

Only eight out of twenty kings of Judah were actually considered as "doing what was right in the eyes of the LORD," and some of those still did not tear down the high places of worship, but continued to offer sacrifices and burn incense. The other twelve kings of Judah "did evil in the sight of the LORD." The evil kings worshiped foreign gods and the stars and the heavens. They married pagan wives and practiced divinatioin, sorcery, and witchcraft, consulting with spiritists and mediums. They practiced sodomy, and some even sacrificed their children to the god Molech.

# As the King Goes, so Goes the Kingdom

When the kings rebelliously turned their backs on the Lord, and did not obey His commands or decrees, they fell into, and adopted, the same ungodly customs and lifestyles as the pagan kings and nations around them. They worshiped their worthless, lifeless gods. Whatever way the king chose to walk, the people of Israel and Judah followed. The evil kings and tribe leaders literally caused the people to sin. Consequently, the tribes of Israel lost their identity as a holy nation. A horrible time of moral and national decline had begun, and it would continue to decline for over another three hundred years, but God would never forsake them.

He told them over and over again that if they would repent and turn from their sins, He would forgive them and bring blessings to them. He would do this because He was in covenant with them, and His mercy is everlasting. So if a king was devoted to the Lord and obeyed His commands and decrees, he honored and pleased God. With God's help, he had the ability to lead his kingdom in righteousness and receive the blessings of protection and prosperity for his kingdom. A king completely devoted to God was referred to as "walking as David." Only two kings of Judah were given that honor—Hezekiah and Josiah. Good kings, who were still dabbling with pagan religions, and who did not destroy the high places, caused their people to sin.

Kings were great inquirers when it came to reigning over their kingdoms. They inquired of the elders, wise men, witches, sorcerers, men of God, and prophets. They wanted to know how things were going to turn out, what decisions they should make, and even sought after the interpretation of their dreams. At various times, the Lord sent prophets to the kings with messages from Him. If the kings were not happy about the prophecies or interpretations, they did not always heed their advice, and sometimes the prophets died. Whether the kings were good or evil, God was involved in their lives and their kingdoms, orchestrating His plan of redemption and salvation for all people, which would come in God's perfect timing.

## The Time of the Prophets

The Bible has shown us that God is a personal God. He loves to communicate with us, and He lets us know what He is going to do in the future. Besides speaking through prophets, He spoke to the people of the Old Testament in various ways, for example: through a donkey, in a burning bush, personally and directly, through angels, and through visions and dreams.

A prophet or a prophetess was a messenger from God, one who delivered a message of truth from the Holy Spirit of God. Their messages contained guidance, promises, and warnings, which would be fulfilled in the near or distant future, depending upon the circumstances. These messages were God's proclamations, which would always come to pass. The Apostle Peter, in the New Testament, spoke to the early Christians about these Old Testament prophets who had *Christ's Spirit* in them (see 1 Peter 1:10–12). The Spirit of Christ was in the Old Testament Jewish prophets, even before Jesus Christ was born, crucified and resurrected.

Many prophets had prophesied throughout the Old Testament days, but during the time of the forty kings, God's use of the prophets began to accelerate. Evil was becoming more prevalent among His chosen people, and He was about to bring His judgment upon them so that there would remain a godly remnant. Even in this dark time of idol worship and a lack of love for God, He would keep the promises He had made to their forefathers, Abraham, Isaac, and Jacob.

A true prophecy literally comes from God, whether directly from Him, or through a prophet; and it comes to pass. "When a prophet speaketh in the name of the LORD, if the thing follow not, nor come to pass, that is the thing which the LORD hath not spoken, but the prophet hath spoken it presumptuously: thou shalt not be afraid of him" (Deuteronomy 18:22). Messages that are contrary to the Scriptures and lead us away from God, comes from a false prophet.

Besides prophesying and interceding through prayer for people, the prophets in the Old Testament came alongside to help and encourage the people in times of need and crisis. With the Spirit of God in them and upon them, they were given boldness to be able to put their lives on the line when it came to speaking the messages of God. They spoke to whomever God sent them to, whether it was to the common man or to the king. One thing was for sure, the prophet of God delivered the message that repentance and obedience were the answer to receiving God's promises, blessings, and hope. Disobedience (rebelling against Him) would bring His wrath.

The prophets were not very popular people with those who did not want to hear the truth or with those who did not want to change their ways to honor God, and they led a very isolated, lonely life. They were called by God to carry out His purposes in both kingdoms, and often times, they became the major players that changed and guided the turn of events according to the will of God. They spoke about God's love, provisions and blessings; and they spoke about His mercy and justice, which included

THE KING IS COMING

judgment for sin. They also spoke about a time in the future when God would send "One" to deliver and redeem them. This "One" would be called Yeshua, Messiah, Jesus Christ—God's Son, who would come to earth to be born in the womb of a young Jewish virgin. This "One" was called by many different names by the prophets and men of old:

Ancient of Days (Daniel 7:9)

Lord our righteousness (Jeremiah 23:6)

BRANCH (The) (Zechariah 3:8)

Lord, your Redeemer (Isaiah 43:14)

Branch of righteousness (Jeremiah 33:15)

Man of Sorrows (Isaiah 53:3)

Branch of the root of Jesse (Isaiah 11:1)

Messiah (Daniel 9:25)

Chiefest Among Ten Thousand (Song of Solom. 5:10)

Mighty God (Isaiah 9:6)

Counselor (Isaiah 9:6)

Mighty one of Jacob (Isaiah 60:16)

Diadem (Isaiah 28:5)

Most Holy (Daniel 9:24)

Everlasting Father (Isaiah 9:6)

Most Mighty (Psalm 45:3)

First-born (Psalm 89:27)

Prince of Peace (Isaiah 9:6)

Foundation Laid in Zion (Isaiah 28:16)

Prophet (Deuteronomy 18:15, 18)

God of Israel (Isaiah 45:15)

Redeemer (Isaiah 59:20)

Headstone of the corner (Psalm 118:22)

Righteous servant (Isaiah 53:11)

Holy One of Israel (Isaiah 37:23)

Root of Jesse (Isaiah 11:10)

Immanuel (Psalm 130:8)

Rose of Sharon (Song of Solomon 2:1)

Judge of Israel (Micah 5:1)

Seed of the woman (Genesis 3:15)

King of Glory (Psalm 24:7)

Stone (Daniel 2:45)

King of Zion (Zechariah 9:9)

Sun of righteousness (Malachi 4:2)

King over all the earth (Zechariah 14:8-9)

Sure foundation (Isaiah 28:16)

Lily of the valleys (Song of Solomon 2:1)

Wonderful (Isaiah 9:6)

Lord of hosts (Isaiah 54:5)

God knows the hearts of men today, and He knew them in the Old Testament times. Nothing was done that took Him by surprise, and nothing that was done foiled what He had planned.

What a time of conflict for the kingdoms of the north (Israel) and the south (Judah)! Between the dates of 931-586 BC, there were many major wars and battles between Israel and Judah and other nations, such as Egypt,

Syria, Arman, Edom, Assyria, Chaldea, Moab, Ammon, and Babylonia. The wars and battles were harsh, with many dying by the sword—kings, priests, men, women, and children. Israel was the forerunner of evil, and Israel would have to be dealt with first, because Judah, the Davidic line, was quickly following in Israel's footsteps. Something must be done to stop this evil that was spreading, and God knew exactly what to do.

## In Conclusion

There was now a divided kingdom—the Southern Kingdom was Judah, which included Benjamin; and the Northern Kingdom was Israel, which included the remaining ten tribes of Jacob. God had changed Jacob's name to Israel, and these twelve tribes were all his descendants.

King Solomon's decision to turn from God and worship other gods began the downward trend toward idolatry with Israel and Judah. After the kingdoms were divided, King Jeroboam I reigned over the Northern Kingdom of Israel, bringing full-blown idolatry to the people, blaspheming God. He did this to keep them from going back to Jerusalem to worship, fearing they would not return to his kingdom. Not only did he promote idolatry, but he also perverted the priesthood and sacrificial system, even adding his own holy feast day. God had established these systems for the Hebrews, and no one had the right to establish new ones, or even make changes, to them. Sadly, all of Israel's kings, and most of Judah's kings, would follow the wicked sins of idolatry that Jeroboam I had started.

In the next few chapters, we will see how God intervened by sending a flurry of His prophets to try and turn the people back to Him. The prophets will preach to them, warn them, and point out their need for repentance to avoid impending judgment. How will they respond to His prophets?

## Deeper Insights:

1. Most of the kings followed after the sins of Jeroboam I. What were those sins that caused God's judgment to fall on so many

kings and people? Read the following Scriptures and list the sins of Jeroboam: 1 Kings 12:25–33.

What was sinful about the high places? Read Deuteronomy 12:1–6, 13–14.

Why was it wrong for King Jeroboam to ordain a feast? Read Leviticus 23:2, 4.

What was wrong with Jeroboam ordaining his own high priests? Read Numbers 18:1–7.

2. How does the Old Testament say we can recognize a false prophet? Read Deuteronomy 18:20–22.

3. "As the king goes, so goes the kingdom." Do you think that is a fair analysis? Why or why not?

4. Why do you think God felt it was urgent to send a surge of prophets to these nations during this period of time of the divided kingdoms?

5. What made it possible for the prophets of old to prophesy? Read 2 Peter 1:21.

6. What does the New Testament have to say about false prophets? Read the following Scriptures: Matthew 7:15–20, 22–23; 24:11–12, 24–28; Mark 13:22–23; 2 Peter 2:1–3; 1 John 4:1–6.

7. How is it that we, as Christians, are able to prophesy? Read the following Scriptures: John 16:13–15; Acts 19:6; 1 Corinthians 2:9–16.

8. What will happen if anyone tries to change the prophecies of God that are written in the Bible? Read Revelation 22:18–20.

# CHAPTER 3

## HOW THE PROPHETS INFLUENCE THE KINGS

### The Prophets and the Kings

Jacob's (Israel's) descendants are in trouble, especially the Northern Kingdom of Israel at this time. Israel has fallen into full-blown rebellion, following the evil ways of idolatry and pagan sacrifice that King Jeroboam I had established. Judah, the Southern Kingdom, is not doing a whole lot better. Idolatry was not new to the Israelites—they had slipped into it before in various times of their history, but this was becoming mass scale. King Jeroboam I had established it as the norm, and King Rehoboam had allowed it to take place in Judah as well.

Between 911-721 BC, until Israel fell, the Bible records that God sent at least fourteen prophets and other men of God to both the good and evil kings of Israel and Judah. He sent them to remind them of God's Law that brings peace and blessings, and to persuade them to return to Him and become godly kings over Israel and Judah. In this chapter, we will be talking about ten of these men.

## Azariah, Hanani, and King Asa of Judah

Information about King Asa can be found in 1 Kings 15; 2 Chronicles 14–16; Matthew 1:7.

King Asa, Judah's third king, was a "lamp" the Lord set had set up in Jerusalem, and he was a good king for most of his reign. He abolished altars used for idols, and took down images and groves, and he commanded Judah to follow the Law of Moses. God gave King Asa ten years of rest and peace. When it was time for him to go to war with the Ethiopians, he remembered God and prayed for help; and the Lord gave him victory. The Lord sent the prophet Azariah to him with this message:

> The LORD is with you, while ye be with him; and if ye seek him, he will be found of you; but if ye forsake him, he will forsake you. ... Be ye strong therefore, and let not your hands be weak: for your work shall be rewarded. (2 Chronicles 15:2–7)

All of the tribes of Judah and Benjamin, and those with them from Ephraim, Manasseh, and Simeon, came to live in King Asa's kingdom. Encouraged by the Lord, King Asa removed all the idols out of Judah and Benjamin that had been taken from Ephraim. The tribes made a covenant with the Lord, and anyone who chose not to be in covenant, was put to death. He put all the gold and silver in the temple that he and his father had dedicated, and he renewed the sacrificial altar. He even removed his mother, Maachah, from being queen because she worshiped idols, and he destroyed her idols. The Bible says he had a perfect heart, although he did not remove all the high places.

Later, evil King Baasha of Israel, who was in league with Ben-Hadad of Syria, began to surround Judah by building a fort around them. Being afraid, King Asa sent the silver and gold treasures that had been housed in the temple and his palace as a present to Ben-Hadad to try to persuade him to break his league with King Baasha. Asa's strategy worked, but the Lord sent Hanani the prophet to rebuke him for relying on the Syrian king instead of Him. Had he relied on the Lord, the king of Syria would have been delivered into his hands. Now he would be plagued with wars.

King Asa was angry with the prophet and threw him in prison. He also began oppressing some of his own people. As time went on, Asa was afflicted with a terrible disease in his feet, and once again, turned to someone other than God for his help.

LOUISE A. FUGATE

## Jehu and King Baasha of Israel

Information about King Baasha can be found in 1 Kings 15–16.

King Baasha had attained his position as king over Israel after he killed King Nadab, taking his place as king. He was evil and caused Israel to sin. While he was king, he killed the whole house of Jeroboam I, fulfilling the prophecy of Ahijah in 1 Kings 14:10–11. Then the Lord sent Hanani's son Jehu to Baasha with this prophecy:

> Behold, I will take away the posterity of Ba´-ash-a, and the posterity of his house; and will make thy house like the house of Jer-o-bo´-am the son of Ne´-bat. Him that dieth of Ba´-asha-a in the city shall the dogs eat; and him that dieth of his in the fields shall the fowls of the air eat. (1 Kings 16:3–4)

## Elijah and King Ahab of Israel

Information about King Ahab can be found in 1 Kings 16–18; 20–22; 2 Kings 10.

Elijah was a prophet from Gilead, who was deeply committed to obeying the commandments of the living God of Abraham, Isaac, and Jacob. He hated idolatry, and he aggressively came against it. While evil King Ahab was reigning over Israel, he married Jezebel, daughter of the king of Sidon. She was a worshiper of Baal and a priest of Astarte, influencing the king to build a Baal temple in Samaria, the capital of Israel, from where he reigned. Ahab was also a Baal worshiper. The following story shows the intense faith Elijah had in the Lord, and it shows the nonsense of worshiping a lifeless god.

One day God sent Elijah to King Ahab and told the king to bring the people of Israel, his 450 Baal prophets, and Jezebel's four hundred Asherah prophets to Mount Carmel. When he did, Elijah asked them, "How long halt ye between two opinions? If the LORD be God, follow him: but if Ba´-al, then follow him. And the people answered him not a word" (1 Kings 18:21).

So Elijah built a case for God and proved to them that their god of Baal could do nothing for them. He told them to go and get two bulls, one for him and one for the Baal prophets. He told them to cut up their bull into pieces to be used as a sacrifice and lay the pieces upon the wood, and he would do the same with the other bull. Neither altar would have fire. When the altars were completed, Elijah told them, "Call ye on the name of your gods, and I will call on the name of the LORD: and the God that answereth by fire, let him be God. And all the people answered and said, It is well spoken" (1 Kings 18:24).

After the Baal prophets prepared their bulls first, they called out to Baal for a half a day:

> O Ba'al, hear us. But there was no voice, nor any that answered. And they leaped upon the altar which was made. And it came to pass at noon, that E-li′-jah mocked them, and said, Cry aloud: for he is a god; either he is talking, or he is pursuing, or he is on a journey, or peradventure he sleepeth, and must be awaked. (1 Kings 18:26–27)

The Baal prophets shouted and even cut themselves with their weapons, right up until evening, but Baal would not answer them.

> And E-li′-jah said unto all the people, Come near unto me. And all the people came near unto him. And he repaired the altar of the LORD that was broken down. And E-li′-jah took twelve stones, according to the number of the tribes of the sons of Jacob, unto whom the word of the LORD came, saying, Israel shall be thy name: And with the stones he built an altar in the name of the LORD: and he made a trench about the altar, as great as would contain two measures of seed. And he put the wood in order, and cut the bullock in pieces, and laid him on the wood, and said, Fill four barrels with water, and pour it on the burnt sacrifice, and on the wood. And he said, Do it the second time. And they did it the second time. And he said, Do

it the third time. And they did it the third time. And the water ran round about the altar; and he filled the trench also with water.

And it came to pass at the time of the offering of the evening sacrifice, that E-li´-jah the prophet came nearer, and said, LORD God of Abraham, Isaac, and of Israel, let it be known this day that thou art God in Israel, and that I am thy servant, and that I have done all these things at thy word. Hear me, O LORD, hear me, that this people may know that thou art the LORD God, and that thou hast turned their heart back again. Then the fire of the LORD fell and consumed the burnt sacrifice, and the wood, and the stones, and the dust, and licked up the water that was in the trench. And when all the people saw it, they fell on their faces: and they said, The LORD, he is the God; the LORD, he is the God. (1 Kings 18:30–39)

After that, Elijah ordered the prophets of Baal to be killed by the sword.

Later on, King Ahab had another encounter with Elijah when he offered money to Naboth, a Jezreelite, for the land his vineyard was planted on. This was Naboth's allotted land from his forefathers. When Naboth refused the king's offer, his wife Jezebel devised a deceptive plan to falsely accuse Naboth of blaspheming God and the king. After the king ordered Naboth be stoned to death, the fate of him and Jezebel was sealed. Then Elijah gave this prophecy to King Ahab from the Lord:

Thus saith the LORD ... In the place where dogs licked the blood of Naboth shall dogs lick thy blood, even thine. ... I will bring evil upon thee, and will take away thy posterity, and will cut off from Ahab him that pisseth against the wall, and him that is shut up and left in Israel, And will make thine house like the house of Jer-o-bo´-am ... like the house of Ba´-ash-a ... thou hast provoked me to anger, and made Israel to sin. ... The dogs shall eat Jez´-e-bel by the wall of Jez´-reel. Him that dieth of Ahab in the city the dogs shall eat; and him that dieth in the field shall the fows of the air eat. (1 Kings 21:19–24)

When King Ahab heard that prophecy, he humbled himself before the Lord, and the Lord temporarily withheld the judgment He had promised him until the days of his son.

## Micaiah and King Ahab

On one occasion, King Ahab of Israel asked King Jehoshaphat of Judah to join him in taking back Ramoth-gilead, which Syria had taken. Before he would do that, Jehoshaphat wanted to inquire of the Lord. King Ahab asked his four hundred men if he should go to war, and they all said he should go, but King Jehoshaphat still wanted to hear from a prophet of the Lord. So the king sent for the prophet Micaiah. In the meantime, other prophets came forward and also told the king to go. When Micaiah arrived, he was told to tell the king the same thing that the other prophets had said, but instead, he spoke what God said to him: "I saw all Israel scattered upon the hills, as sheep that have not a shepherd: and the LORD said, These have no master: let them return every man to his house in peace" (1 Kings 22:17).

King Ahab became angry at Micaiah's words, and Micaiah told him that the Lord had put a lying spirit in each of his own prophets. With those words, King Ahab threw Micaiah in prison, and the two kings went up to battle with Ramoth-gilead. King Ahab was wounded by the Syrians and died in his chariot, fulfilling part of the prophecy given to him earlier by Elijah in 1 Kings 21:19–24: "And one washed the chariot in the pool of Sa-mar´-i-a; and the dogs licked up his blood; and they washed his armor; according unto the word of the LORD which he spake" (1 Kings 22:38).

After the battle was over, and King Jehoshaphat had gone home, God sent the prophet Jehu to him to rebuke him for helping the ungodly, but he did acknowledge him for taking away the groves out of his land.

The Hebrew word translated *groves is* "'ăshêyrâh."The meaning of the word is "Phoenician goddess...image of the same."[1]

## Jahaziel and King Jehoshaphat of Judah

Information about King Jehoshaphat can be found in 1 Kings 15, 22; 2 Chronicles 17, 19–21; Matthew 1:8.

When King Jehoshaphat was King of Judah, he walked in the ways of David and did not worship idols. God honored him and increased his wealth and honor, and he received gifts from all over Judah. He sent out his princes to the people in Judah and taught them from the book of the Law—the written Law that Moses had placed in the ark, and he drove the Sodomites out of his land. God put His fear upon those around Judah, so there was rest from war.

King Jehoshaphat set up righteous judges, Levites, priests, and leaders to judge the people and to help them with their controversies. One day when the Moabites, Ammonites, and others came to invade Judah, King Jehoshaphat became afraid and asked God for Judah's deliverance. God sent His Spirit upon Jahaziel, a Levite, and he gave the king this prophecy:

> Thus saith the LORD unto you, Be not afraid nor dismayed by reason of this great multitude; for the battle is not yours, but God's. ... Ye shall not need to fight in this battle: set yourselves, stand ye still, and see the salvation of the LORD with you, O Judah and Jerusalem: fear not, nor be dismayed; tomorrow go out against them: for the LORD will be with you. And Je-hosh´-a-phat bowed his head with his face to the ground: and all Judah and the inhabitants of Jerusalem fell before the LORD, worshiping the LORD. (2 Chronicles 20:15–18)

On the day of battle, King Jehoshaphat told the people of Jerusalem:

> Believe in the LORD your God, so shall ye be established; believe his prophets, so shall ye prosper. ... he appointed

singers unto the LORD, and that should praise the beauty of holiness, as they went out before the army, and to say, Praise the LORD; for his mercy endureth for ever. ... And when Judah came toward the watch tower in the wilderness, they looked unto the multitude, and, behold, they were dead bodies fallen to the earth, and none escaped. (2 Chronicles 20:20–24)

It took three days for Judah to carry away the spoils from that battle, and the countries around them knew that the Lord was with them. The Lord gave them peace during the remainder of Jehoshaphat's reign. Even though King Jehoshaphat obeyed God, he still did not take away the high places of worship.

## Elijah and King Ahaziah of Israel

Information about King Ahaziah can be found in 1 Kings 22; 2 Kings 1.

After King Ahab of Israel died in battle at Ramoth-gilead, his son Ahaziah became king, and he was an evil king who worshiped Baal. One day, King Ahaziah of Israel fell down through some lattice from an upper room and became sick. He sent his messengers to inquire of the god of Ekron, whose name was Baalzebub, as to whether or not he would recover from his sickness. God knew it, and he sent Elijah to meet these messengers on their way. Elijah gave them this prophecy from the Lord: "Is it not because there is not a God in Israel, that ye go to inquire of Ba´-al-ze´-bub the god of Ek´-ron? Now therefore thus saith the LORD, Thou shalt not come down from that bed on which thou art gone up, but shalt surely die" (2 Kings 1:3–4).

## Elisha Asks for Elijah's Spirit

A time came when Elijah and his attendant, Elisha, both knew that God was getting ready to take Elijah away. Just before the Lord took him, he asked Elisha what he could do for him. "E-li´-sha said, I pray thee, let a double portion of thy spirit be upon me. And he said, ...if thou see me when I am taken from thee, it shall be so unto thee; but if not, it shall not be so" (2 Kings 2:9-10).

> And it came to pass, as they still went on, and talked, that, behold, there appeared a chariot of fire, and horses of fire, and parted them both asunder; and E-li´-jah went up by a whirlwind into heaven. And E-li´-sha saw it, and he cried, my father, my father, the chariot of Israel, and the horsemen thereof. And he saw him no more: and he took hold of his own clothes, and rent (tore) them in two pieces. He took up also the mantle of E-li´-jah that fell from him, and went back, and stood by the bank of Jordan; And he took the mantle of E-li´-jah that fell from him, and smote the waters, and said, Where is the LORD God of E-li´-jah? And when he also had smitten the waters, they parted hither and thither: and E-li´-sha went over. (2 Kings 2:11–14)

The Hebrew word translated *mantle* is "'addereth." The meaning of the word is "garment, glory, goodly...robe."[2] The prophets, who were watching said, "The Spirit of E-l´-jah doth rest on E-li´-sha" (2 Kings 2:15). They sent for fifty men, who searched for three days to find Elijah, but he was nowhere to be found. Just as God had worked miracles through Elijah by His Spirit, He would do the same through Elisha.

## Elisha and King Joram (Jehoram) of Israel

Information about King Joram can be found in 2 Kings 1, 3, 5–6, 8–9.

King Joram, the son of King Ahab, put away Baal's image, but practiced the same sins as evil King Jeroboam I. Earlier, after King Ahab's death, the king of Moab began to rebel against Israel. So King Joram of Israel asked King Jehoshaphat of Judah to go to war with him against the king of Moab, and the king of Edom joined them. After they had journeyed for a week, there was no water for them or their cattle, and they began to believe among themselves that the Lord was going to deliver them into Moab's hands.

King Jehoshaphat wanted to consult with one of the Lord's prophets as to what they were to do about not having any water. So they went to see Elisha the prophet. Elisha was not happy to see King Joram of Israel and told him to go to the prophets of his parents; but because of King Jehoshaphat of Judah, Elisha listened. Then Elisha told them to bring him a minstrel, and when the minstrel played, "the hand of the Lord came upon him" (2 Kings 3:15), and he told them what the Lord said:

> Make this valley full of ditches. ... Ye shall not see wind, neither shall ye see rain; yet that valley shall be filled with water, that ye may drink, both ye, and your cattle, and your beasts. And this is but a light thing in the sight of the LORD: he will deliver the Mo´-abites also into your hand. And ye shall smite every fenced city, and every choice city, and shall fell every good tree, and stop all wells of water, and mar every good piece of land with stones. (2 Kings 3:16–19)

The next morning after they finished sacrificing to the Lord, the country was filled with water that came from Edom. When the Moabites heard that the kings had come to fight with them, they geared up for battle and went to the border. It was early in the morning, and the sun was shining on the water and the water looked red like blood, making them think that the kings had killed each other. When the Moabites went down into the Israelite camp, the Israelites, who were waiting for them, killed many of them. They chased them home and killed them in their own land.

## Elisha and King Jehoram of Judah

Information about King Jehoram can be found in 1 Kings 22; 2 Kings 8–9; 2 Chronicles 21–22.

After King Jehoshaphat of Judah died, his son Jehoram succeeded him as the fifth King over Judah. King Jehoram was evil just like the Kings of

Israel. He married wicked King Ahab's daughter Athaliah and killed all of his brothers to gain more power. Even so, the Lord was faithful to Judah "because of the covenant that he had made with David" (2 Chronicles 21:7).

King Jehoram influenced Judah to worship in the high places. The Lord sent a message to the King from Elijah:

> Because thou hast not walked in the ways of Je-hosh´-a-phat thy father, nor in the ways of A´-sa king of Judah, But hast walked in the way of the kings of Israel, and hast made Judah and the inhabitants of Jerusalem to go a whoring ... with a great plague will the LORD smite thy people, and thy children, and thy wives, and all thy goods: And thou shalt have great sickness by disease of thy bowels, until thy bowels fall out by reason of the sickness day by day. (2 Chronicles 21:12–15)

Before King Jehoram of Judah died of the Lord's plague, the Lord sent the Philistines and the Arabians to Judah. They robbed the king of everything he had, including his wives and all but one son; and he died of the Lord's plague two years later. After his death, his son, Ahaziah, reigned in his place as King of Judah.

## Elisha and Jehu

Information about Jehu can be found in 1 Kings 19; 2 Kings 9–10.

One day, King Ahaziah of Judah teamed up with King Joram of Israel to go to war against Hazael, King of Syria. During the battle, King Joram of Israel was wounded and went to Jezreel to heal. So King Ahaziah of Judah went to see him there. While Ahaziah was gone, God gave Elisha, the prophet, a message for King Jehoshaphat's son Jehu in Ramoth-gilead. The prophets' children were there, and Elisha sent one of them with a message for Jehu and a box of oil to pour on Jehu's head. When the prophet's child found Jehu, he poured the oil on his head and gave him Elisha's message:

Thus saith the LORD God of Israel, I have anointed thee king over the people of the LORD, even over Israel. And thou shalt smite the house of Ahab thy master, that I may avenge the blood of my servants the prophets, and the blood of all the servants of the LORD, at the hand of Jez´-e-bel. For the whole house of Ahab shall perish ... And I will make the house of Ahab like the house of Jer-o-bo´-am the son of Ne´-bat, and like the house of Ba´-asha the son of A-hi´-jah: And the dogs shall eat Jez´-e-bel. (2 Kings 9:6–10)

Jehu killed Jezebel's son, King Joram of Israel, and succeeded him as king. He killed King Ahaziah of Judah and everyone in Jezreel and Samaria who were related to Ahab, including Ahab's seventy sons, his priests, and all the people associated with Ahab. Then he killed Jezebel, King Joram's mother, by ordering her to be thrown down and trodden under by horses. There was not enough left of her body to bury, fulfilling the prophecy of Elijah in 1 Kings 21:19–24 and the prophecy of Elisha in 2 Kings 9:6–10.

Jehu also ordered all Baal worshipers to come into the temple of Baal, where he killed them all. He abolished Baal worship in Israel, but he still committed the sins of Jeroboam I, causing Israel to sin by worshiping the golden calves at Bethel and Dan. The Lord told Jehu:

Because thou hast done well in executing that which is right in mine eyes, and hast done unto the house of Ahab according to all that was in mine heart, thy children of the fourth generation shall sit on the throne of Israel. But Jehu took no need to walk in the law of the LORD God of Israel with all his heart: for he departed not from the sins of Jer-o-bo´-am, which made Isarel to sin. (2 Kings 10:30–31)

# Zechariah, Elisha, and King Joash (Jehoash) of Judah

Information about King Joash can be found in 2 Kings 11–12; 2 Chronicles 24; and Matthew 23.

When Athaliah, King Ahaziah's mother, found out that her son Ahaziah had been killed, she started killing the royal family of Judah. Jehosheba, King Ahaziah's sister, took King Ahaziah's son Joash, and hid him away so that he could one day be king of Judah. While he was in hiding, Athaliah reigned over Judah for six years. Then Joash, at seven years old, was brought out of hiding and was crowned king of Judah. At that time, the people of Judah destroyed the temple of Baal and its altars and images; and they also killed the priest of Baal. Then they killed Athaliah with the sword. "And Je-hoi´-a-da (the priest) made a covenant between the LORD and the King and the people, that they should be the LORD'S people; between the King also and the people" (2 Kings 11:17).

King Joash didn't abolish the high places where the people burnt their incense and sacrificed their offerings, but he did set up a system to collect money to repair the damaged places of the Lord's house. Later, when King Hazael of Syria began attacking all Israel's coastline, captured Gath, and was headed for Jerusalem, King Joash became afraid and sent the sacred items and the gold items that were in the temple and in his palace to King Hazael, hoping that he would turn from Jerusalem, which he did.

King Joash acted as a good king as long as Jehoiada, the priest, was with him; but when Jehoiada died, things changed. He began to listen to the princes of Judah, and they began worshiping idols. Still, God sent men of God to them to bring them back to Him.

And the spirit of God came upon Zech-a-ri´-ah the son of Je-hoi´-a-da the priest, which stood above the people, and said unto them, Thus saith God, Why transgress ye the commandments of the LORD, that ye cannot prosper? Because ye have forsaken the LORD, he hath laso forsaken you. And they conspired against him, and stoned him with stones at the commandment of the king in the court of the house of the LORD. Thus Jo´-ash the king remembered not the kindness which Je-hoi´-a-da his father had done to him, but slew his son. (2 Chronicles 24:20–22)

King Joash of Judah died when his servants conspired against him and killed him.

## The Man of God and King Amaziah of Judah

Information about King Amaziah can be found in 2 Kings 14; 2 Chronicles 25.

King Amaziah, son of King Jehoash of Judah, was a good king over Judah for a while, but he left the high places where the people sacrificed and offered burnt offerings. He killed those who had killed his father, King Jehoash of Judah; he killed ten thousand Edomites in the Valley of Salt, and he captured Selah (in Edom).

When he built up a great army, hiring one hundred thousand mighty men from Israel, God sent a man of God to him to tell him not to do that, because God was not with Israel. So King Amaziah sent the men from Israel home and went on to fight his battle with Seir, which he won. However, while he had been at war, the mighty men he had sent back to Israel invaded Judah, killing three thousand of his people. On top of everything else, King Amaziah had brought idols to his home from Seir and began to worship them. God sent a man of God to him again, only this time with a message about his own death:

> Why hast thou sought after the gods of the people, which could not deliver their own people out of thine hand? ... Then the prophet forbare, and said, I know that God hath determined to destroy thee, because thou hast done this, and hast not hearkened unto my counsel. (2 Chronicles 25:15–16)

Later, King Amaziah of Judah was engaged in battle in Judah with King Jehoash of Israel, which had been planned by God. Judah was defeated, and King Amaziah was captured and taken to Jerusalem. The king of Israel attacked Jerusalem, breaking down a large section of its wall. He took the gold and silver and vessels from the temple; and he took treasures and hostages from the palace. Amaziah lived for fifteen more years, but fled from Jerusalem to Lachish when a conspiracy was formed against him. The conspirators chased him down at Lachish and killed him.

## Jonah the Prophet

Information can be found in the Book of Jonah; Matthew 12.

It was probably some time during the reign of King Jeroboam II that God called Jonah to go to Nineveh, the Assyrian capital. Nineveh was a wicked city, and God told Jonah to go to them and warn them of His impending judgment. Jonah was to tell them to repent. At first, Jonah did not go, and because of his disobedience, God arranged for a whale to swallow him for three days until Jonah submitted to God and agreed to go to Nineveh. Some think of this as a myth or fairy tale, but in the Book of Matthew, we find Jesus referring back to this story in the Old Testament, when He was speaking about His own death and resurrection three days later:

> For as Jonah was three days and three nights in the whale's belly; so shall the Son of man be three days and three nights in the heart of the earth. The men of Nin´-e-veh shall rise in judgment with this generation, and shall condemn it: because they repented at the preaching of Jonah; and, behold, a greater than Jonah is here. (Matthew 12:40–41)

## In Conclusion

Israel, for the most part, had forgotten their Maker; and now they were living like all the pagans that surrounded them. As you can see, idolatry was the norm for the kings of Israel, which kept their people in bondage to idolatry as well. Judah, however, was still the light between the two nations. God was constantly sending His prophets and men of God to the kings to guide them into doing the right things, and He also sent those godly men to prophesy of their fate, if they did not obey. It is easy to see how willing God was to help the kings when they would turn from their sins and partner with Him.

Israel, as a nation, was rejecting God, and now we will see how God will send His prophets to tell them of their impending doom. Will they turn to Him and repent of their sins, or will they keep living in rebellion and suffer the consequences?

# Deeper Insights:

1. Read 1 Kings 19:18. God told Elijah, "Yet I have left me seven thousand in Israel, all the knees which have not bowed unto Ba´-al, and every mouth which hath not kissed him?"

   After reading Romans 9:25–29 and 11:1–11, what do you think God meant by the "seven thousand"?

2. When the Spirit of God was upon Elijah, he performed miracles. Read the following Scriptures to learn how God miraculously empowered him: 1 Kings 17:14–24; 2 Kings 2:1–8

3. When the Lord took Elijah up from the earth, Elisha was given Elijah's mantle (see 2 Kings 2:9–10), and he was also given "supernatural" abilities through the Spirit of God. Read the following Scriptures below to see how the Spirit of God miraculously moved in his life:

   2 Kings 2:9–25      2 Kings 5
   2 Kings 4:1–44      2 Kings 6:1–7

4. Read Jonah, chapters 1–4. Why did God tell Jonah to go to Nineveh? How did Nineveh respond when Jonah gave them God's message?

# CHAPTER 4

## THE FALL OF THE NORTHERN
## KINGDOM OF ISRAEL

### Why Do Israel and Judah Become Wicked?

To get a grasp on this question, we can once again look at Romans 1:20–27, where Paul is talking to the Romans in his letter to them. Paul is telling them that God has made Himself known to man since Creation—"even His eternal power and Godhead; so that they are without excuse" (v. 20). The problem is that humans forget to praise God and thank Him for what He has done. Then they become "vain in their imaginations" and begin to think they are wise within themselves. When they think they are wise, they become foolish, and "their foolish heart was darkened" (v. 21). That is what happened to King Solomon and the Jewish nation back then. Paul says they changed "the glory of the incorruptible God" (v. 23) into images of man and animals, and other creatures. "[They] changed the truth of God into a lie, and and worshiped and served the creature more than the Creator" (v. 25). God "gave them up unto vile affections: for even their women did change the natural use into that which is against nature" (v. 26). Women were having sex with women and men were having sex with men. They knew that what they were doing was "worthy of death" (v. 32) according to God's Law, but they continued to do what they wanted to do.

> Even as they did not like to retain God in their knowledge, God gave them over to a reprobate mind, to do those things which are not convenient; Being filled with all unrighteousness, fornication, wickedness, covetousness, maliciousness; full of envy, murder,

debate, deceit, malignity; whisperers, Backbiters, haters of God, despiteful, proud, boasters, inventors of evil things, disobedient to parents, Without understanding, covenantbreakers, without natural affection, implacable, unmerciful. (Romans 1:28–31)

## Amos the Prophet and King Jeroboam II

Information about King Jeroboam II can be found in 2 Kings 13–14; Amos 7.

As time went on, and wickedness worsened in Israel and Judah, God began to send more prophets who pointed out the sins they were commiting, warning them that judgment was coming, if they did not repent.

Amos was a shepherd from Judah, who was called by God to be a prophet to the Northern Kingdom of Israel. Sometime during the evil reign of King Jeroboam II, Amos was given a prophetic message of Israel's future. God gave him symbolic visions about Israel's sinful condition and the judgment of God that would be coming upon Israel (see Amos 7–9). He preached about their spiritual corruption, sexual perversion, violence, robbery, and justice for the needy and poor who had been oppressed. He also announced judgment on Judah because they were not keeping God's commandments either. Israel's neighbors: Damascus, Gaza, Tyrus, Edom, Ammon, and Moab wouldn't be exempt either. They would be judged for their part in the captivity of Israel when it came to pass. The Lord had punished Israel in many ways over the years by bringing hardships upon them so they would return to Him in their hour of need, but now they seemed to be in all-out rebellion. Amos relayed God's messages to them:

> The virgin of Israel is fallen; she shall no more rise: she is forsaken upon her land; there is none to raise her up. …
> Forasmuch therefore as your treading is upon the poor, and ye take from him burdens of wheat: ye have built houses of hewn stone, but ye shall not dwell in them; ye have planted pleasant vineyards, but ye shall not drink

wine of them. For I know your manifold transgressions and your mighty sins: they afflict the just, they take a bribe, and they turn aside the poor in the gate from their right. (Amos 5:2–12)

The Lord pleaded with them to come back to Him: "Seek good, and not evil, that ye may live: and so the LORD, the God of hosts, shall be with you, as ye have spoken" (Amos 5:14).

The Lord gave prophecies to Amos about the downfall of both Israel and King Jeroboam II, which were not well received.

The high places of Isaac shall be desolate, and the sanctuaries of Israel shall be laid waste; and I will rise against the house of Jer-o-bo´-am with the sword. Then Am-a-zi´-ah the priest of Beth-el sent to Jer-o-bo´-am king of Israel, saying, Amos hath conspired against thee in the midst of the house of Israel: the land is not able to bear all his words. For thus Amos saith, Jer-o-bo´-am shall die by the sword, and Israel shall surely be led away captive out of their own land. (Amos 7:9–11)

Amaziah told Amos to stop prophesying about Israel and to leave their land, "for it is the king's chapel, and it is the king's court" (Amos 7:13). Amos gave this prophetic response:

The LORD … said unto me, Go prophesy unto my people Israel. Now therefore hear thou the word of the LORD: Thou sayest, Prophesy not against Israel, and drop not thy word against the house of Isaac. Therefore thus saith the LORD; Thy wife shall be a harlot in the city, and thy sons and thy daughters shall fall by the sword, and thy land shall be divided by line; and thou shalt die in a polluted land: and Israel shall surely go into captivity forth of his land. (Amos 7:15–17)

# Isaiah the Prophet

In the same year that King Azariah died, the Lord gave to Isaiah, a man who lived in Jerusalem, a vision of Judah's sinful condition: "I have nourished and brought up children, and they have rebelled against me" (Isaiah 1:2). "From the sole of the foot even unto the head there is no soundness in it; but wounds, and bruises, and putrifying sores: they have not been closed, neither bound up, neither mollified with ointment" (Isaiah 1:6).

Isaiah calls Judah to repentance and gives him a vision of the Lord in heaven:

> Wash you, make you clean, put away the evil of your doings from before mine eyes; cease to do evil; Learn to do well; seek judgment, relieve the oppressed, judge the fatherless, plead for the widow. Come now, and let us reason together, saith the LORD: though your sins be as scarlet, they shall be as white as snow; though they be red like crimson, they shall be as wool. (Isaiah 1:16–18)

> I saw also the Lord sitting upon a throne, high and lifted up, and his train filled the temple. Above it stood the ser´-a-phim: each one had six wings; with twain he covered his face, and with twain he covered his feet, and with twain he did fly. And one cried unto another, and said, Holy, holy, holy, is the LORD of hosts: the whole earth is full of his glory. And the posts of the door moved at the voice of him that cried, and the house was filled with smoke. (Isaiah 6:1–4)

> Then said I, Woe is me! For I am undone; because I am a man of unclean lips, and I dwell in the midst of a people of unclean lips: for mine eyes have seen the king, the LORD of hosts. Then flew one of the ser´-a-phim unto me, having a live coal in his hand, which he had taken with the tongs from off the altar: And he laid it upon

my mouth, and said, Lo, this hath touched thy lips; and thine iniquity is taken away, and thy sin purged. Also I heard the voice of the Lord, saying, Whom shall I send, and who will go for us? Then said I, Here am I; send me. And he said, Go, and tell this people, Hear ye indeed, but understand not; and see ye indeed, but perceive not. (Isaiah 6:5–9)

## The Prophets Hosea and Micah

Hosea was called by the Lord to be a prophet to the lost people in the Northern Kingdom, because Israel had turned their backs on God to practice pagan religions. They had forgotten their husband, the Lord, and had gone after other lovers. So that Hosea could understand that Israel was as an unfaithful wife, or a harlot to God, He told Hosea to marry a harlot who would be unfaithful to him. Hosea pointed out the sins of Israel to the people:

> No truth, nor mercy, nor knowledge of God in the land. By swearing, and lying, and killing, and stealing, and committing adultery, they break out and blood toucheth blood. ... the spirit of whoredoms hath caused them to err and they have gone a whoring from under their God. (Hosea 4:1–13)

> "Israel hath forgotten his Maker and buildeth temples; and Judah hath multiplied fenced cities: but I will send a fire upon his cities, and it shall devour the palaces thereof" (Hosea 8:13–14).

> When E´-phra-im spake trembling, he exalted himself in Israel; but when he offended in Ba´-al, he died. And now they sin more and more, and have made them molten images of their silver, and idols according to their own understanding, all of it the work of the craftsmen: they

say of them, Let the men that sacrifice kiss the calves.
(Hosea 13:1–2)

The Hebrew word translated *Ephraim* is "'E'phrayim." The meaning
of the word is "a son of Joseph; also the tribe descended from him, and
its territory."[1]

The prophets Hosea and Micah spoke primarily to Judah. They
prophesied what was about ready to happen to Israel:

> E'-phra-im is smitten, their root is dried up, they shall
> bear no fruit: yea, though they bring forth, yet will I
> slay even the beloved fruit of their womb. My God will
> cast them away, because they did not hearken unto him:
> and they shall be wanderers among the nations. (Hosea
> 9:16–17)

> My people are destroyed for lack of knowledge: because
> thou hast rejected knowledge, I will also reject thee, that
> thou shalt be no priest to me: seeing thou hast forgotten
> the law of thy God, I will also forget thy children. As they
> were increased, so they sinned against me: therefore will
> I change their glory into shame. (Hosea 4:6–7)

> I will make Sa-mar'-i-a as a heap of the field, and as
> plantings of a vineyard: and I will pour down the stones
> thereof into the valley, and I will discover the foundations
> thereof. And all the graven images thereof shall be beaten
> to pieces, and all the hires thereof shall be burned with
> the fire, and all the idols thereof will I lay desolate: for she
> gathered it of the hire of a harlot, and they shall return to
> the hire of a harlot. (Micah 1:6–7)

Even with the promises of judgment, God in His love for them, still
cried out and pleaded for them to come back to Him before He brought
judgment. "O Israel thou hast destroyed thyself; but in me is thine help. I
will be thy King: where is any other that may save thee in all thy cities?"

(Hosea 13:9–10). "O Israel, return unto the LORD thy God; for thou hast fallen by thine iniquity. … say unto him, Take away all iniquity, and receive us graciously: so will we render the calves [offerings] of our lips" (Hosea 14:1–2).

## Hope for Israel in the Last Days

At that time, it was clear that the people of Israel would fall under God's judgment, and they would become wanderers; however, a day will come in our future when Israel will be gathered and restored by Jesus, their Messiah, to live with Him forever. Someday in the future, they will receive mercy and forgiveness when Jesus makes His second return to the earth in the last days. It will not be because they deserve it, but because God made an everlasting covenant with their forefathers Abraham, Isaac, and Jacob; and He is faithful. His name will be glorified. Hosea continued to give Israel God's promises: "I will betroth thee unto me for ever; yea, I will betroth thee unto me in righteousness, and in judgment, and in loving-kindness, and in mercies. I will even betroth thee unto me in faithfulness: and thou shalt know the LORD" (Hosea 2:19–20).

> I will heal their backsliding, I will love them freely: for mine anger is turned away from him. … E´-phra-im shall say, What have I to do any more with idols? I have heard him, and observed him: I am like a green fir tree. From me is thy fruit found. (Hosea 14:4–8)

The Hebrew word translated *betroth* is "'âras." The meaning of the word is "to engage for matrimony…espouse."[2]

In those days, Assyria was busy conquering nations and requiring payment of tribute money from each of them. During this time, Micah was concerned about the poor people, who were being oppressed by the wealthy leaders, prophets, and priests of Judah. "They covet fields and take them by violence; and houses, and take them away: so they oppress a man and his house, even a man and his heritage" (Micah 2:2).

Hear this, I pray you, ye heads of the house of Jacob, and princes of the house of Israel, that abhor judgment and pervert all equity. They build up Zion with blood, and Jerusalem with iniquity. The heads thereof judge for reward, and the priests thereof teach for hire, and the prophets thereof divine for money. (Micah 3:9–11)

Micah was concerned because now the same sins that had infected Israel had spread to Judah "for her wound is incurable; for it is come unto Judah; he is come unto the gate of my people, even to Jerusalem" (Micah 1:9).

Micah prophesied that Judah would be exiled into Babylon, but he also gave promises that the Lord would deliver them from Babylon as well:

Be in pain, and labor to bring forth, O daughter of Zion, like a woman in travail: for now shalt thou go forth out of the city, and thou shalt dwell in the field, and thou shalt go even to Babylon; there shalt thou be delivered; there the LORD shall redeem thee from the hand of thine enemies. (Micah 4:10)

Micah prophesied that one day a ruler would come from Bethlehem. He was speaking of the birth of Jesus Christ, the Son of God, Who would be coming soon.

But thou Beth-lehem Eph´-ra-tah, though thou be little among the thousands of Judah, yet out of thee shall he come forth unto me that is to be ruler in Israel; whose goings forth have been from of old, from everlasting. Therefore will he give them up, until the time that she which travaileth hath brought forth: then the remnant of his brethren shall return unto the children of Israel. (Micah 5:2–3)

He will turn again, he will have compassion upon us; he will subdue our iniquities; and thou wilt cast all their sins

into the depths of the sea. Thou wilt perform the truth to
Jacob, and the mercy to Abraham, which thou hast sworn
unto our fathers from the days of old. (Micah 7:19–20)

## Isaiah and King Ahaz of Judah

Information can be found in 2 Kings 16; 2 Chronicles 27–28.

King Ahaz, the twelfth king of Judah, was not a good king. He kept
the high places and offered sacrifices, including his own children, and
he burned offerings in places other than the temple, as had been set up
by God with Moses. At that time, King Rezin of Syria and King Pekah
of Israel allied together to attack Jerusalem and set up a king there. The
Lord sent Isaiah, the prophet to go and speak to King Ahaz about them:

> Take heed, and be quiet; fear not, neither be fainthearted
> for the two tails of these smoking firebrands, for the
> fierce anger of Re´-zin with Syria, and of the son of Rem-
> a-li´-ah [King Pekah] … It [the evil alliance] shall not
> stand, neither shall it come to pass. … If ye will not
> believe, surely ye shall not be established. (Isaiah 7:4–9)

Then Isaiah, trying to encourage King Ahaz to trust in God, gave him
a prophetic sign He prophesied about the birth of Jesus Christ:

> Therefore the Lord himself shall give you a sign: Behold,
> a virgin shall conceive, and bear a son, and shall call his
> name Im-man´-u-el. Butter and honey shall he eat, that
> he may know to refuse the evil, and choose the good. For
> before the child shall know to refuse the evil, and choose
> the good, the land that thou abhorrest shall be forsaken
> of both her kings. (Isaiah 7:14–16)

The plan of King Pekah of Israel and King Rezin of Syria failed, and
they were defeated.

One day, King Ahaz, who was fearful of the Syrians, called King Tiglathpileser III to come and help Judah. He sent presents of silver and gold from the Lord's temple and from his palace. So King Tiglathpileser captured Damascus, a large city in Syria, taking the residents to the city of Kir, and he killed King Rezin.

Later, King Ahaz went to see King Tiglathpileser. When he saw the king's altar, he liked it so much, that he sent a pattern to his priest Urijah to build one for him. When he arrived back at his palace and saw the new altar, he began making offerings on it and sprinkling it with the blood from his peace offerings. He also brought in the Altar of Burnt Offering that was used at the Lord's house and put it north of his new altar that Urijah built. He commanded Urijah to use the new altar instead of the bronze altar, which he would use for consultation. He modified the bronze stands and bowls and removed the covered area and the king's entry of the Lord's house. He destroyed the vessels in the Lord's house and closed it up, setting up shrines in all the cities. He did all of this for the king of Assyria.

Later, after the Edomites came and defeated Judah, and the Philistines invaded the lower part of Judah, King Ahaz became fearful again and sent a message to King Tiglathpileser of Assyria. King Tiglathpileser refused to help him, which only kindled more anger inside King Ahaz towards the Lord, and he began to worship the foreign gods. He brought further destruction to the things of the Lord and closed down the temple, setting up altars throughout the city. This downhill slide into idolatry would follow him to his death.

He sacrificed unto the gods of Damascus, which smote him: and he said, Because the gods of the kings of Syria help them, therefore will I sacrifice to them, that they may help me. But they were the ruin of him, and of all Israel. And Ahaz gathered together the vessels of the house of God, and cut in pieces the vessels of the house of God, and shut up the doors of the house of the LORD, and he made him altars in every corner of Jerusalem. And in every several city of Judah he made high places to burn incense unto other gods, and provoked to anger the LORD God of his fathers. (2 Chronicles 28:23–25)

# The Lord Sends Israel into Exile

Hoshea became the last king of Israel, reigning from Samaria, and he was an evil king. King Shalmaneser of Assyria came to attack Hoshea. He discovered Hoshea was a traitor to him, for he no longer paid tribute to him, but instead had sent envoys to king So of Egypt. King Shalmaneser threw him into prison and invaded his land, besieging Samaria for three years. Then later, Shalmaneser came and deported the Israelites to Assyria in 721 BC. He settled them in "Ha´-la and in Ha´-bor by the river of Go´-zan, and in the cities of the Medes" (2 Kings 18:11).

Why did the Lord do this? "Because they obeyed not the voice of the LORD their God, but transgressed his covenant, and all that Moses the servant of the LORD commanded, and would not hear them, not do them" (2 Kings 18:12). "The children of Israel walked in all the sins of Jer-o-bó-am" (2 Kings 17:22).

The exile of Israel was the fulfillment of the prophecy given to Jeroboam I by Ahijah:

> For the LORD shall smite Israel, as a reed is shaken in the water, and he shall root up Israel out of this good land, which he gave to their fathers, and shall scatter them beyond the river [Euphrates], because they have made their groves, provoking the LORD to anger. And he shall give Israel up because of the sins of Jer-o-bo´-am, who did sin, and who made Israel to sin. (1 Kings 14:15–16)

The Lord, out of His love for Israel and Judah, had sent prophets to them to try and turn their hearts to Him before His judgment would fall upon them; but Israel, the Northern Kingdom, rejected Him and would not turn back to Him.

> They would not hear, but hardened their necks ... did not believe in the LORD their God. ... they rejected his statutes, and his covenant that he made with their fathers ... they followed vanity, and became vain, and went after the heathen that were round about them ...

and made them molten images … worshiped all the host of heaven, and served Ba´-al. … they caused their sons and their daughters to pass through the fire, and used divination and enchantments, and sold themselves to do evil in the sight of the LORD, to provoke him to anger. Therefore the LORD was very angry with Israel, and removed them out of his sight: there was none left but the tribe of Judah only. (2 Kings 17:14–18)

When the king of Assyria took over Samaria, the capital of Israel, he brought people in from other countries to live there "from Babylon, and from Cu´-thab, and from A´-va, and from Ha´-math, and from Se-phar-va´-im" (2 Kings 17:24).

The Lord sent lions to kill some of these people because they did not worship Him. So the king of Assyria gave an order to bring a priest back from exile that had been taken captive from Samaria to instruct the people in the requirements of the God of the land. Even though the priest came and taught them how to worship the Lord, each national group made their own gods in the towns where they settled. These were the names of their gods:

Suc´-coth-be´-noth … Ner´-gal … A-shi´-ma … Nib´-haz … Tartak … and the Seph´-ar-vites burnt their children in fire to A-dram´-me-lech … and A-nam´-me-lech. So they feared the LORD, and made unto themselves of the lowest of them priests of the high places, which sacrificed for them in the houses of the high places. They feared the LORD, and served their own gods. (2 Kings 17:30–31)

# In Conclusion

Israel had forsaken the living God Who had created them and made them into a great nation. Now He would reject them. The ten tribes of the Northern Kingdom would never return to Samaria from exile. They would become known as "the lost tribes of Israel." They had lost their love for God. He had allowed them to be swallowed up by the mixed nations in Assyria to serve their gods and to be isolated from the rest of their Hebrew family that God had set apart as His own.

Yet, God, in His mercy, will someday restore them in our future, which is yet to come. Israel's sins will be forgiven because of Christ's death and resurrection and God's faithfulness to His covenant with their forefathers. God keeps His word!

God also had His watchful eye on Judah, who was not doing much better than Israel; however, unlike Israel, Judah still had a few good kings who loved Him. These kings would lead the people in righteousness. As we shall see, God will accelerate His use of the prophets in Judah, giving many more warnings and prophesies than He had in Israel. The nation of Judah has watched the Northern Kingdom fall. The Lord has rejected the ten tribes of their father, Jacob, and sent them away to Assyria. Will this have an impact on them? They, too, were turning away from God to live the same lifestyles as Israel.

## Deeper Insights:

1. Read Amos 7–8 to learn about the visions God gave Amos regarding Israel's condition.

2. The Bible is very clear that the kings of Israel were evil. What were the sins of Israel? Read 2 Kings 17:7–17, 22.

3. What does the Lord say is good? Read Micah 6:8.

4. Why do you think it was necessary for God to reject Israel?

   Some of the people from Israel did escape, but why do you think it was necessary for some of them to die and the rest of them to be swallowed up in the nations of Assyria?

5. Even though they would not return to Samaria from exile, God did promise them a day of restoration in the "last days." Read Isaiah 45:18–25, 54; Hosea 2:14–23; Amos 9:11–15.

# CHAPTER 5

## REVIVALS IN THE SOUTHERN KINGDOM OF JUDAH

## King Hezekiah Brings Revival

Information about King Hezekiah can be found in 2 Chronicles 29; 2 Kings 18–20; Isaiah 38.

There were some kings in Judah who still loved the Lord, and they would do what they could to spiritually rally Judah for God. King Hezekiah, Judah's thirteenth king, was one of those kings. He feared and respected the Lord, and he was completely devoted to Him. He was determined to swing Judah, and those left in Israel, back to the Lord. The Bible says he "walked as David." He told them, "Now it is in mine heart to make a covenant with the LORD God of Israel, that his fierce wrath may turn away from us. ... the LORD has chosen you to stand before him, to serve him, and that ye should minister unto him, and burn incense" (2 Chronicles 29:10–11).

King Hezekiah wrote letters to everyone in Judah, and to those who had escaped captivity in Israel, urging them to return to the God of their forefathers, and He invited them to come to Jerusalem to celebrate the Passover, which God had commanded them to continually do to remember how He had delivered them from the plague of death in Egypt. He and the princes sent out this proclamation to all the cities, including people in Israel who had escaped.

> Ye children of Israel, turn again unto the LORD God
> of Abraham, Isaac, and Israel, and he will return to the

remnant of you, that are escaped out of the hand of the kings of Assyria. ... Now be ye not stiffnecked, as your fathers were, but yield yourselves unto the LORD, and enter into his sanctuary, which he hath sanctified for ever: and serve the LORD your God, that the fierceness of his wrath may turn away from you. For if ye turn again unto the LORD, your brethren and your children shall find compassion before them that lead them captive, so that they shall come again into this land: for the LORD your God is gracious and merciful, and will not turn away his face from you, if ye return unto him. (2 Chronicles 30:6–9)

Some in Israel who read the proclamation laughed and made fun of it, but some felt drawn in their hearts to go. At that time, God unified the people of Judah to follow their king as he re-established the Feast of Unleavened Bread (the Passover). Music, worship, and praise were heard in the Lord's house, and blood was again sprinkled upon the Altar to bring reconciliation between the people and the Lord, making atonement for all the people of Judah. The Jews, who came seeking God from Israel, were in need of being cleansed. The king prayed for them, and God healed them. Two thousand bullocks and seventeen thousand sheep were given for the sacrifices, and the celebration lasted for seven days. It was the greatest celebration since the days of King Solomon.King Hezekiah went on to destroy the idols and places of idol worship "and brake in pieces the brazen serpent that Moses had made: for unto those days the children of Israel did burn incense to it: and he called it Ne-hush´-tan" (2 Kings 18:4).

The Hebrew word translated *Nehushtan* is "ne-hush´-tan." The meaning of the word is "something made of copper, i.e. the copper serpent of the Desert."[1]

In looking back in Numbers 21, when the Israelites were wandering in the desert those forty years, we find information about this "brazen serpent." The Israelites had begun to speak against God and complain about not having food or water instead of trusting Him to provide it for them. God had sent poisonous snakes into their camp, which killed many of them. When the people acknowledged their sin, and Moses prayed, God instructed Moses to make the "brazen serpent." Anyone who was bitten by a snake could look up at the serpent and live. The Israelites had been using this old "brazen serpent" for an idol.

King Hezekiah also re-established the tithing system. The people brought in oil, honey, wine, corn, crops, sheep, and oxen until there was much more than needed. He told them to build storehouses, and he assigned the Levites and the priests to be in charge of distributing the contributions to God and other priests, which included their families, and all those who were in charge of serving in God's house.

[King Hezekiah] trusted in the LORD God of Israel; so that after him was none like him among all the kings of Judah, nor any that were before him. For he clave to the LORD, and departed not from following him, but kept his commandments, which the LORD commanded Moses. And the LORD was with him; and he prospered whithersoever he went forth: and he rebelled against the king of Assyria, and served him not. (2 Kings 18:5–7)

As time went on, King Sennacherib of Assyria came to fight with Jersualem. King Hezekiah cut off the water supply outside the city and fortified the broken walls and towers. He built another wall around the first wall and made many weapons and shields, organizing men from his military to take charge of the people. While King Sennacherib was besieging Lachish, another town in Judah, King Hezekiah sent some of his servants to give his people this message:

Be strong and courageous, be not afraid nor dismayed for the king of Assyria, nor for all the multitude that is with him: for there be more with us than with him: With him is an arm of flesh; but with us is the LORD our God to help us, and to fight our battles. (2 Chronicles 32:7–8)

However, in his own attempt to turn King Sennacherib away from Judah, King Hezekiah agreed to pay him silver and gold. He also gave him the silver in his palace and the silver in the temple of the Lord. Hezekiah even stripped the gold off the pillars, doors, and doorposts of the temple. He sent his priest, scribe, and elders of the priests to Isaiah to ask for prayer. Isaiah gave them this message for the king from the Lord:

> Be not afraid of the words which thou hast heard, with which the servants of the king of Assyria have blasphemed me. Behold, I will send a blast upon him, and he shall hear a rumor, and shall return to his own land; and I will cause him to fall by the sword in his own land. (2 Kings 19:6–7)

King Sennacherib sent commanders with a large army to Jerusalem to deliver a message to King Hezekiah and Judah to convince them that their own king could not protect them and that they should serve him instead. He even told them that the Lord had sent him against Judah and that no god could save them from him. King Hezekiah refused to serve the evil king of Assyria and turned to God for help.

> O LORD, God of Israel, which dwellest between the cher´-u-bim [in the most holy place], thou art the God, even thou alone, of all the kingdoms of the earth; thou hast made heaven and earth. LORD, bow down thine ear, and hear: open, LORD, thine eyes, and see: and hear the words of Sen-nach´-er-ib, which hath sent him to reproach the living God. Of a truth, LORD, the kings of Assyria have destroyed the nations and their lands … I beseech thee, save thou us out of his hand, that all the kingdoms of the earth may know that thou art the LORD God, even thou only. (2 Kings 19:15–19)

Then Isaiah sent a prophecy to King Hezekiah regarding King Sennacherib:

> Therefore thus saith the LORD concerning the king of Assyria, He shall not come into this city, nor shoot an arrow there, nor come before it with shield, nor cast a bank against it. … For I will defend this city, to save it,

for mine own sake, and for my servant David's sake. (2 Kings 19:30–34)

In fulfillment of the prophecy against King Sennacherib, the Lord sent out his angel to Sennacherub's camp and killed one hundred eighty-five thousand of his men. When Sennacherib returned to Nineveh, the capital of Assyria at that time, and was worshiping his own god Nisroch his sons came and killed him with their swords.

Later on, when King Hezekiah became sick and was preparing to die, he prayed, and Isaiah came to see him to give him this message from the Lord:

> Thus saith the LORD, Set thine house in order; for thou shalt die, and not live. Then Hez-e-ki´-ah turned his face toward the wall, and prayed unto the LORD, And said, Remember now, O LORD, I beseech thee, how I have walked before thee in truth and with a perfect heart, and have done that which is good in thy sight. And Hez-e-ki´-ah wept sore. (Isaiah 38:1–3)

The Lord answered Hezekiah's prayer:

> I have heard thy prayer, I have seen thy tears: behold, I will add unto thy days fifteen years. And I will deliver thee and this city out of the hand of the king of Assyria: and I will defend this city. And this shall be a sign unto thee from the LORD, that the LORD will do this thing that he hath spoken. … I will make the shadow cast by the sun go back the ten steps it has gone down on the stairway of Ahaz. So the sunlight went back the ten steps it had gone down. (Isaiah 38:7–8, NIV®)

This sign was speaking of a type of sundial using a staircase.

Even after all God had done and promised, King Hezekiah later became proud and brought God's anger to Judah and himself. Then he humbled himself, and the Lord withheld His wrath upon them while he was alive; but the Lord left him for a while to test him to see what was in his heart.

## Judah's Future Foretold

When Merodach-Baladan was King of Babylon, he sent King Hezekiah letters and a gift because he had heard he was sick. When King Merodach-Baladan's messengers came to find out more about the sign that the Lord had given King Hezekiah, he showed them all he had in his storehouse, including gold, spices, oil, and armory. When Isaiah heard that Hezekiah had showed the Babylonians everything he had, he prophesied to King Hezekiah about their captivity, which would come by Babylon:

> Hear the word of the LORD. Behold, the days come, that all that is in thine house, and that which thy fathers have laid up in store unto this day, shall be carried into Babylon: nothing shall be left, saith the LORD. And of thy sons that shall issue from thee, which thou shalt beget, shall they take away; and they shall be eunuchs in the palace of the king of Babylon. (2 Kings 20:16–18)

## Isaiah Speaks Hope for Judah

During Isaiah's time of prophesying, he gave much hope to Judah. Even though the prophetic messages and warnings had declared that Judah would eventually go into captivity, Isaiah also prophesied of a time when they would return from captivity; and he spoke of a time of salvation. In the Scriptures below, Isaiah records the language of the Lord, which speaks of a beautiful love He has for them. It speaks of *Christ their Redeemer*, Who would someday bring a hope to them and to all nations:

> And there shall come forth a rod out of the stem of Jesse, and a *Branch* shall grow out of his roots: And the spirit of

the LORD shall rest upon him, the spirit of wisdom and understanding, the spirit of counsel and might, the spirit of knowledge and of the fear of the LORD ... and he shall not judge after the sight of his eyes, neither reprove after the hearing of his ears: But with righteousness shall he judge the poor, and reprove with equity for the meek of the earth: and he shall smite the earth with the rod of his mouth, and with the breath of his lips shall he slay the wicked. And righteousness shall be the girdle of his loins, and faithfulness the girdle of his reins. (Isaiah 11:1–5; emphasis added)

Behold, the Lord GOD will come with strong hand, and his arm shall rule for him: behold, his reward is with him, and his work before him. He shall feed his flock like a shepherd: he shall gather the lambs with his arm, and carry them in his bosom, and shall gently lead those that are with young. (Isaiah 40:10–11)

The Hebrew word translated *arm* is "zᵉrôʿâh."[2] The meaning of the word is "the arm (as stretched out) ... force ... help, mighty, power." Interestingly, this word is derived from "zâraʿ," which means "to sow ... disseminate ... conceive seed."[3] The "arm" Isaiah is speaking about is *Christ the Son of God*. Isaiah continued his message from the Lord:

Fear thou not; For I am with thee: be not dismayed; for I am thy God: I will strengthen thee; yea, I will help thee; yea, I will uphold thee with the right hand of my righteousness. Behold, all they that were incensed against thee shall be ashamed and confounded: they shall be as nothing; and they that strive with thee shall perish. (Isaiah 41:10–11)

I the LORD have called thee in righteousness, and will hold thine hand, and will keep thee, and give thee for a covenant of the people, for a light to the Gentiles; To open the blind eyes, to bring out the prisoners from the prison, and them that sit in darkness out of the prison house. (Isaiah 42:6–7)

"Thou shalt also be a crown of glory in the hand of the LORD, and a royal diadem in the hand of thy God" (Isaiah 62:3).

# Evil King Manasseh Is Transformed

Information about King Manasseh can be found in 2 Kings 21 and 2 Chronicles 33.

King Hezekiah had brought a beautiful reformation to Judah, but when he died, his son Manasseh became one of the most evil kings in the Southern Kingdom of Judah. He followed the evil practices of the pagan nations that the Lord had already driven out of their Promised Land. He restored idolatry, the worship of the starry hosts in the temple, and he sacrificed his own son in the fire. He practiced sorcery and divination, consulted mediums and spiritists, and he put the Asherah pole he had made in God's house. Earlier, the Lord had told David and his son Solomon: "In this house and in Jerusalem, which I have chosen out of all the tribes of Israel, I will put my name forever" (2 Kings 21:7). The temple was the house of the God of Abraham, Isaac, and Jacob—not the house of a false god.

> And the LORD spake by his servants the prophets, saying, Because Ma-nas´-seh King of Judah hath done these abominations, and hath done wickedly above all that the Am´-orites did, which were before him, and hath made Judah also to sin with his idols ... I am bringing such evil upon Jerusalem and Judah, that whosoever heareth of it, both his ears shall tingle. ... And I will forsake the remnant of mine inheritance, and deliver them into the hand of their enemies; and they shall become a prey and a spoil to all their enemies ... Manasseh shed innocent blood very much, till he had filled Jerusalem from one

end to another; beside his sin wherewith he made Judah to sin, in doing that which was evil in the sight of the LORD. (2 Kings 21:10–16)

The king of Assyria came and captured King Manasseh and took him away to Babylon in chains, where in his trouble, he humbled himself and called upon the Lord. Then the Lord sent him back to Jerusalem, where he built a high wall around the city of David, destroyed the idols and pagan altars in the Lord's house, and repaired the Altar. He sacrificed "peace offerings and "thank offerings" upon it and commanded the people of Judah "to serve the LORD God of Israel" (2 Chronicles 33:16).

Later, Amon, Manasseh's son, who succeeded him, was just as evil as his father had been in the beginning of his reign. So the sins of idolatry and violence continued after he became king. Eventually, Amon's servants conspired against him and killed him in his home.

## Jeremiah the Prophet and King Josiah

Information about King Josiah can be found in 1 Kings 13; 2 Kings 21–23; 2 Chronicles 35.

King Josiah, son of King Amon, became King of Judah at the age of eight years old and he "walked in all the way of David his father" (2 Kings 22:2). Remember, earlier a man of God had prophesied about Josiah to King Jeroboam I.

During his reign, the Lord told Jeremiah His plans of judgment for Judah and Jerusalem:

> I am about to summon all the peoples of the northern kingdoms, declares the LORD. Their kings will come and set up their thrones in the entrance of the gates of Jerusalem; they will come against all her surrounding walls and against all the towns of Judah. I will pronounce my judgments on my people because of their wickedness in forsaking me, in burning incense to other gods and in worshiping what their hands have made. (Jeremiah 1:14-16, NIV®)

When the people of Israel had forsaken God, God had called it adultery. This was the reason He had divorced Himself from Israel.

> And it came to pass through the lightness of her [Israel's] whoredom, that she defiled the land, and committed adultery with stones and with stocks. And yet for all this her treacherous sister Judah hath not turned unto me with her whole heart, but feignedly, saith the LORD. (Jeremiah 3:9–10)

The Hebrew word translated *feignedly* is "sheh´-ker." The meaning of the word is "an untruth ... a sham ... deceit (-ful)."[4] Judah's heart was not devoted to the Lord. Jeremiah called Israel and Jerusalem to repentance, because God wanted to give them His mercy: "O Jerusalem, wash thine heart from wickedness, that thou mayest be saved" (Jeremiah 4:14).

God gave the people every opportunity to change. He told Jeremiah to stand at the gate of the temple and give this message urging the people to change their evil ways:

> Amend your ways and your doings, and I will cause you to dwell in this place. Trust ye not in lying words, saying, The temple of the LORD, The temple of the LORD, The temple of the LORD, are these. For if ye thoroughly amend your ways and your doings; if ye thoroughly execute judgment between a man and his neighbor; If ye oppress not the stranger, the fatherless, and the widow, and shed not innocent blood in this place, neither walk after other gods to your hurt:

> Then will I cause you to dwell in this place, in the land that I gave to your fathers, for ever and ever. ... Will ye steal, murder, and commit adultery, and swear falsely, and burn incense unto Ba´-al, and walk after other gods whom ye know not; And come and stand before me in this house, which is called by my name, and say, We are delivered to do all these abominations? Is this house,

which is called by my name, become a den of robbers in your eyes? Behold, even I have seen it, saith the LORD. (Jeremiah 7:3–11)

Judah was devoted to other gods and worshiped them. "The children gather wood, and the fathers kindle the fire, and the women knead their dough, to make cakes to the queen of heaven, and to pour out drink offerings unto other gods, that they may provoke me to anger" (Jeremiah 7:18).

What had God told the Israelites in the days of Moses when He delivered them out of Egypt at a time before He had given them the Law?

Obey my voice, and I will be your God, and ye shall be my people: and walk ye in all the ways that I have commanded you, that it may be well unto you. But they hearkened not, nor inclined their ear, but walked in the counsels and in the imagination of their evil heart. (Jeremiah 7:23–24)

The house of Israel had been no different than the pagan nations who lived around them.

Since the day that your fathers came forth out of the land of Egypt unto this day I have even sent unto you all my servants the prophets, daily rising up early and sending them: Yet they hearkened not unto me…but hardened their neck: they did worse than their fathers. (Jeremiah 7:25–26)

Behold, the days come, saith the LORD, that I will punish all them which are circumcised with the uncircumcised; Egypt, and Judah, and E´-dom, and the children of Ammon, and Moab, and all that are in the utmost corners, that dwell in the wilderness: for all these nations are uncircumcised, and all the house of Israel are uncircumcised in the heart. (Jeremiah 9:25–26)

The covenant had been broken between God and the house of Israel and the house of Judah. "Thus saith the LORD God of Israel; Cursed be the man that obeyeth not the words of this covenant, Which I commanded your fathers in the day that I brought them forth out of the land of Egypt" (Jeremiah 11:3–4).

The men who were from the Levite city of Anahoth in Benjamin were there listening to Jeremiah. They commanded him to stop prophesying in the Lord's name or they would kill him. So the Lord declared that they and their families would die by the sword, and they would not have a continuing family line. Jeremiah continued to prophesy and speak the words given to him by the Lord.

## The Valley of Hinnom

The Valley of Hinnom was a place where Judah worshiped idols and sacrificed their children. God sent Jeremiah there to prophesy against it in the presence of the king of Judah and the people of his kingdom:

> I will bring evil upon this place ... Because they have forsaken me, and have estranged this place, and have burned incense in it unto other gods, whom neither they nor their fathers have known, nor the kings of Judah, and have filled this place with the blood of innocents; They have built also the high places of Ba´-al, to burn their sons with fire for bunt offerings unto Ba´-al, which I commanded not, nor spake it, neither came it into my mind ... This place shall no more be called To´-phet, nor The valley of the son of Hin´-nom, but The valley of slaughter. And I will make void the counsel of Judah and Jerusalem in this place; and I will cause them to fall by the sword before their enemies, and by the hands of them that seek their lives: and their carcases will I give to be meat for the fowls of the heaven, and for the beasts of the earth.

And I will make this city desolate, and a hissing; every one that passeth thereby shall be astonished and hiss because of all the plagues thereof. And I will cause them to eat the flesh of their sons and the flesh of their daughters, and they shall eat every one the flesh of his friend in the siege and straitness, wherewith their enemies, and they that seek their lives, shall straiten them. (Jeremiah 19:3–9)

Even their homes would be defiled, as Tophet would be, because they worshiped the heavens on their rooftops.

One day, King Josiah ordered that the money the people had contributed to the temple be used to pay workers to repair the temple. During the restoration, the high priest, Hilkiah, the found the book of the Law and gave it to the secretary, Shaphan, to read. This was the Law of Moses (see Exodus 19:24). After he read it, he took it to King Josiah and read it to him. King Josiah was extremely upset when he heard the words of the book of the Law and tore his clothes. "Great is the wrath of the LORD that is kindled against us, because our fathers have not hearkened unto the words of this book, to do according unto all that which is written concerning us" (2 Kings 22:13).

The king sent his men to inquire of the prophetess Huldah in Jerusalem, and she told them:

> Thus saith the LORD, Behold, I will bring evil upon this place, and upon the inhabitants thereof … Because they have forsaken me, and have burned incense unto other gods…. But to the king of Judah [King Josiah] … thus shall ye say to him … Because thine heart was tender, and thou hast humbled thyself before the LORD … and hast rent thy clothes, and wept before me; I also have heard thee, saith the LORD. Behold therefore, I will gather thee unto thy fathers, and thou shalt be gathered into thy grave in peace; and thine eyes shall not see all the evil which I will bring upon this place. (2 Kings 22:16–20)

# King Josiah Brings Revival to Judah

King Josiah called everyone in Judah to come to him while he read the book of the Law.

> And the king stood by a pillar, and made a covenant before the LORD, to walk after the LORD, and to keep his commandments and his testimonies and his statutes with all their heart and all their soul, to perform the words of this covenant that were written in this book. And all the people stood to the covenant. (2 Kings 23:3)

Then Josiah cleaned house. He ordered everything that had been used in idol worship to be taken outside of Jerusalem and burned in the Kidron Valley, with the ashes taken to Bethel. He burned the Asherah pole (having to do with female goddesses), which had been placed in the temple. He ground the ashes to powder, casting the powder on the children's graves. He also tore down the houses of the sodomites, which were by the temple of the Lord and where women wove hangings for the wooden idols. He destroyed Topheth in the Valley of Ben Hinnom so it could no longer be used to sacrifice sons and daughters by fire to the god Molech. He removed the statues of horses and chariots that had been placed at the temple entrance that the evil kings had dedicated to the sun. He tore down and destroyed altars that the kings had built on their roofs and in the temple court yards, and he threw their remains into the Kidron Valley. Josiah also destroyed the high places that Solomon had built for the Sidonian, Moabite, and Ammonite goddesses on the Hill of Corruption, smashing them and tearing down the Asherah poles there. When he was done, he filled the sites with human bones. He destroyed the altar, the high place, and the Asherah pole built by the very evil King Jeroboam I, and ground them to powder.

> As Jo-si´-ah turned himself, he spied the sepulchers that were there in the mount, and sent, and took the bones out of the sepulchers, and burned them upon the altar, and polluted it, according to the word of the LORD which

the man of God proclaimed ... Then he said, What title is that that I see? And the men of the city told him, it is the sepulcher of the man of God, which came from Judah, and proclaimed these things that thou hast done against the altar of Beth-el. And he said, Let him alone; let no man move his bones. So they let his bones alone, with the bones of the prophet that came out of Sa-mar´-i-a. (2 Kings 23:16–18)

This had been prophesied in Kings 13:1–2.

Josiah got rid of the mediums and spiritists, the household gods, the idols and all the other detestable things seen in Judah and Jerusalem. This he did to fulfill the requirements of the law written in the book that Hilkiah the priest had discovered in the temple of the LORD. Neither before nor after Josiah was there a king like him who turned to the LORD as he did—with all his heart and with all his soul and with all his strength, in accordance with all the Law of Moses. (2 Kings 23:24–25, NIV®)

## The Prophet Nahum

Earlier, God had sent Jonah to warn Ninevah, which was the capital of Assyria, to repent of its sins. It did at that time, and judgment was withheld. Now the prophet Nahum was being sent to prophesy against Ninevah to pronounce its judgment. Even though God had used Assyria to carry away Israel, its wicked capital will fall in 612 BC by the hands of the "medes, Babylonians and Scythians."[5]

Behold, I am against thee, saith the LORD of hosts, and I will burn her chariots in the smoke, and the sword shall devour thy young lions: and I will cut off thy prey from the earth, and the voice of thy messengers shall no more be heard. (Nahum 2:13)

What were the sins of Nineveh?

> It is all full of lies and robbery; the prey departeth not ...
> The horseman lifteth up both the bright sword and the
> glittering spear: and there is a multitude of slain, and a
> great number of carcases; and there is no end of their
> corpses ... Because of the multitude of the whoredoms
> of the well-favored harlot, the mistress of witchcrafts,
> that selleth nations through her whoredoms, and families
> through her witchcrafts. (Nahum 3:1–4)

## The Prophet Zephaniah

During Josiah's reign, Zephaniah called Jerusalem to repentance:

> Woe to her that is filthy and polluted, to the oppressing
> city! She obeyed not the voice; she received not correction;
> she trusted not in the LORD; she drew not near to her
> God. Her princes within her are roaring lions; her judges
> are evening wolves; they gnaw not the bones till the
> morrow. Her prophets are light and treacherous persons:
> her priests have polluted the sanctuary, they have done
> violence to the law. (Zephaniah 3:1–4)

"Seek ye the LORD, all ye meek of the earth, which have wrought his judgment; seek righteousness, seek meekness: it may be ye shall be hid in the day of the LORD'S anger" (Zephaniah 2:3).

Even though God's judgment was getting ready to come, Zephaniah prophesied of a hope of restoration for God's remnant in the "last days"—a time in our own future when Jesus will come for them:

> Therefore wait ye upon me, saith the LORD, until the
> day that I rise up to the prey: for my determination is to
> gather the nations, that I may assemble the kingdoms,

to pour upon them mine indignation, even all my fierce anger: for all the earth shall be devoured with the fire of my jealousy.

For then will I turn to the people a pure language that they may call upon the name of the LORD to serve him with one consent. From beyond the rivers of E-thi-o´-pi-a my suppliants, even the daughter of my dispersed, shall bring mine offering. In that day shalt thou not be ashamed for all thy doings, wherein thou hast transgressed against me; for then I will take away out of the midst of thee them that rejoice in thy pride, and thou shalt not more be haughty because of my holy mountain. I will also leave in the midst of thee an afflicted and poor people, and they shall trust in the name of the LORD. (Zephaniah 3:8–12)

"I bring you again, even in the time that I gather you: for I will make you a name and a praise among all people of the earth, when I turn back your captivity before your eyes, saith the LORD" (Zephaniah 3:20).

## Judah Will Fall

Regardless of the reformation of King Josiah, God's judgment would still come to Judah.

> Notwithstanding the LORD turned not from the fierceness of his great wrath, wherewith his anger was kindled against Judah, because of all the provocations that Ma-nas´-seh had provoked him withal. And the LORD said, I will remove Judah also out of my sight, as I have removed Israel, and will cast off this city Jerusalem which I have chosen, and the house of which I said, my name shall be there. (2 Kings 23:26–27)

LOUISE A. FUGATE

# The Death of Josiah

When Pharoah Necho of Egypt went to fight Carchemish (Eastern Capital of the Hittites on the Euphrates),[6] Jo-si´-ah went out against him. But he sent ambassadors to him, saying, "What have I to do with thee, thou king of Judah? I come not against thee this day, but against the house wherewith I have war: for God commanded me to make haste: forbear thee from meddling with God, who is with me, that he destroy thee not" (2 Chronicles 35:20–21).

King Josiah ignored King Necho. He was wounded by Necho's archers and carried back to Jerusalem, where he died.

# Kings Jehoahaz (Shallum) and King Jehoiakim

Information about King Jehoahaz can be found in 1 Chronicles 3.

Information about King Jehoiakim can be found in 2 Kings 23–24; 2 Chronicles 36; Jeremiah 22, 26, 36.

After King Josiah died, his evil son Jehoahaz reigned over Judah for about three months. Pharaoh Necho of Egypt came and put him in chains and sent him to the Levitical city of Hamath, where he stayed until his death.

After taking King Jehoahaz away, Pharaoh Necho quickly replaced him with his brother Eliakim and changed his name to Jehoiakim (Judah's eighteenth king). He was a promoter of idol worship, and he did all the evil things his fathers had done. Judah became a tribute nation under Pharaoh Necho for three years, and King Jehoiakim paid Necho with the gold and silver he collected from the people by heavily taxing them.

# In Conclusion

The times were evil, and most of the hearts of Judah had become as evil as the hearts of Israel, who had been taken away into exile. Through the prophets, the Lord continued to send messages of judgment to those who were disobedient and hope to those who would repent.

Over and over and over again, God reminded them of their lack of obedience, but why? Was it because God was a dictator or a harsh judge? There seems to be a far *deeper reason* than that for this extreme command of obedience. Jesus said it this way: "He that hath my commandments, and keepeth them, *he it is that loveth me*" (John 14:21–24; emphasis added).

God was saving a godly remnant, a faithful family line, from which Jesus would be born, but He was also looking for a people who would love Him with their hearts. He did not want obedience from uncircumcised hearts (those who did not love Him). Circumcision was required in the written Law, and it was a physical sign of God's chosen people. It meant nothing, though, if their hearts were far from Him; and God is always watching the hearts of men. God knew that true transformation of the heart could only come from the Holy Spirit, which is given through faith in Jesus Christ, and He knew that soon He was going to send Jesus through the family line of Judah to make that possible.

Even though Kings Hezekiah and Josiah had brought revival and reformation to the people, God would not turn from His judgment because of the sins of Manasseh.

As we have read about the kings and the prophets, there can be no doubt that God had been persistent, patient, and merciful to the people of Judah, but now the people of Judah were at the threshold of exile. Judah will have three more kings, and Jeremiah will play a major role during their reigns. In this next chapter, we will see the first exiles taken captive, and we will see Jeremiah standing bold and strong for the Lord in spite of his suffering and persecution.

## Deeper Insights:

1. During the time of Moses, after the book of the Law was written, where was it kept and why? Read Deuteronomy 31:24–27.

   Besides judgments and statutes, what was the major key component in the book of the Law? Read Exodus 20:1–17.

   What other names were given to the Ten Commandments? Read Exodus 34:28–29.

According to Moses, when should the book of the Law be read to the Israelites and why? Read Deuteronomy 31:10–13.

Moses had told the Israelites that there would be consequences if they disobeyed what was written in the book of the Law. In regards to the remnant of Judah at this time, what had Moses prophesied would happen to them? Read Deuteronomy 28:63–68.

2. What was Josiah's immediate response after reading the book of the Law? Read 2 Kings 23:3.

Why would God still bring His judgment? Read 2 Chronicles 34:25.

Why did God say Josiah would be spared from this judgment? Read 2 Chronicles 34:26–28.

3. Judgment was coming to Judah and to Jerusalem, because the kings and the people had forsaken the Lord God of their fathers, and they had disobeyed His commands. Read Isaiah 5:1–7, a parable, which God gave to Isaiah regarding His judgment that was coming upon them.

4. Read Jeremiah 7:32. What did God rename the valley of Hinnom? Why?

Can you think of behaviors in our society that could compare to what was being done at Tophet? In what ways, as a nation and personally, are we responsible for sacrificing our own children, mentally, physically, and spiritually?

5. God calls all who forsake Him, adulterous. How have we, as Christians—the Bride of Christ, become adulterous to God? How has our nation become an adulterous nation?

# CHAPTER 6

## NEBUCHADNEZZAR ATTACKS JERUSALEM

## Jeremiah and King Jehoiakim

Information about King Jehoiakim can be found in 2 Kings 23–24; 2 Chronicles 36; Jeremiah 22, 26, 36.

There would be no more revivals or reformations before Judah's fall. God had sent many prophets with many messages, but Judah had not listened and was now on a downhill slide to exile. Jeremiah, who had been prophesying, would now be ringing in Judah's last days as he bravely and boldly obeyed the voice of God. He would continue to warn of judgment and preach repentance to Judah until he would also be taken away.

In the Bible there are fifty-two chapters in the Book of Jeremiah containing messages and prophecies, which he gave over a forty-year period during the time of Judah's decline; and he delivered those messages with an impact. His ear was always open to God's voice. He was willing to do whatever God commanded him to do, and most of the time, he was not very popular. Jeremiah's words often offended people because he spoke God's truth about His love, mercy, and judgment. People did not want to hear about God's judgment.

Today we are living in the same sinful conditions as Judah was then. God has promised that someday He will bring judgment to those who reject Jesus. There are many signs that point to the nearness of His return. While it is called today, we need to respond to His call to repent, and receive Christ and His forgiveness.

Listen as Jeremiah spoke boldly to King Jehoiakim to point out his sins, and what to do about them shortly after he became king:

> Woe unto him that buildeth his house by unrighteousness, and his chambers by wrong; that useth his neighbor's service without wages, and giveth him not for his work. ...Thine eyes and thine heart are not but for thy covetousness, and for to shed innocent blood, and for oppression, and for violence, to do it. (Jeremiah 22:13–17)

> Execute ye judgment and righteousness, and deliver the spoiled out of the hand of the oppressor: and do no wrong, do no violence to the stranger, the fatherless, nor the widow, neither shed innocent blood in this place. For if ye do this thing indeed, then shall there enter in by the gates of this house kings sitting upon the throne of David, riding in chariots and on horses, he, and his servants, and his people. But if ye will not hear these words, I swear by myself, saith the LORD, that this house shall become a desolation. (Jeremiah 22:3–5)

The Lord sent Jeremiah to the potter's house where He gave him the analogy of God being the potter and the people of Judah being the clay. Then He sent him out to the people of Judah with this warning:

> Return ye now every one from his evil way, and make your ways and your doings good. And they said, There is no hope: but we will walk after our own devices, and we will every one do the imagination of his evil heart. (Jeremiah 18:11–12)

The Lord said, "I will scatter them as with an east wind before the enemy; I will show them the back, and not the face, in the day of their calamity" (Jeremiah 18:17).

Later, the Lord sent Jeremiah to the temple courtyard where he warned the people about the upcoming desolation of Judah, which would come because they had not listened to God's words. The priests and false prophets were there and also heard the warning.

> Thus saith the LORD; If ye will not hearken to me, to walk in my law, which I have set before you, To hearken to the words of my servants the prophets, whom I send unto you ... Then will I make this house like Shi´-loh, and will make this city a curse to all the nations of the earth. (Jeremiah 26:4–6)

Shiloh had been the religious center for the Jews in Ephraim, upon which God had brought His judgment. The Philistines had attacked the Israelites, killing thirty thousand footmen, took the ark, and killed Eli's (the priest's) two unrighteous sons who were priests (see Jeremiah 7:12; 1 Samuel 4:10-11).

The people wanted to kill Jeremiah when he told them what would happen to them. When King Jehoiakim heard what Jeremiah had said, he asked Jeremiah why he had prophesied that the house of Judah would become like Shiloh. Jeremiah boldly gave him this answer:

> The LORD sent me to prophesy against this house and against this city all the words that ye have heard. Therefore now amend your ways and your doings, and obey the voice of the LORD your God; and the LORD will repent him of the evil that he hath pronounced against you. As for me, behold, I am in your hand: do with me as seemeth good and meet unto you. But know ye for certain, that if ye put me to death, ye shall surely bring innocent blood upon yourselves, and upon this city, and upon the inhabitants thereof: for of a truth the LORD hath sent me unto you to speak all these words in your ears. (Jeremiah 26:12–15)

## Jeremiah Is Persecuted

Jeremiah's words were offensive to the people of Judah and Jerusalem because they exposed their sins and revealed the evil in their hearts. They did not want to change, and they did not want to hear that God would punish them if they did not turn back to Him. Defiance and rebellion was raging, and as Jeremiah continued to preach, he began to be persecuted. Pashur, the temple governor, put Jeremiah in stocks near the temple. After he was released, Jeremiah prophesied against Pashur and Judah, giving them these words from the Lord:

> I will deliver all the strength of this city, and all the labors thereof, and all the precious things thereof, and all the treasures of the kings of Judah will I give into the hand of their enemies, which shall spoil them, and take them, and carry them to Babylon. And thou, Pash´-ur, and all that dwell in thine house shall go into captivity: and thou shalt come to Babylon, and there thou shalt die, and shalt be buried there, thou, and all thy friends, to whom thou hast prophesied lies. (Jeremiah 20:5–6)

After having been threatened to be beaten and murdered, and having been put in stocks, Jeremiah continued to preach God's words to the people of Judah and Jerusalem; and he predicted their seventy-year exile.

> Because ye have not heard my words, Behold, I will send and take all the families of the north, saith the LORD, and Neb-u-chad-rez´-zar the king of Babylon, my servant, and will bring them against this land, and against the inhabitants thereof, and against all these nations round about, and will utterly destroy them, and make them an astonishment, and a hissing, and perpetual desolations. (Jeremiah 25:8–9)

> And this whole land shall be a desolation, and an astonishment; these nations shall serve the king of

Babylon seventy years. And it shall come to pass, when seventy years are accomplished, that I will punish the king of Babylon, and that nation, saith the LORD, for their iniquity, and the land of the Chal-de´-ans, and will make it perpetual desolations. (Jeremiah 25:11–12)

# Jeremiah's Rolls Are Burned

One day the Lord told Jeremiah to write down all His judgments against Israel, Judah, and the other nations. So Jeremiah spoke God's words, and Baruch wrote down all that he said. Jeremiah was not allowed to go to the temple, but he told Baruch to take the roll and read it to the people in the temple and to the people of Judah who would be there on the day of fasting. Then they would have a chance to repent before the judgments would come.

> Then read Bar´-uch in the book the words of Jeremiah in the house of the LORD, in the chamber of Gem-a-ri´-ah the son of Sha´-phan the scribe, in the higher court at the entry of the new gate of the LORD'S house, in the ears of all the people. (Jeremiah 36:10)

After Micaiah (not the prophet) went to the king's house and told all the officials what Baruch had read from the rolls, Baruch was brought to read the roll to them. After he read the roll to them, they became afraid and Jehudi read it to the king. As Jehudi read the pages, the king cut off pieces, one by one, and burned them in his firepot until he had burned the entire roll. No one who listened to the reading was afraid or repentant. The king wanted to capture Jeremiah and Baruch, but the Lord had hidden them. Since Jeremiah's words had been burned up by the king, the Lord told Jeremiah to tell Baruch to write them again. Then Jeremiah delivered this message to the king from the Lord:

> Thou hast burned this roll, saying, Why has thou written therein, saying, The king of Babylon shall certainly come

and destroy this land, and shall cause to cease from thence man and beast? Therefore, thus saith the LORD of Je-hoi´-a-kim king of Judah; he shall have none to sit upon the throne of David: and his dead body shall be cast out in the day to the heat, and in the night to the frost. And I will punish him and his seed and his servants for their iniquity; and I will bring upon them, and upon the inhabitants of Jerusalem, and upon the men of Judah, all the evil that I have pronounced against them; but they hearkened not. (Jeremiah 36:29–31)

## Nebuchadnezzar's First Attack on Jerusalem

After Nebuchadnezzar (Nebuchadrezzar) won the battle at Carchemish in 605 BC, he gained control of the trade routes and the Middle East. God made him to be His servant to bring judgment to Judah and Jerusalem and to all the nations who had either helped bring their judgment, or stood by without compassion. In 604 BC, Nebuchadnezzar, joined by Syria, Moab, and Amnon, destroyed Ashkelon, a nearby city, which was only the beginning of Judah's doom.

In his days Neb-u-chad-nez´-zar king of Babylon came up, and Je-hoi´-a-kim became his servant three years: then he turned and rebelled against him. And the LORD sent against him bands of the Chal´-dees, and bands of the Syrians, and bands of the Mo´-abites, and bands of the children of Ammon, and sent them against Judah to destroy it, according to the word of the LORD, which he spake by his servants the prophets. (2 Kings 24:1–2)

Then King Nebuchadnezzar plundered the temple in Jerusalem and carried all the articles to his own temple in Babylon. He also bound King Jehoiakim with the intention of taking him to Babylon, but Jehoiakim died on the way. Earlier, Jeremiah had prophesied of Jehoiakim's death and of the deportation of his son, Coniah (Jehoiachin): "He shall be buried with the burial of an ass, drawn and cast forth beyond the gates of Jerusalem." (Jeremiah 22:19)

> I will give thee into the hand of them that seek thy life, and into the hand of them whose face thou fearest, even into the hand of Neb-u-chad-nez´-zar king of Babylon, and into the hand of the Chal-de´-ans. And I will cast thee out, and thy mother that bare thee, into another country, where ye were not born; and there shall ye die. But to the land whereunto they desire to return, thither shall they not return. ... Write ye this man childless, a man that shall not prosper in his days: for no man of his seed shall prosper, sitting upon the throne of David, and ruling any more in Judah. (Jeremiah 22:25–30)

## Nebuchadnezzar's Second Attack on Jerusalem

Information about King Jehoiachin can be found in 2 Kings 24; Jeremiah 52.

Jehoiachin, son of King Jehoiakim, became King of Judah at the age of eighteen, but his reign was short, lasting only three months. In 597 BC, King Nebuchadnezzar and his servants came back and attacked Jerusalem again, and King Jehoiachin and his household were taken captive, as Jeremiah had prophesied.

> [Nebuchadnezzar] carried out thence all the treasures of the house of the LORD, and the treasures of the king's house, and cut in pieces all the vessels of gold which Solomon king of Israel had made in the temple of the LORD, as the LORD had said. And he carried away all Jerusalem, and all the princes, and all the mighty men of valor, even ten thousand captives, and all the craftsmen and smiths: none remained, save the poorest sort of the people of the land. And he carried away Je-hoi´-a-chin

to Babylon, and the king's mother, and the king's wives, and his officers, and the mighty of the land, those carried he into captivity from Jerusalem to Babylon. (2 Kings 24:13–15)

## Jeremiah and King Zedekiah

Information about King Zedekiah can be found in 2 Kings 24; 2 Chronicles 36; Jeremiah 34, 37–39, 52; Ezekiel 17.

After King Nebuchadnezzar sent King Jehoiachin to Babylon, he made Mattaniah, King Josiah's son, the last king of Jerusalem and Judah; and he changed his name to Zedekiah.

God gave Jeremiah a vision of two baskets of figs—one basket of *good* figs and one basket of *evil* figs. The *good* figs represented God's remnant of the line of Judah, who would carry on the everlasting covenant with David's line. It didn't seem like it now, but God had sent them away for their own good, and He would restore them. Through them, there would be a king forever upon David's throne—King Jesus! The evil figs that were left would meet their demise.

> Like these *good* figs, so will I acknowledge them that are carried away captive of Judah, whom I have sent out of this place into the land of the Chal-de´-ans for their good. For I will set mine eyes upon them for good, and I will bring them again to this land: and I will build them, and not pull them down; and I will plant them, and not pluck them up. And I will give them a heart to know me, that I am the LORD: and they shall be my people, and I will be their God: for they shall return unto me with their whole heart. (Jeremiah 24:5–7; emphasis added)

The *evil* figs represented those who would remain in Jerusalem and those who would go to Egypt.

And I will deliver them to be removed into all the
kingdoms of the earth for their hurt, to be a reproach and
a proverb, a taunt and a curse, in all places whither I shall
drive them. And I will send the sword, the famine, and
the pestilence, among them, till they be consumed from
off the land that I gave unto them and to their fathers.
(Jeremiah 24:9–10)

King Zedekiah was not interested in Jeremiah's words; however, one
day he did send his servants to ask Jeremiah to pray for them because of
Nebuchadnezzar's military presence. "Then Pharaoh's army was come
forth out of Egypt: and when the Chal-de´-ans that besieged Jerusalem
heard tidings of them, they departed from Jerusalem" (Jeremiah 37:5).

Even though the Chaldeans had left, Jeremiah gave the king this
warning: "The Chal-de´-ans shall come again, and fight against this city,
and take it, and burn it with fire" (Jeremiah 37:8).

## The Corrupt Priests and False Prophets

The Lord gave Jeremiah these messages for the priests:

Woe be unto the pastors that destroy and scatter the sheep
of my pasture! saith the LORD. ... Ye have scattered my
flock, and driven them away, and have not visited them:
behold, I will visit upon you the evil of your doings, saith
the LORD. (Jeremiah 23:1–2)

God had not sent the false prophets. Even though Jeremiah had
rebuked them, they continued to deceive the people and live corrupt lives.
God said this about them:

I have seen also in the prophets of Jerusalem a horrible
thing: they commit adultery, and walk in lies: they
strengthen also the hands of evildoers, that none doth
return from his wickedness: they are all of them unto me

as Sodom, and the inhabitants thereof as Go-mor´-rah. ... Behold, I will feed them with wormwood, and make them drink the water of gall: for from the prophets of Jerusalem is profaneness gone forth into all the land. ... Hearken not unto the words of the prophets that prophesy unto you: they make you vain: they speak a vision of their own heart, and not out of the mouth of the LORD. They say still unto them that despise me, The LORD hath said, Ye shall have peace; and they say unto every one that walketh after the imagination of his own heart, No evil shall come upon you. (Jeremiah 23:14–17)

God had given so many promises to Judah that He would not forget them, that He loved them, and that He would restore them. God gave them promises of King Jesus and a new covenant:

Behold, the days come, saith the LORD, that I will raise unto David a righteous Branch, and a King shall reign and prosper, and shall execute judgment and justice in the earth. In his days Judah shall be saved, and Israel shall dwell safely: and this is his name whereby he shall be called, THE LORD OUR RIGHTEOUSNESS. (Jeremiah 23:5–6)

Behold, the days come, saith the LORD, that I will make a new covenant with the house of Israel, and with the house of Jacob: Not according to the covenant that I made with their fathers in the day that I took them by the hand to bring them out of the land of Egypt; which my covenant they brake, although I was a husband unto them, saith the LORD: But this shall be the covenant that I will make with the house of Israel; After those days, saith the LORD, I will put my law in their inward parts, and write it in their hearts; and will be their God, and they shall be my people. (Jeremiah 31:31–33)

"For Israel hath not been forsaken, nor Judah of his God, of the LORD of hosts; though their land was filled with sin against the Holy One of Israel" (Jeremiah 51:5).

The Lord had told Jeremiah, "Houses and fields and vineyards shall be possessed again in this land" (Jeremiah 32:15). He gave Jeremiah a sign to show him that they would: His uncle came and asked him to buy his land in Anthoth. After Jeremiah bought the land, he gave the sealed deed to Baruch to keep in a jar of pottery. Jeremiah asked the Lord why He had told him to buy the field since the Chaldeans were going to be taking over, and the Lord told him what He was going to do:

> Behold, I will gather them out of all countries, whither I
> have driven them in mine anger, and in my fury, and in
> great wrath; and I will bring them again unto this place,
> and I will cause them to dwell safely: And they shall be
> my people, and I will be their God: And I will give them
> one heart, and one way, that they may fear me for ever,
> for the good of them, and of their children after them:
> And I will make an everlasting covenant with them, that
> I will not turn away from them, to do them good; but I
> will put my fear in their hearts, that they shall not depart
> from me. (Jeremiah 32:37–40)

One day Jeremiah left to go to Benjamin to claim his portion of land. A guard saw him in Benjamin and thought he was deserting to go to the Chaldeans and arrested him. The princes beat him and threw him into a prison dungeon; however, Jeremiah continued to prophesy about the judgment coming to those who will remain in Jerusalem.

The princes wanted Jeremiah to die, so they conferred with King Zedekiah; and he ordered that Jeremiah be lowered down into a dungeon where he sank in the mud. Ebedmelech, one of the king's slaves, came to Jeremiah's rescue when he convinced the king that Jeremiah would starve to death in the dungeon. King Zedekiah gave orders for him to be brought up out of the dungeon, and he resided in the prison's court. While he was there, King Zedekiah met secretly with him and conferred with him, and Jeremiah again reminded him to submit to King Nebuchadnezzar. On one occasion, when King Zedekiah asked Jeremiah if he had anything from the Lord for him, Jeremiah answered him: "There is: for, said he, thou shalt be delivered into the hand of the king of Babylon" (Jeremiah 37:17).

## Jeremiah's Letter to the Jews in Babylon

Jeremiah wrote a letter of encouragement from the Lord to the Jews who had already gone into exile with King Jehoiachin to Babylon. He gave them a message about how to live and carry on for the next seventy years in their present situation of captivity and grief. He also gave them the Lord's promises:

> Build ye houses, and dwell in them; and plant gardens, and eat the fruit of them; Take ye wives, and beget sons and daughters; and take wives for your sons, and give your daughters to husbands, that they may bear sons and daughters; that ye may be increased there, and not diminished. And seek the peace of the city whither I have caused you to be carried away captives, and pray unto the LORD for it: for in the peace thereof shall ye have peace. (Jeremiah 29:5–7)

> Let not your prophets and your diviners, that be in the midst of you, deceive you, neither hearken to your dreams which ye cause to be dreamed. For they prophesy falsely unto you in my name: I have not sent them, saith the LORD. (Jeremiah 29:8–9)

> After seventy years be accomplished at Babylon I will visit you, and perform my good word toward you, in causing you to return to this place. For I know the thoughts that I think toward you, saith the LORD, thoughts of peace, and not of evil, to give you an expected end. Then shall ye call upon me, and ye shall go and pray unto me, and I will hearken unto you. And ye shall seek me, and find

me, when ye shall search for me with all your heart. And I will be found of you, saith the LORD: and I will turn away your captivity, and I will gather you from all the nations, and from all the places whither I have driven you, saith the LORD; and I will bring you again into the place whence I caused you to be carried away captive. (Jeremiah 29:10–14)

King Zedekiah knew it was just a matter of time before he would be warring with Nebuchadnezzar, and he sent Pashur to ask Jeremiah if the Lord would come and fight against Nebuchadnezzar with them. Not only would God not help him, but, He would deliver the king and his city into Nebuchadnezzar's hands. The Lord told Jeremiah to give this message to King Zedekiah from Him:

Thus saith the LORD God of Israel ... I myself will fight against you with an outstretched hand and with a strong arm, even in anger, and in fury, and in great wrath. ... I will deliver Zed-e-ki´-ah king of Judah, and his servants, and the people, and such as are left in this city from the pestilence, from the sword, and from the famine, into the hand of Neb-u-chad-rez´-zar king of Babylon, and into the hand of their enemies, and into the hand of those that seek their life: and he shall smite them with the edge of the sword; he shall not spare them, neither have pity, nor have mercy. ... He that abideth in this city shall die by the sword, and by the famine, and by the pestilence: but he that goeth out, and falleth to the Chal-de´-ans that besiege you, he shall live, and his life shall be unto him for a prey. (Jeremiah 21:5–9)

Behold, I will give this city into the hand of the king of Babylon, and he shall burn it with fire: And thou shalt not escape out of his hand, but shalt surely be taken, and delivered into his hand; and thine eyes shall behold the eyes of the king of Babylon, and he shall speak with thee mouth to mouth, and thou shalt go to Babylon. ... Thou shalt not die by the sword: But thou shalt die in peace. (Jeremiah 34:2–5)

# In Conclusion

The reformations and revivals were over for Judah, but God chose Jeremiah, a strong and courageous prophet, to speak the truth through the last days before Judah's fall. His words of warnings brought persecution and imprisonment to him, but he would continue to deliver God's messages to try and turn the people from their sins. He spoke about sin, judgment, and repentance to all facets of society. With every warning came God's promises of love, mercy, and a hope for their future. Jeremiah also spoke about the judgment that would be coming to the nations who would capture Judah and to those who would stand by watching and do nothing.

In 604 BC, Nebuchadnezzar made his first attack on Jerusalem, capturing King Jehoiakim, who died on his way to Babylon. Then about seven years later, in 597 BC, he attacked Jerusalem again, this time taking King Jehoiachin, his family, and all that were strong and mighty. Nebuchadnezzar assigned Mattaniah to be the next king, changing his name to Zedekiah. King Zedekiah had no interest in Jeremiah's messages or in his God.

The people who had gone into exile in Babylon had gone into a country that had no regard whatsoever for the living God of the Hebrews, and they were a nation of idolatry. Even though most of the Jews had left God to do as they pleased, they felt empty and abandoned by Him when they realized what had happened to them. God had removed them from the land that He had given their forefathers. Now there was no longer anything to identify them as a Jewish nation, except poverty, loss, and their shame. Jeremiah sent them a letter of encouragement about how to carry on for the next seventy years and to give them a hope for the future.

Nebuchadnezzar was not through with Jerusalem yet. Jerusalem will come to total devastation, just as God had warned the Jews of Judah time and time again through his prophets.

## Deeper Insights:

1. Why do you think, after hearing the prophesies, and seeing Israel fall, it was so easy for the people of Judah to stay in idolatry, rather than to put their trust in the God of their forefathers?

2. What do you think God meant when he said that the Jews "have hardened their necks, that they might not hear my words?" Read Jeremiah 17:23 and 19:15. What is another word for this kind of action?

3. Why did God send Nebuchadnezzar to attack Jerusalem the first time in 604 BC? What had King Manesseh done? Read 2 Kings 21:1–7, 16.

   What did Jeremiah prophesy would happen to those who would not stay and serve Nebuchadnezzar? Read Jeremiah 27:8.

4. Read Jeremiah 24:5–10.

   What did God promise would happen in the future (still yet to come) for the *good* figs?" What did God promise would happen to the *bad* figs?"

5. What did God have against the priests and pastors? Read Jeremiah 2:8, 10:21; 23:1–2.

   What did God have against the prophets? Read Jeremiah 23:14, 21, 31–32.

   What were the false prophets telling the people in Judah? Read Jeremiah 27:9–11, 14–15. Read Jeremiah 28, which tells about the false prophet, Hananiah.

   What did Jeremiah say identifies a true prophet who is sent from God? Read Jeremiah 28:9. What does the Bible say about false prophets of our day? Read Matthew 7:22–23; 2 Peter 2.

# CHAPTER 7

## THE LAST DAYS OF JERUSALEM

## The Call of the Prophet Ezekiel

Ezekiel was a man of God who had also been exiled to Babylon in 597 BC, along with King Jehoiachin. One day the Spirit of the Lord entered into Ezekiel and gave him a vision of heaven. He saw "the appearance of the likeness of the glory of the Lord" (Ezekiel 1:28). Then He spoke to Ezekiel:

> Son of man, I send thee to the children of Israel, to a rebellious nation that hath rebelled against me: they and their fathers have transgressed against me, even unto this very day. For they are impudent children and stiffhearted. (Ezekiel 2:3–4)

Ezekiel was transported by the Spirit to the exiles in Babylon where he sat with them for seven days. Then the Lord told him: "Son of man, I have made thee a *watchman* unto the house of Israel: therefore hear the word at my mouth, and give them warning from me." (Ezekiel 3:17; emphasis added)

What did God mean, when He told Ezekiel He was calling him to be a "watchman?" We find the answer in the Book of Ezekiel. Ezekiel will be held responsible for warning the people to turn from their sins.

> When I say unto the wicked, Thou shalt surely die; and thou givest him not warning, nor speakest to warn the

wicked from his wicked way, to save his life; the same wicked man shall die in his iniquity; but his blood will I require at thine hand. Yet if thou warn the wicked, and he turn not from his wickedness, nor from his wicked way, he shall die in his iniquity; but thou hast delivered thy soul.

Again, When a righteous man doth turn from his righteousness, and commit iniquity, and I lay a stumbling block before him, he shall die: because thou hast not given him warning, he shall die in his sin, and his righteousness which he hath done shall not be remembered; but his blood will I require at thine hand. Nevertheless if thou warn the righteous man, that the righteous sin not, and he doth not sin, he shall surely live, because he is warned; also thou hast delivered thy soul. (Ezekiel 3:18–21)

One day the Lord transported Ezekiel by the Spirit from Babylon to Jerusalem where He set him down beside the temple. The Lord showed him the evil idolatry and other abominations that had been going on in the house of the Lord.

And he brought me to the door of the court ... And he said unto me, Go in, and behold the wicked abominations that they do here. So I went in and saw; and behold every form of creeping things, and abominable beasts, and all the idols of the house of Israel, portrayed upon the wall round about. And there stood before them seventy men of the ancients of the house of Israel, and in the midst of them stood Ja-az-a-ni´-ah the son of Sha´-phan, with every man his censer in his hand; and a thick cloud of incense went up. Then said he unto me, Son of man, hast thou seen what the ancients of the house of Israel do in the dark, every man in the chambers of his imagery? for they say, The LORD seeth us not; the LORD hath forsaken the earth. (Ezekiel 8:7–12)

"The nation's leaders are secretly practicing animal worship."[1] "There sat women weeping for Tam´-muz [god of flocks]"[2] (Ezekiel 8:14).

> And he brought me into the inner court of the LORD'S house, and, behold, at the door of the temple of the LORD, between the porch and the altar, were about five and twenty men, with their backs toward the temple of the LORD, and their faces toward the east; and they worshiped the sun toward the east. (Ezekiel 8:16)

In Ezekiel 9, the Lord gave Ezekiel a vision of the great slaughter that was getting ready to take place in Jerusalem. In the vision, the Lord told a man who was dressed in linen to go out into the city and put a mark on the foreheads of those who loved the Lord—those who grieved over the wickedness in Jerusalem. Everyone else in the city of Jerusalem would die. He told him:

> Slay utterly old and young, both maids, and little children, and women: but come not near any man upon whom is the mark; and begin at my sanctuary, Then they began at the ancient men which were before the house. … And they went forth, and slew in the city. … The iniquity of the house of Israel and Judah is exceeding great, and the land is full of blood, and the city full of perverseness: for they say, The LORD hath forsaken the earth, and the LORD seeth not. (Ezekiel 9:6–9)

God showed Ezekiel that Jerusalem would fall, but that He would send a remnant to him in Babylon:

> Yet, behold, therein shall be left a remnant that shall be brought forth, both sons and daughters: behold, they shall come forth unto you, and ye shall see their way and their doings: and ye shall be comforted concerning the evil that I have brought upon Jerusalem, even concerning all that I have brought upon it. And they shall comfort you, when

ye see their ways and their doings: and ye shall know that
I have not done without cause all that I have done in it,
saith the Lord GOD. (Ezekiel 14:22–23)

## The Fall of Jerusalem

Even though Jeremiah had warned King Zedekiah many times to submit
to Nebuchadnezzar, he still rebelled against him.

> In the ninth year of his reign … Neb-u-chad-nez´-zar king
> of Babylon came, he, and all his host, against Jerusalem,
> and pitched against it; and they built forts against it round
> about. And the city was besieged unto the eleventh year
> of King Zed-e-ki´-ah. (2 Kings 25:1–2)

> And in the fourth month, in the ninth day of the month,
> the famine was sore in the city, so that there was no bread
> for people of the land. Then the city was broken up, and
> all the men of war fled, and went forth out of the city
> by night by the way of the gate between the two walls,
> which was by the king's garden; (now the Chal-de´-ans
> were by the city round about:) and they went by the way
> of the plain. But the army of the Chal-de´-ans pursued
> after the king, and overtook Zed-e-ki´-ah in the plains of
> Jericho; and all his army was scattered from him. Then
> they took the king, and carried him up unto the king of
> Babylon to Rib´-lah in the land of Ha´-math; where he
> gave judgment upon him. And the king of Babylon slew
> the sons of Zed-e-ki´-ah before his eyes: he slew also all
> the princes of Judah in Rib´-lah. Then he put out the eyes
> of Zed-e-ki´-ah; and the king of Babylon bound him in
> chains, and carried him to Babylon, and put him in prison
> till the day of his death. (Jeremiah 52:6–11)

The prophets had been warning the people to turn back to the Lord for years, but they had not listened. The *good* figs had gone to Babylon. The *bad* figs were the people that were left in the city, which Jeremiah had prophesied about. The Book of Lamentations gives us a glimpse of what life was like for those who had been left in the besieged city of Jerusalem:

"Her gates are sunk into the ground; he hath destroyed and broken her bars: her king and her princes are among the Gentiles; the law is no more; her prophets also find no vision from the LORD" (Lamentations 2:9).

> The LORD done that which he hath devised; he hath fulfilled his word that he had commanded in the days of old: He hath thrown down, and hath not pitied: and he hath caused thine enemy to rejoice over thee, he hath set up the horn of thine adversaries. (Lamentations 2:17)

"The young and the old lie on the ground in the streets: my virgins and my young men are fallen by the sword; thou hast slain them in the day of thine anger; thou hast killed, and not pitied" (Lamentations 2:21).

"They that be slain with the sword are better than they that be slain with hunger" (Lamentations 4:9).

> The LORD hath accomplished his fury; he hath poured out his fierce anger, and hath kindled a fire in Zion, and it hath devoured the foundations thereof. The kings of the earth, and all the inhabitants of the world, would not have believed that the adversary and the enemy should have entered into the gates of Jerusalem. (Lamentations 4:11–12)

To better understand the horror that was taking place in the city, one can read Lamentations 4 in its entirety, which records in detail the terrible effects of the famine and starvation within Jerusalem.

# Jerusalem Is Demolished (587 BC–586 BC)

Information can be found in 2 Kings 25; Jeremiah 39

> In ... the nineteenth year of King Neb-u-chad-nez´-zar
> king of Babylon, came Neb´-u-zar-ad´-an, captain of the
> guard, a servant of the king of Babylon, unto Jerusalem:
> And he burnt the house of the LORD, and the king's
> house, and all the houses of Jerusalem, and every great
> man's house burnt he with fire. And all the army of the
> Chal´-dees, that were with the captain of the guard,
> brake down the walls of Jerusalem round about. (2 Kings
> 25:8–10)

Nebuzaradan, Nebuchadnezzar's captain of the guard, took those who
remained in the city to Babylon, while the very poor remained in Judah
to take care of the crops. He also took some temple servers, a scribe, the
king's attendees, and thirty men of the people to Babylon, where the king
had them killed. Before he left, Nebuzaradan robbed the temple, carrying
away the brass pillars and vessels made of gold, silver, and brass.

# Ezekiel Hears of Judah's Demise

"And it came to pass in the twelfth year of our captivity, in the tenth
month, in the fifth day of the month, that one that had escaped out of
Jerusalem came unto me, saying, The city is smitten" (Ezekiel 33:21).

# The Prophet Obadiah

The LORD raised up Obadiah the prophet to rebuke the Edomites (Esau's
descendants)[3] for proudly rejoicing over the sad misfortunes of Judah and
aiding in their demise. Someday God's judgement would be coming to
them as well. Earlier, when King Jehoram had reigned, the Edomites
had allied with the Philistines and Arabians against Jerusalem. Now they

had allied with Babylon against Jerusalem, and the Lord prophesied to Obadiah of their demise that is still to come in our future:

> For the day of the LORD is near upon all the heathen: as thou hast done, it shall be done unto thee: thy reward shall return upon thine own head. ... But upon mount Zion shall be deliverance, and there shall be holiness; and the house of Jacob shall possess their possessions. And the house of Jacob shall be a fire, and the house of Joseph a flame, and the house of Esau for stubble, and they shall kindle in them, and devour them; and there shall not be *any* remaining of the house of Esau; for the LORD hath spoken it. (Obadiah 1:15–18)

## Governor Gedaliah

Information about Governor Gedaliah can be found in 2 Kings 25; Jeremiah 40–41.

Nebuchadnezzar appointed Gedaliah to be governor over the remnant of the poor people who had been left in Judah. Since Jerusalem had been destroyed, he governed them from Mizpah. Nebuchadnezzar was good to Jeremiah and ordered his release from his chains in the prison court, giving him permission to go to Mizpah and live under Gedaliah with the people who were left there.

The captains in the fields and their men, including Ishmael, Johanan, Jonathan, Seraiah, the sons of Ephai, and Jezaniah heard that Nebuchadnezzar had appointed Gedaliah to be governor of the poor who had been left in the land. So they went to see him. Gedaliah told them not to be afraid to submit to and live with the Chaldeans, although he would stay in Mizpah to govern. He told them to take wine, fruit, and oil to put in their storage and to settle in the cities they had taken. When the other Jews who lived around Mizpah heard the news, they returned to Judah and gathered wine and summer crops as well.

At that time, King Baalis of the Ammonites conspired to kill Gedaliah, and he had sent Ishmael, who had been an officer of the king, to do the job. When Johanan heard about it, he and the captains warned Gedaliah, but he did not believe them. Johanan even offered to go and kill Ishmael himself so that Gedaliah would remain governor, and the remnant of Jews would not be scattered and destroyed; but Gedaliah refused his offer.

Just as Johanan had said, Ishmael and ten other men went to Gedaliah's house and killed him, along with the Jews and Chaldeans that were with him. The next day, a band of men from Shechem, Shiloh, and Samaria came up to bring offerings to the Lord. Ishmael met them and told them to go to Gedaliah's house where he killed them all, except for ten who begged to be set free to tend to their crops. He then threw the dead bodies into a pit. Then Ishmael captured and took away the remainder of the captives in Mizpah and left to go to the Ammonites; however, Johanan and the captains got wind of Ishmael's terrible crime and his plan; and he took men to fight Ishmael. When they caught up with him, the captives were so happy to see Johanan and his men that they joined up with them; and Ishmael, with eight of his men, ran away to the Ammonites. So Johanan took the captains and the remnant of people to Chimham, a place just outside of Bethlehem.

## No Remnant in Egypt

The captives were afraid of the Chaldeans because Ishmael had killed the governor who had been appointed by Nebuchadnezzar. Johanan and the small remnant asked Jeremiah to inquire of the Lord as to where they should go and how they should live, and they told him they would obey whatever the Lord would tell Jeremiah. After ten days, the Lord answered Jeremiah's prayer and told him to give them these *conditional* choices:

> *If ye will still abide in this land,* then will I build you, and
> not pull you down, and I will plant you, and not pluck
> you up: for I repent me of the evil that I have done unto
> you. Be not afraid of the king of Babylon, of whom ye are
> afraid ...for I am with you to save you, and to deliver you

from his hand. And I will show mercies unto you, that he may have mercy upon you, and cause you to return to your own land.

*But if ye say, We will not dwell in this land,* neither obey the voice of the LORD your God, Saying, No; but we will go into the land of Egypt, where we shall see no war, nor hear the sound of the trumpet, nor have hunger of bread; and there will we dwell. ... Then it shall come to pass, that the sword, which ye feared, shall overtake you there in the land of Egypt, and the famine, whereof ye were afraid, shall follow close after you there in Egypt; and there ye shall die. (Jeremiah 42:10–16; emphasis added)

They had been warned, but Azariah, Johanan, and some of the prideful men with them did not believe God had told them not to go to Egypt. They accused Jeremiah of lying to them. They believed that he was setting them up to be exiled into Babylon to be killed. Johanan and all the army officers led the remnant of Judah off to Egypt, including Jeremiah and Baruch, who were forced to go. When they arrived in Tahpanhes, the Lord showed Jeremiah that He would send Nebuchadrezzar, king of Babylon, to destroy Egypt.

God gave this message to Jeremiah to give to the Jews who had chosen to flee into Egypt, those living in Egypt in "Mig´-dol, Tah´-pan-hes and Noph and Path´-ros" (Jeremiah 44:1):

Wherefore commit ye this great evil against your souls, to cut off from you man and woman, child and suckling, out of Judah, to leave you none to remain; In that ye provoke me unto wrath with the works of your hands, burning incense unto other gods in the land of Egypt, whither ye be gone to dwell, that ye might cut yourselves off, and that ye might be a curse and a reproach among all the nations of the earth? (Jeremiah 44:7–8)

I will punish them that dwell in the land of Egypt, as I have punished Jerusalem, by the sword, by the famine, and by the pestilence: So that none of the remnant of Judah, which are gone into the land of Egypt to sojourn there, shall escape or remain, that they should return into the land of Judah, to the which they have a desire to return to dwell there: for none shall return but such as shall escape. (Jeremiah 44:13–14)

The Jews seriously believed they had been better off before. They angrily told Jeremiah:

We will certainly do whatsoever thing goeth forth out of our own mouth, to burn incense unto the queen of heaven, and to pour out drink offerings unto her, as we have done, we, and our fathers, our kings, and our princes, in the cities of Judah, and in the streets of Jerusalem: for then had we plenty of victuals, and were well, and saw no evil. (Jeremiah 44:17)

Jeremiah reminded them that it was because of the sins of idolatry that the Lord had brought this judgment upon them, and then he gave them this message from the Lord:

Ye and your wives have both spoken with your mouths, and fulfilled with your hand, saying, We will surely perform our vows that we have vowed, to burn incense to the queen of heaven, and to pour out drink offerings unto her: ye will surely accomplish your vows, and surely perform your vows.

Therefore hear ye the word of the LORD, all Judah that dwell in the land of Egypt; behold, I have sworn by my great name, saith the LORD, that my name shall no more be named in the mouth of any man of Judah in all the land of Egypt, saying, The LORD GOD liveth. Behold,

I will watch over them for evil, and not for good: and all the men of Judah that are in the land of Egypt shall be consumed by the sword and by the famine, until there be an end of them. Yet a small number that escape the sword shall return out of the land of Egypt into the land of Judah, and all the remnant of Judah, that are gone into the land of Egypt to sojourn there, shall know whose words shall stand, mine, or theirs.

And this shall be a *sign* unto you, saith the LORD, that I will punish you in this place, that ye may know that my words shall surely stand against you for evil: Thus saith the LORD; behold, I will give Phar´-aoh-hoph´-ra king of Egypt into the hand of his enemies, and into the hand of them that seek his life; as I gave Zed-e-ki´-ah king of Judah into the hand of Neb-u-chad-rez´-zar king of Babylon, his enemy, and that sought his life. (Jeremiah 44:25–30; emphasis added)

## Judgment of the Heathen Nations

After the fall of Jerusalem, God did bring judgment on Ammon, Moab, Edom, and Philistia, for "all took a vengeful delight in Israel's downfall ... Shortly after this, Ammon, Moab and Edom were overrun by Nabataean tribesmen. The Philistines disappeared from history a century before the birth of Jesus."[4] However, the end of God's final judgment on all wicked nations is still to come. There will be a final day of God's wrath after the day of the great tribulation in the future.

What we have been reading about in this period of history should startle us, because right now our own governmental leaders are leading us into the same ungodly lifestyles as what we have just seen with Israel and Judah. Just because our leaders make ungodly decisions and laws, doesn't make it right with God. There will be a day of reckoning for all who do not bend their knee to Christ and His holiness.

# In Conclusion

Like Israel, Judah had fallen, and can't you imagine the smile on Satan's face! The Israelite nation, whom God had chosen and established to be a holy nation, had succumbed to all the wiles of the Devil. He had enticed and deceived them, causing them to stop worshiping the living God and to give their allegiance and worship to other gods made of stone, wood, and metal. Every sin imaginable had been committed by God's holy nation, and now God had turned His back on them. With Satan's hatred of God, he probably thought if he could destroy God's people, he could destroy God's plan to bring the Savior Jesus Christ into the world. Without Jesus, salvation for humanity would be foiled. What he hadn't counted on was that God's love and mercy, His sovereignty, and His faithfulness were promised to those who were in His covenant; and God is a promise keeper.

Satan had underestimated God! It was true that the people of Judah had been removed because of their sin and that the Jews, who had fled to Egypt, would never return; but God would still bring about His plan of salvation. He would still save a remnant of Jews who would be delivered from exile after seventy years. Also, someday in the future, Judah and Israel would enter into a new blood covenant with God through Jesus Christ. God was still watching and would care for those taken captive to Babylon. In fact, God called the prophet Ezekiel to be a watchman and to minister to the captives in Babylon.

In the ancient days, Job, Satan, and the Lord were having a discussion about Job, who was a righteous man. Satan was sure that if God brought physical hardship to Job, he would turn away from God. Satan told the Lord, "Skin for skin, yea, all that a man hath will he give for his life. But put forth thine hand now, and touch his bone and his flesh, and he will curse thee to thy face" (Job 2:4–5).

Judah had not been righteous before the Lord as Job had been, but you can be sure that Satan was counting on their hearts to become forever hardened against the Lord because of the punishment He was inflicting upon them. Now we are going to leave the demolished and desolated city of Jerusalem and go to Babylon to visit the land of the exiled remnant of Judah, where we will be able to find out a little about their physical, emotional, and spiritual condition. Will they harden their hearts towards God, or will they listen to Ezekiel who God had called to be their "watchman"?

## Deeper Insights:

1. God gave Ezekiel a vision of His glory in heaven right before He called him to go to the captives. Read Ezekiel 1 to get a glimpse of what he saw.

2. God told Ezekiel He was sending him "to the children of Israel...a rebellious nation" (Ezekiel 2:3).

   What did God tell Ezekiel that helped him prepare for this mission? Read Ezekiel 2:5–10.

3. God called Ezekiel to be a "watchman" to those who were in captivity in Babylon. Read Ezekiel 3:18–21; 33:1–7 to see what the responsibility of a watchman is.

   What do you think God meant when He said, "his blood will I require at thine hand?"

   Read Acts 20:17–26, which is Paul's account to the elders in Ephesus.

   As believers in Christ, do you think we are called to be watchmen to others?

   Read the following Scriptures: Matthew 28:19–20; Galatians 6:1; Ephesians 4:15; 2 Timothy 4:2; 1 Thessalonians 5:14; James 5:20; Jude 21–23; Proverbs 11:30

   Can you think of a time when you felt God's Spirit urging you to take the responsibility of a watchman for someone else? Did you obey? What were the results?

4. What did God promise would happen to those who did not go with them into captivity in Babylon? Read Jeremiah 29:17–19; 43:8–13.

# CHAPTER 8

## BABYLON

## The City of Idols

What was life like in this place called Babylon—the place where God had sent the Jews into exile? Excavations give us a clue of what the city of Babylon was like. It was located in what we now know as Iraq, along the Euphrates River. It is the same general area in which the Garden of Eden was located, and from where Abraham once lived before his family left the idolatrous city of Ur.

The following paraphrase is taken from information found in the Holman Bible Atlas[1]:

> After its devastation by Sennacherib in 689 BC, Nahopolassur and Nebuchadnezzar rebuilt Babylon in two sections—the ancient city was on the east side of the river, and the newer section, which housed the palace and residential areas, was on the west side of the river. Nebuchadnezzar built a bridge over the river, which connected both sections. It was a busy trade center with caravans traveling through, bringing their goods to trade and sell.

Babylon was a city of manmade gods and symbols, and statues of these gods were everywhere throughout the city and the palace: "bulls (symbol of the weather god Adad)," and "dragons (symbol of Marduk)."[2] Marduk was the patron god of Babylon. The city had nine gates, and each gate had a name of a Babylonian god—"Ishtar, Marduk, Sin, Enlil, Urash, Shamash, Adad, Zababa, and Lugalgirra."[3] Another huge structure in Babylon was the "ziggurat [temple-tower] known as Etemenanki—'Building of the foundation of Heaven and Earth.' ... A temple to Marduk crowned the top of the ziggeraut."[4]

Ezekiel gives us an indication of the vicinity of the exiled Jews in Babylon. He said, "I was among the captives by the river of Che´-bar" (Ezekiel 1:1).

Che´-bar "ran from the Euphrates north of Babylon, close to the city of Nippur."[5] "Several sites settled by the deportees bear the name 'Tel' (Tel-abib, Tel-melah, Tel-harsha), a term designating an abandoned ruin. This suggests that the Babylonians may have selected abandoned villages for some of the settlements."[6] Cherub, Addan, and Immer (see Ezra 2:59) were other sites in which the Jews would eventually settle.

During the early years of their captivity, the Jews experienced emotional and spiritual anguish. They were separated from their families, friends, and temple; and were thrown into and unfamiliar world that was totally encompassed with idol worship. It was a world that did not recognize the Lord they had once been devoted to. They were now living in a world that did not understand their divine background, their covenant with the Lord, and the depth of sorrow in their hearts. Even though they had also worshiped idols, they still remembered their God and their temple worship, though they had perverted it. Having that taken away from them, they now felt the effects of godly sorrow, rejection, and abandonment by the living God. They wrote:

> By the rivers of Babylon, there we sat down, yea, we wept, when we remembered Zion. We hanged our harps upon the willows in the midst thereof. For there they that carried us away captive required of us a song; and they that wasted us required of us mirth, saying, Sing us one of the songs of Zion. How shall we sing the LORD'S song in a strange land? (Psalm 137:1–4)

It had been prophesied by the prophets that one day in the future, the Lord would destroy idolatrous Babylon. The exiles now remembered that

God had promised justice would be coming: "O daughter of Babylon, who art to be destroyed; happy shall he be, that rewardeth thee as thou hast served us. Happy shall he be, that taketh and dasheth thy little ones against the stones" (Psalm 137:8–9).

## Judah's Nativity and Marriage to God

God gave Ezekiel this message to show the exiled Jews that He had chosen them. The following Scriptures truly show God's deepest love for Jacob's (Israel's) children. They also speak of how Christ seeks and saves all sinners from our lives of sin. Listen to the Lord's words:

> On the day you were born your cord was not cut, nor were you washed with water to make you clean, nor were you rubbed with salt or wrapped in cloths. No one looked on you with pity or had compassion enough to do any of these things for you. Rather, you were thrown out into the open field, for on the day you were born you were despised.
>
> Then I passed by and saw you kicking about in your blood, and as you lay there in your blood I said to you, "Live!" I made you grow like a plant of the field. You grew and developed and entered puberty. Your breasts had formed and your hair had grown, yet you were stark naked.
>
> Later I passed by, and when I looked at you and saw that you were old enough for love, I spread the corner of my garment over you and covered your naked body. I gave you my solemn oath and entered into a covenant with you, declares the Sovereign LORD, and you became mine.
>
> I bathed you with water and washed the blood from you and put ointments on you. I clothed you with an

embroidered dress and put sandals of fine leather on you. I dressed you in fine linen and covered you with costly garments. I adorned you with jewelry: I put bracelets on your arms and a necklace around your neck, and I put a ring on your nose, earrings on your ears and a beautiful crown on your head. So you were adorned with gold and silver; your clothes were of fine linen and costly fabric and embroidered cloth. Your food was honey, olive oil and the finest flour. You became very beautiful and rose to be a queen. And your fame spread among the nations on account of your beauty, because the splendor I had given you made your beauty perfect, declares the Sovereign LORD. (Ezekiel 16:4–14, NIV®)

## Judah's Adultery

God wanted Judah to fully understand why they had been sent into exile so they would turn to Him and repent.

You took some of your garments to make gaudy high places, where you carried on your prostitution. You went to him, and he possessed your beauty. You also took the fine jewelry I gave you, the jewelry made of my gold and silver, and you made for yourself male idols and engaged in prostitution with them. And you took your embroidered clothes to put on them, and you offered my oil and incense before them. Also the food I provided for you—the flour, olive oil and honey I gave you to eat— you offered as fragrant incense before them. That is what happened, declares the Sovereign LORD.

And you took your sons and daughters whom you bore to me and sacrificed them as food to the idols. Was your prostitution not enough? You slaughtered my children and sacrificed them to the idols. In all your detestable practices and your prostitution you did not remember the days of your youth, when you were naked and bare, kicking about in your blood.

Woe! Woe to you, declares the Sovereign LORD. In addition to all your other wickedness, you built a mound for yourself and made a lofty shrine in every public square. At every street corner you built your lofty shrines and degraded your beauty, spreading your legs with increasing promiscuity to anyone who passed by. You engaged in prostitution with the Egyptians, your neighbors with large genitals, and aroused my anger with your increasing promiscuity. So I stretched out my hand against you and reduced your territory; I gave you over to the greed of your enemies, the daughters of the Philistines, who were shocked by your lewd conduct. You engaged in prostitution with the Assyrians too, because you were insatiable; and even after that, you still were not satisfied. Then you increased your promiscuity to include Babylonia, a land of merchants, but even with this you were not satisfied.

I am filled with fury against you, declares the Sovereign LORD, when you do all these things, acting like a brazen prostitute! When you built your mounds at every street corner and made your lofty shrines in every public square, you were unlike a prostitute, because you scorned payment.

You adulterous wife! You prefer strangers to your own husband! (Ezekiel 16:15–32)

God reminded them of His own faithfulness, in spite of their condition: "Nevertheless I will remember my covenant with thee in the days of thy youth, and I will establish unto thee an everlasting covenant" (Ezekiel 16:60).

Ezekiel told them to look to the Lord for their salvation. Listen as you read the promises Ezekiel prophesied to the people of Israel, to those God called His sheep. You will hear the Lord's promises of the future Shepherd, who would be coming to gather them, feed them, and bring them peace. This event is still to come in our future.

> I, will both search my sheep, and seek them out. ... and will deliver them out of all places where they have been scattered in the cloudy and dark day. ... I will feed my flock, and I will cause them to lie down, saith the Lord GOD. I will seek that which was lost, and bring again that which was driven away, and will bind up that which was broken, and I will strengthen that which was sick: but I will destroy the fat and the strong; I will feed them with judgment. (Ezekiel 34:11–16)

> I will set up one Shepherd over them, and he shall feed them, even my Servant David: he shall feed them, and he shall be their shepherd. And the LORD will be their God, and my Servant David a prince among them; I the LORD have spoken it. (Ezekiel 34:23–24)

One day, when they see Jesus, they will recognize Him as their long-awaited Messiah and will receive Him as their King. Read these beautiful promises of hope for their future that the Lord gave them to sustain them during their exile.

> I will make with them a covenant of peace, and will cause the evil beasts to cease out of the land: and they shall dwell safely in the wilderness and sleep in the woods. And I will make them and the places round about my hill a blessing: and I will cause the shower to come down in his season; there shall be showers of blessing. And the tree of the field shall yield her fruit, and the earth shall yield her increase, and they shall be safe in their land, and shall know that I am the LORD, when I have broken the bands

of their yoke, and delivered them out of the hand of those that served themselves of them. ... they shall know that I the LORD their God am with them, and that they, even the house of Israel, are my people, saith the Lord GOD. And ye my flock, the flock of my pasture are men, and I am your God. (Ezekiel 34:25–31)

Then will I sprinkle clean water upon you, and ye shall be clean: from all your filthiness, and from all your idols, will I cleanse you. A new heart also will I give you and a new spirit will I put within you, and I will take away the stony heart out of your flesh, and I will give you a heart of flesh. And I will put my spirit within you and cause you to walk in my statutes and ye shall keep my judgments, and do them. And ye shall dwell in the land that I gave to your fathers, and ye shall be my people, and I will be your God. ... Then shall ye remember your own evil ways, and your doings that were not good, and shall loathe yourselves in your own sight for your iniquities and for your abominations. (Ezekiel 36:25–31)

Therefore thus saith the Lord GOD; Now will I bring again the captivity of Jacob, and have mercy upon the whole house of Israel, and will be jealous for my holy name; After that they have borne their shame, and all their trespasses whereby they have trespassed against me, when they dwelt safely in their land, and none made them afraid. (Ezekiel 39:25–26)

## Daniel's Life in Babylon

When King Nebuchadnezzar besieged Jerusalem the first time and took the first exiles to Babylon, Daniel, a young godly Jewish man, had gone, too. During that time, Nebuchadnezzar began looking for some strong, healthy young men to serve him in the palace—men who came from the seed of King Jehoiakim, the children of Israel, and of the princes. He ordered Ashpenaz, who was in charge of his eunuchs, to choose young men with these characteristsics: "no blemish ... well-favored ... skillful in all wisdom ... cunning in knowledge ... understanding science ... had ability in them to stand in the king's palace, and whom they might teach the learning and the tongue of the Chal-de´-ans" (Daniel 1:4).

Some of the young men chosen from Judah were Daniel, Hananiah, and Mishael. These four young men were given new names: Belteshazar (Daniel); Shadrach (Hananiah); Mishael (Meshach); and Azariah (Abednego).

For three years, the king provided them with the same meat and wine that was used in the palace for himself so that they would be strong and healthy in his sight at the end of the three years; however, the Babylonians did not follow the Jewish food laws, and that meant that the laws about what was clean and unclean were not being practiced. Daniel asked permission for himself, Shadrach, Meshach, and Abednego to be given only pulse to eat and water to drink, with the promise that they would look and be just as healthy as the others.

The Hebrew word translated *pulse* is "zêrâ'ôn." The meaning of the word is "something sown... i.e. a vegetable (as food)."[7]

After being given a ten-day trial period of eating the food on their Jewish diet, these four young men looked even better than those who had eaten the king's food. So Daniel was granted his request for them to continue eating pulse and drinking water. God began to fill them with His knowledge and wisdom, and He gave Daniel the ability to interpret dreams and visions. At the end of the time set by the king, the young Jewish men surpassed all the magicians and enchanters in the king's kingdom with knowledge and understanding.

During the next year, Nebuchadnezzar began to have troubling dreams and commanded all of his so-called experts in magical arts to tell him what he had dreamed and asked them to interpret the dreams, which of course, they could not. The king gave an order to kill all the wise men in Babylon, Daniel included. Daniel went before the king and told him that he would interpret his dream if he could have some time. Shadrach, Meshach, and Abednego prayed and asked God for His mercies regarding this dream. God gave Daniel a vision in the night. Then Daniel went to the man who had been ordered to kill the wise men. He told him not to carry out the order, but to take him in to see the king so he could give his interpretation of the king's dream. Daniel told the king that his experts in magical arts would not be able to help him, but the "God in heaven" could.

Daniel not only told Nebuchadnezzar what he had dreamed, but he also gave him God's interpretation of it, which had to do with a prophecy of "four world empires, beginning in the present and stretching into the future."[8]

The king was so grateful that he appointed Daniel to rule the province of Babylon and to take charge of his wise men. He also appointed the other three men that were with Daniel to be administrators over Babylon.

## The Firey Furnace

Everything was good for the four young men from Judah until 585 BC, when the king made a ninety foot golden statue of himself and ordered everyone to bow down to it or be thrown into a firey furnace. Shadrach, Meshach, and Abednego refused to bow and were brought before the furious king. They told the king:

> King Nebuchadnezzar, we do not need to defend ourselves before you in this matter. If we are thrown into the blazing furnace, the God we serve is able to deliver us from it, and he will deliver us from Your Majesty's hand. But even if he does not, we want you to know, Your Majesty, that we will not serve your gods or worship the image of gold you have set up. (Daniel 3:16–18, NIV®)

Then the king ordered the furnace to be heated up to seven times hotter than it normally was. While the soldiers were throwing the three men, who were bound in their clothes, into the furnace, the soldiers died from the heat. Shadrach, Meshach, and Abednego fell down into the fire. When the king looked into the fire, he saw four men walking around in the fire, not three. He told his counselors, "I see four men loose, walking in the midst of the fire, and they have no hurt; and the form of the fourth is like the Son of God" (Daniel 3:25).

When the king ordered the three men to come out of the furnace, there was no sign that they had been near the fire or the heat, not even the smell of smoke was on them. The king made this announcement:

> Blessed be the God of Sha´-drach, Me´-shach, and A-bed´-ne-go, who hath sent his angel, and delivered his servants that trusted in him, and have changed the king's word, and yielded their bodies, that they might not serve nor worship any god, except their own God.
>
> Therefore I make a decree, That every people, nation, and language, which speak any thing amiss against the God of Sha´-drach, Me´-shach, and A-bed´-ne-go, shall be cut in pieces, and their houses shall be made a dunghill: because there is no other God that can deliver after this sort. (Daniel 3:28–29)

## King Nebuchadnezzar's Downfall

Later on, King Nebuchadnezzar had another dream which could not be interpreted by his wise men; and he asked Daniel to interpret it. He told Daniel, "The spirit of the holy gods is in thee" (Daniel 4:18). When the king told Daniel his dream about a tree (see Daniel 4:10–17), Daniel was troubled by the dream, and after one hour, gave the king this interpretation from the Lord:

> They shall drive thee from men, and thy dwelling shall be with the beasts of the field, and they shall make thee to eat grass as oxen, and they shall wet thee with the dew of heaven, and seven times shall pass over thee, till thou know that the most High ruleth in the kingdom of men, and giveth it to whomsoever he will. And whereas they commanded to leave the stump of the tree roots; thy

kingdom shall be sure unto thee, after that thou shalt have known that the heavens do rule. (Daniel 4:25–26)

After that, Daniel advised the king to quit sinning, to live right, and to be merciful to the poor; however, a year later, the king began to boast about himself:

> Is not this great Babylon, that I have built for the house of the kingdom by the might of my power, and for the honor of my majesty? While the word was in the king's mouth, there fell a voice from heaven, saying, O King Neb-u-chad-nez´zar, to thee it is spoken; The kingdom is departed from thee. (Daniel 4:30–31).

> The same hour was the thing fulfilled upon Neb-u-chad-nez´zar: and he was driven from men, and did eat grass as oxen, and his body was wet with the dew of heaven, till his hairs were grown like eagles' feathers, and his nails like birds' claws. (Daniel 4:33)

## God Transforms King Nebuchadnezzar

> And at the end of the days, I, Neb-u-chad-nez´-zar, lifted mine eyes unto heaven, and mine understanding returned unto me, and I blessed the most High, and I praised and honored him that liveth for ever, whose dominion is an everlasting dominion, and his kingdom is from generation to generation: And all the inhabitants of the earth are reputed as nothing: and he doeth according to his will in the army of heaven, and among the inhabitants of the earth: and none can stay his hand, or say unto him, What doest Thou?

> At the same time my reason returned unto me; and for the glory of my kingdom, mine honor and brightness returned

unto me; and my counselors and my lords sought unto me; and I was established in my kingdom, and excellent majesty was added unto me. Now I Neb-u-chad-nez´-zar praise and extol and honor the King of heaven, all whose works are truth, and his ways judgment: and those that walk in pride he is able to abase. (Daniel 4:34–37)

## The Time of King Belshazzar

After Nebuchadnezzar died, Nabonidus became king; but he left to go to another country, leaving his son Belshazzar to be the king of Babylon in his absence. King Belshazzar, like King Nebuchadnezzar, also had an encounter with Daniel. He was holding a big banquet and ordered the gold and silver wine goblets that had been stolen from the temple in Jerusalem to be brought in so that he and others with him could drink wine from them. When they were drinking from them, they began to praise the gods of metal, wood, and stone. All of a sudden, a hand appeared, and its fingers began to write on the palace wall.

The king was terrified, and called in all his wise men of Babylon to interpret the writing on the wall, offering lavish gifts to them, but none of them could read or understand the writing on the wall. The queen told King Belshazzar about Daniel who had helped his grandfather when he was king. So the king sent for Daniel. Daniel reminded King Belshazzar about how arrogant his grandfather Nebuchadnezzar had been towards God and how God had humbled him to the point that he acknowledged God and worshiped him. He told the king:

> And thou … hast not humbled thine heart, though thou knowest all this; But hast lifted up thyself against the Lord of heaven; and they have brought the vessels of his house before thee, and thou, and thy lords, thy wives, and thy concubines, have drunk wine in them; and thou hast praised the gods of silver, and gold, of brass, iron, wood, and stone, which see not, nor hear, nor know: and the

God in whose hand thy breath is, and whose are all thy ways, hast thou not glorified. (Daniel 5:22–23)

Then Daniel interpreted the writing on the wall: "ME´-NE; God hath numbered thy kingdom, and finished it. TE´-KEL; Thou art weighed in the balances, and art found wanting. PE´-RES; Thy kingdom is divided, and given to the Medes and Persians" (Daniel 5:26–28).

That very night, someone killed King Belshazzar, and Darius became king of Babylon.

## King Darius the Median

King Darius made Daniel one of his administrators over his satraps. The king planned to place Daniel over his kingdom because of his faithfulness and good qualities. The other administrators and satraps tried to find fault with him because they resented Daniel, but they could not. So they urged the king to issue an edict that anyone who prayed to any god or man, except to the king, in the next thirty days should be thrown into the lions' den; so the king issued the edict.

The edict only spurred Daniel on: "He went into his house; and his windows being open in his chamber toward Jerusalem, he kneeled upon his knees three times a day, and prayed, and gave thanks before his God, as he did aforetime" (Daniel 6:10).

The jealous men went and told the king that Daniel was praying to his God three times a day. The king, who favored Daniel, did not want to hurt him and tried to find a way to save him; but his men reminded him that once a king decrees an edict, the edict cannot be changed. When the king realized that what they said was true, he had Daniel thrown into the lions' den and he sealed the opening. He told Daniel, "Thy God whom thou servest continually, he will deliver thee" (Daniel 6:16).

The next morning the king got up early to check on Daniel and called out to him to find out if his God had rescued him. Daniel answered:

O king, live forever! My God hath sent his angel, and hath shut the lions' mouths, that they have not hurt me:

117

forasmuch as before him innocency was found in me; and also before thee, O king, have I done no hurt" (Daniel 6:21–22).

The king was happy about this, and then he threw the jealous men into the lions' den; and the lions destroyed them. After that, King Darius issued a decree about Daniel's God:

> I make a decree, That in every dominion of my kingdom men tremble and fear before the God of Daniel: for he is the living God, and steadfast for ever, and his kingdom that which shall not be destroyed, and his dominion shall be even unto the end. He delivereth and rescueth, and he worketh signs and wonders in heaven and in earth, who hath delivered Daniel from the power of the lions. So this Daniel prospered in the reign of Da-ri´-us, and in the reign of Cyrus the Persian. (Daniel 6:26–28)

## Daniel Intercedes for Judah

In the first year of Darius (538–539 BC), Daniel read Jeremiah's written words about why God sent the Jews into exile for seventy years; and he prayed for God's mercy:

> O Lord, according to all thy righteousness, I beseech thee, let thine anger and thy fury be turned away from thy city Jerusalem, thy holy mountain: because for our sins, and for the iniquities of our fathers, Jerusalem and thy people are become a reproach to all that are about us. ... hear the prayer of thy servant, and his supplications, and cause thy face to shine upon thy sanctuary that is desolate, for the Lord's sake. ... we do not present our supplications before thee for our righteousness, but for thy great mercies. ... O Lord, hear; O Lord, forgive; O Lord, hearken and do;

defer not, for thine own sake, O my God: for thy city and thy people are called by thy name. (Daniel 9:16–19)

While Daniel was praying and confessing his sins and the sins of Israel, the angel Gabriel came and gave him a prophetic timetable about the future of Israel. It includes a prophecy about the coming of the Messiah and the "last days."

Seventy 'sevens' are decreed for your people and your holy city to finish transgression, to put an end to sin, to atone for wickedness, to bring in everlasting righteousness, to seal up vision and prophecy and to anoint the most holy.

Know and understand this: From the issuing of the decree to restore and rebuild Jerusalem until the Anointed One, the ruler, comes, there will be seven 'sevens,' and sixty-two 'sevens.' It will be rebuilt with streets and a trench, but in times of trouble. After the sixty-two 'sevens,' the Anointed One will be cut off and will have nothing. The people of the ruler who will come will destroy the city and the sanctuary.

The end will come like a flood: War will continue until the end, and desolations have been decreed. He will confirm a covenant with many for one 'seven.' In the middle of the 'seven' he will put an end to sacrifice and offering. And on a wing of the temple, he will set up an abomination that causes desolation, until the end that is decreed is poured out on him. (Daniel 9:24–27, NIV®)

In the third year of Cyrus of Persia, Daniel had been mourning for three weeks; and he had a vision of a man who came to see him:

A certain man clothed in linen, whose loins were girded with fine gold of U´-phaz: His body also was like the beryl, and his face as the appearance of lightning, and his eyes as lamps of fire, and his arms and his feet like in color to polished brass, and the voice of his words like the voice of a multitutde. (Daniel 10:5–6)

"Now I am come to make thee understand what shall befall thy people in the latter days: for yet the vision is for many days" (Daniel 10:14).

Daniel's visions in chapters 11–12 have to do with the future of Israel, which is still yet to come.

## In Conclusion

God, out of His mercy and love for the house of Judah, had sent them into Babylon, an idolatrous city, for seventy years; but He had not abandoned His people. He had sent Ezekiel and Daniel there, too. Ezekiel was a "watchman" over them to remind them that God was their Father who had chosen them, and that He would always be faithful to them. He reminded them of their adultery to God, encouraged them to return to Him, and he consoled them.

God used Daniel, an emboldened heralder of faith, to plant seeds of faith into the hearts of Kings Nebuchadnezzar and Darius, which resulted in religious freedom for the Jews. After reading Jeremiah's words about why the Jews went into the seventy-year exile, Daniel interceded for God's mercy over the house of Israel. He prayed, fasted, and mourned over what they had done to cause this judgement of separation from their God and their country.

Through the ministries of Ezekiel and Daniel, the faith of the Jews from Judah had sustained. Will God remember His promise to take them out of exile and return them to their land? If so, will they want to go back to their ravaged city of Jerusalem or remain in Babylon where they have built new lives?

## Deeper Insights:

1. Babylon was a city full of idols, and they were on display at every turn. Can you think of any cities or countries today that are steeped in idolatry?

2. Read Ezekiel 16:15–32. What caused Jerusalem to fall? What did God say Jerusalem played the part of?

   Read Ezekiel 16:45–52. Who does Ezekiel say are Judah's sisters? What were the sins of her sister, Sodom?

   The Bible says Christians are the Bride of Christ. Before we were saved, Christ, in His love and mercy, passed by us and took us from our polluted and naked state. When we turned to Him as our Lord and Savior, repenting of our sins, He washed them away and anointed us with oil. He also gave us fine clothing and jewels (see Ezekiel 16:3–14). Yet, as individuals, we have, at times, played the part of the harlot by leaving Him, even if for a moment, to enjoy the pleasures of this earthly life.

   Can you think of times in your own life, as a Christian, that you played the harlot?

3. God will remember His promises to Judah. Read Ezekiel 16:59–63 and 36:24–38.

4. For what purpose did God abase King Nebuchadnezzar, which was the fulfillment of his prophetic dream about the tree? Read Daniel 4:17.

   What was Nebuchadnezzar's primary sin in this case? Read Daniel 4:37.

5. How did God deliver Daniel from the lions? Read Daniel 6:22.

   How did Daniel's bravery and faith in God change the kingdom? Read Daniel 6:26–27.

6. Why did King Belshazzar, Nebuchadnezzar's grandson, die? Read Daniel 5:22–23.

# CHAPTER 9

## THE EXILES RETURN TO JERUSALEM

### Cyrus the Great

In 539 BC, the Babylonian Empire fell to the Persian king, Cyrus. Isaiah 45:1 says that Cyrus was the Lord's "anointed." The LORD gave Babylon to him so that the Judean exiles could be free to go to Jerusalem to restore the temple. The Lord said of King Cyrus: "I have raised him up in righteousness, and I will direct all his ways: he shall build my city, and he shall let go my captives, not for price nor reward, saith the LORD of hosts" (Isaiah 45:13).

King Cyrus knew why God had given him Babylon, as well. He made a proclamation that all Jews who wanted to go back to Jerusalem to rebuild the temple were free to go:

> Thus saith Cyrus king of Persia, The LORD God of heaven hath given me all the kingdoms of the earth; and he hath charged me to build him a house at Jerusalem, which is in Judah. Who is there among you of all his people? His God be with him, and let him go up to Jerusalem, which is in Judah, and build the house of the LORD God of Israel, (he is the God,) which is in Jerusalem. And whosoever remaineth in any place where he sojourneth, let the men of his place help him with silver, and with gold, and with goods, and with beasts, beside the freewill offering for the house of God that is in Jerusalem. (Ezra 1:2–4)

The Hebrew word translated *sojourneth* is "gûwr." The meaning of the word is "to turn aside from the road (for a lodging or any other purpose)."[1]

Jeremiah 29:10; Daniel 9:2; Zechariah 7:5; and 2 Chronicles 36:21 all indicate that the Jews would be in exile for seventy years—from the time of the fall of Jerusalem in 586 BC until the temple would be restored in 515 BC. King Cyrus made a decree for the temple to be rebuilt and the captives to go free. He brought out the gold and silver articles that King Nebuchadnezzar had stolen from the temple in Jerusalem so they could, once again, be placed in the Lord's house.

## Sheshbazzar Leads the Jews Back to Jerusalem

Information can be found in Ezra 2.

King Cyrus appointed Sheshbazzar, who was of Davidic lineage, to be the governor over the exiles. He would be leading the exiles back to Jerusalem and would personally deliver the temple articles. By this time, the Jews had adapted to the Babylonian culture; and many of them now spoke the language of Babylon. While millions of the exiled Jews decided to stay in Babylon, in about 538 BC, about fifty thousand of them made the decision to return to Jerusalem to live and to help rebuild their temple. They would still be under the reign of the Persian king.

Can you imagine the caravan? With Sheshbazzar leading, there were 42,330 people of the Jewish congregation, along with 7,337 servants and maids, one hundred singers, and 7,536 horses, mules, camels, and asses, all walking out of Babylon to go back to Jerusalem. It reminds us of their two to three million ancestors who left Egypt so long ago when God had delivered them from bondage in Egypt. Before the exile, the Jews were in bondage to sin. Now God had disciplined the people he loved so much, and they had returned to Him with their hearts. Once again, He had set His chosen people free. A recorded list of the individuals who returned to Jerusalem can be found in Ezra 2 and Nehemiah 7.

Beside the temple articles from King Nebuchadnezzar, the people also brought with them the gold, silver, goods, beasts, freewill offerings, and priests' garments for God's house, which had been collected from some of the heads of the families to help pay for the rebuilding of the temple. Everyone settled in their own allotted towns, including the priests, Levites, and everyone else who would serve in the temple.

## Worship Is Restored

When they arrived in Jerusalem, the first thing to be rebuilt was the altar. Jeshua and Zerubbabel were leaders of the Jewish community in Jerusalem. They, their associates, and the priests began to rebuild the altar on its old foundation. When the altar was finished, they immediately began to offer burnt offerings to God because they were afraid of the other nations around them. They also celebrated the Feast of Tabernacles. After being in exile for seventy years, how wonderful it must have been for them to bring their offerings to the Lord and be reconciled back to Him. They could now, once again, live according to the Law of Moses—the Law given to their forefathers.

## Rebuilding the Temple

In the second year after returning, Zerubbabel and Jeshua appointed the Levites, twenty and over, to promote the work on the Temple, beginning with its foundation. The masons and carpenters were given money to begin rebuilding the temple on Mount Zion. They sent money, meat, drink, and oil to Sidon and Tyre in exchange for cedar logs, which were shipped by sea from Lebanon. When the foundation was complete, the priests and the people celebrated and gave thanks to God. They played trumpets and cymbals, shouting and praising the Lord. It was a time of great emotional reflection and thankfulness.

> Many of the priests and Levites and chief of the fathers,
> who were ancient men, that had seen the first house,
> when the foundation of this house was laid before their
> eyes, wept with a loud voice; and many shouted aloud for
> joy: So that the people could not discern the noise of the

shout of joy from the noise of the weeping of the people: for the people shouted with a loud shout, and the noise was heard afar off. (Ezra 3:12–13)

The Jews were excited to start rebuilding a house for God, a place for the priests to serve Him, bringing reconciliation to the people, as it was in the days of Moses. They needed to have a central place to come together as a community to worship and serve their God—a place to restore their spiritual identity and unity as a covenant nation. The temple would also be a sign to the pagan nations that God was with them. The time was drawing closer for the coming of the promised Messiah, their King. For now, though, a faithful remnant must be saved in order for the promises of Abraham to come to pass through this remnant.

When neighboring enemies of Judah and Benjamin heard that the temple was being rebuilt, they came to Zerubbabel and the chief leaders to ask if they could come and help them. This was the answer they heard: "Ye have nothing to do with us to build a house unto our God; but we ourselves together will build unto the LORD God of Israel, as King Cyrus the king of Persia hath commanded us" (Ezra 4:3).

So these enemies began to continuously harass the Jews to try to discourage them from completing their temple, even to the extent of hiring counselors to frustrate and deter them. When Ahasuerus became king of Persia, the enemies of the Jews sent him a letter bringing accusations against the Jews; but apparently nothing came of that letter. When Artaxerxes became the new king of Persia, the adversaries, still worrying about the Jewish city, wrote him a letter accusing the Jews of being rebellious. They told the king that if the Jews were allowed to continue to build their city and to set up the walls again, they would not pay their tribute and revenues to him. They asked the king to search for historical records about these rebellious Jews. This was the king's response:

And I commanded, and search hath been made, and it is found that this city of old time hath made insurrection against kings, and that rebellion and sedition have been made therein. There have been mighty kings also over Jerusalem, which have ruled over all countries beyond the river; and toll, tribute, and custom, was paid unto them. Give ye now commandment to cause these men to cease, and that this city be not builded, until another commandment shall be given from me. (Ezra 4:19–21)

So the adversaries forced the Jews to stop building the walls, and then the adversaries tore down the walls and burned the gates. As time wore on, the Jews became discouraged and grew doubtful, thinking that maybe this wasn't what God had in mind after all. In about 520 BC, God raised up two prophets for the people in Judah and Jerusalem—Haggai and Zechariah, so they would know God was with them and that He wanted them to continue building.

## The Prophet Haggai Proclaims God's Words

"Then came the word of the LORD by Hag´-gai the prophet, saying…Go up to the mountain, and bring wood, and build the house; and I will take pleasure in it, and I will be glorified, saith the LORD" (Haggai 1:3–8).

It was the Lord Who had given them the desire to rebuild the temple.

> I am with you, saith the LORD. And the LORD stirred up the spirit of Ze-rub´-ba-bel the son of She-al´-ti-el, governor of Judah, and the spirit of Joshua the son of Jos´-e-dech, the high priest, and the spirit of all the remnant of the people; and they came and did work in the house of the LORD of hosts, their God. (Haggai 1:13–14)

The following month, the Lord reminded them that His Spirit is still with them.

> Yet now be strong, O Ze-rub´-ba-bel, saith the LORD; and be strong, O Joshua, son of Jos´-e-dech, the high priest; and be strong, all ye people of the land, saith the LORD, and work: for I am with you, saith the LORD of hosts: According to the word that I covenanted with

you when ye came out of Egypt, so my Spirit remaineth among you: fear ye not. (Haggai 2:4–5)

"The glory of this present house will be greater than the glory of the former house,' says the LORD Almighty. 'And in this place I will grant peace,' declares the LORD Almighty" (Haggai 2:9, NIV®). "From this day will I bless you" (Haggai 2:19).

In the following prophetic Scripture, Haggai figuratively illustrated that a day was coming in which the Lord will avenge Israel's enemies; and that Israel will be established as God's community—God's kingdom.

> I will shake the heavens and the earth; And I will overthrow the throne of kingdoms, and I will destroy the strength of the kingdoms of the heathen; and I will overthrow the chariots, and those that ride in them; and the horses and their riders shall come down, every one by the sword of his brother. In that day, saith the LORD of hosts, will I take thee, O Ze-rub´-ba-bel, my servant, the son of She-al´-ti-el, saith the LORD, and will make thee as a signet: for I have chosen thee, saith the LORD of hosts. (Haggai 2:21–23)

The Hebrew word translated *signet* is "Cheber." The meaning of the word is "community."[2]

# The Prophet Zechariah

Zechariah, a priest and descendant of King David, began prophesying shortly after Haggai began his prophetic ministry. Zechariah's Messianic prophecies came by visions and contained messages of salvation, hope of future restoration, and a kingdom in which the coming King would reign. God gave Zechariah a vision in which Joshua the high priest figuratively represented the sin-stained house of Israel.

> And he showed me Joshua the high priest standing before
> the angel of the LORD, and Satan standing at his right
> hand to resist him. And the LORD said unto Satan, The
> LORD rebuke thee, O Satan; even the LORD that hath
> chosen Jerusalem rebuke thee: is not this a brand plucked
> out of the fire? (Zechariah 3:1–2)

The Hebrew word translated *Joshua* is "Yᵉhôwshûwaʿ." The meaning of the word is "Jehovah-saved."[3]

The Hebrew word translated *Jehovah* is "Yᵉhôvâh." The meaning of the word is "the self-Existent or Eternal…Jewish national name of God … the Lord."[4]

> Now Joshua was clothed with filthy garments, and stood
> before the angel. And he answered and spake unto those
> that stood before him, saying, Take away the filthy
> garments from him. And unto him he said, Behold, I
> have caused thine iniquity to pass from thee, and I will
> clothe thee with change of raiment. And I said, Let them
> set a fair mitre upon his head. So they set a fair mitre upon
> his head, and clothed him with garments. And the angel
> of the LORD stood by. (Zechariah 3:3–5)

The Hebrew word translated *mitre* is "tsânîyph." The meaning of the word is "a head-dress, i.e., piece of cloth wrapped around."[5]

In the vision, the Branch is Jesus, Who will take away the sins from the house of Israel. The Branch will spring up from David's family line in the last days.

> And the angel of the LORD protested unto Joshua,
> saying, Thus saith the LORD of hosts, If thou wilt walk
> in my ways, and if thou wilt keep my charge, then thou
> shalt also judge my house, and shalt also keep my courts,
> and I will give thee places to walk among these that stand
> by. Hear now, O Joshua the high priest, thou, and thy
> fellows that sit before thee: for they are men wondered at:

THE KING IS COMING

The Hebrew word translated *BRANCH* is "tsemach." The meaning
of the word is "a sprout ... bud, that which ... grew (upon ... spring)."[6]

The temple will be rebuilt by the Spirit of God through Zerubbabel
and Joshua, God's anointed. Zechariah prophesied about these two men
of God in Zechariah 4:

> This is the word of the LORD unto Ze-rub´-ba-bel,
> saying, *Not by might, nor by power, but by my Spirit*, saith the
> LORD of hosts ... Ze-rub´-ba-bel thou shalt become a
> plain: and he shall bring forth the headstone thereof with
> shoutings, crying, Grace, grace unto it. (vv. 6–7; emphasis
> added)

> The hands of Ze-rub´-ba-bel have laid the foundation of
> this house; his hands shall also finish it; and thou shalt
> know that the LORD of hosts hath sent me unto you.
> (v. 9)

In the following vision, Zechariah figuratively illustrated the coming
of Christ through David's family line. In the future, Jesus will build
His temple; but it will not be made with human hands. The Lord told
Zechariah to go to the exiles from Babylon and take their gold and silver
and make a crown and set it upon Joshua's head as a symbol and say
to him:

> Thus speaketh the LORD of hosts, saying, Behold the
> man whose name is <u>The BRANCH</u>; and he shall grow
> up out of his place, and he shall build the temple of the
> LORD: Even he shall build the temple of the LORD;

and he shall bear the glory, and shall sit and rule upon his throne; and he shall be a priest upon his throne: and the counsel of peace shall be between them both. (Zechariah 6:12–13)

The time for the arrival of Christ the Messiah is getting near, and Zechariah's Messianic prophecies continue, as Zechariah speaks of their future King.

## The King Is Coming

Rejoice greatly, O daughter of Zion; shout, O daughter of Jerusalem: behold, thy King cometh unto thee: he is just, and having salvation; lowly, and riding upon an ass, and upon a colt the foal of an ass. And I will cut off the chariot from E´-phra-im, and the horse from Jerusalem, and the battle bow shall be cut off: and he shall speak peace unto the heathen: and his dominion shall be from sea even to sea, and from the river even to the ends of the earth. As for thee also, by the blood of thy covenant I have sent forth thy prisoners out of the pit wherein is no water. (Zechariah 9:9–11)

And the LORD their God shall save them in that day as the flock of his people: for they shall be as the stones of a crown, lifted up as an ensign upon his land. For how great is his goodness, and how great is his beauty. (Zechariah 9:16–17)

Zechariah also prophesied about the "last days" when Christ will gather His people from all the nations (the houses of Judah and Joseph) and bring them to His earthly kingdom.

*I will* strengthen the house of Judah, and *I will* save the house of Joseph, and *I will* bring them again to place them;

for I have mercy upon them: and they shall be as though
I had not cast them off: for I am the LORD their God,
and will hear them. ... I will bring them again also out
of the land of Egypt, and gather them out of Assyria; and
I will bring them into the land of Gil´-e-ad and Leb´-a-
non; and place shall not be found for them. (Zechariah
10:6–10; emphasis added)

These prophecies rekindled the hope of the promises God had made
so long ago, and the Jews began to rebuild the temple again with the help
of the prophets. When the adversaries saw the Jews had begun building
again, they asked them who had given them permission to start building.
The Jews boldly gave them this answer:

We are the servants of the God of heaven and earth, and
build the house that was builded these many years ago,
which a great king of Israel builded and set up. But after
that our fathers had provoked the God of heaven unto
wrath, he gave them into the hand of Neb-u-chad-nez´-
zar the king of Babylon, the Chal-de´-an, who destroyed
this house, and carried the people away into Babylon. But
in the first year of Cyrus the king of Babylon the same
King Cyrus made a decree to build this house of God.
(Ezra 5:11–13)

The governor, Tat´-nai, and "She´-thar-boz´-nai, and their companions"
(Ezra 5:3) sent King Darius a letter requesting a search be made in the
king's treasure house in Babylon to see, if indeed, King Cyrus had ever
issued a decree that the Jews had permission to build God's house at
Jerusalem. King Darius ordered a search for the rolls, which contained
King Cyrus' decree, and they were found. Yes, earlier, King Cyrus had
made this decree:

Let the house be builded, the place where they offered
sacrifices, and let the foundations thereof be strongly
laid; the height thereof threescore cubits, and the breadth

thereof threescore cubits: With three rows of great stones, and a row of new timber: and let the expenses be given out of the king's house: And also let the golden and silver vessels of the house of God, which Neb-u-chad-nez´-zar took forth out of the temple which is at Jerusalem, and brought unto Babylon, be restored, and brought again unto the temple which is at Jerusalem, every one to his place, and place them in the house of God. (Ezra 6:3–5)

So King Darius wrote the governor a letter, ordering that the building continue:

Let the work of this house of God alone; let the governor of the Jews and the elders of the Jews build this house of God in his place. Moreover I make a decree what ye shall do to the elders of these Jews for the building of this house of God: that of the king's goods, even of the tribute beyond the river, forthwith expenses be given unto these men, that they be not hindered. (Ezra 6:7–8)

He also ordered that all animals that would be needed for burnt offerings as well as wheat, salt, wine, and oil be supplied to them for their sacrifices in the temple. The punishment for interfering with the Jew's temple project would be death by hanging. A board from one's own house would be used to hang a person, and then his house would be destroyed. Needless to say, the adversaries that had been opposing the Jews quickly changed their ways!

Encouraged by Haggai and Zechariah, and confirmed by King Darius, Zerubbabel continued to lead the Jews in rebuilding the temple. It was completed in 515 BC, and they held a huge dedication celebration. They offered hundreds of animal sacrifices and restored the priesthood to serve in God's house. They also celebrated the Passover and the Feast of Unleavened Bread for seven days, eating with all people who had made a decision to follow the Lord. They were grateful that the Lord had given them joy and had changed the heart of the king of Persia so that he stepped in to help with the rebuilding of the temple. What a joyous time for the Jews! They knew the Lord God still loved them, and that one day, He would send a King to them.

## The Plan to Exterminate the Jews

Over in Persia, King Ahasuerus ruled over 127 provinces stretching from India to Ethiopia. He was giving a big banquet for those in the palace when he ordered Queen Vashti, his wife, to come and show off her beauty to those at the party. Vashti refused. In order to avoid setting a precedence of disrespect with wives to their husabands, he punished her disobedience. The king made a decision to ban her from his presence and to replace her with another woman. He made that decree to his kingdom so that it would be known "that every man should bear rule in his own house" (Esther 1:22). Then the king sent out a search for a woman to replace Vashti as the new queen.

There was a man named Mordecai from the tribe of Benjamin who had been exiled at the same time as King Jeconiah. He lived under the reign of King Ahasuerus, and he had raised his cousin Hadassah (Esther) whose parents had died. After a period of time, the king ordered that "fair young virgins" (Esther 2:2) be brought to the palace so he could select one to be the next queen; and that included Esther.

Hegai, the king's eunuch, was in charge of giving beauty treatments for one year to the girls who had been selected to meet the king. Esther found favor with him, and she was placed in the best position among the virgins. At the end of the year, King Ahasuerus chose Esther to be queen; but he did not know that Esther was a Jew, because Mordecai had told her not to say anything about it.

Mordecai would visit everyday outside the courtyard to check on Esther. One day, while waiting to see Esther, he overheard two of the king's chamberlains, Bigthan and Teresh, conspiring to kill the king. Of course Mordecai told Esther, and she told the king. The two men were hung on the gallows.

Later on, King Ahasuerus gave honor to a man named Haman, to whom all of the king's men bowed down, except Mordecai who refused. This made Haman angry with him. Having found out that Mordecai was a Jew, Haman spitefully conspired to exterminate the whole Jewish nation in Babylon. Haman told the king about the customs of the Jews and their disobedience to the king in bowing down to royal officials, and suggested the king send out an order to have all the Jews in the kingdom exterminated. The king accepted his idea and sent out an order that he would pay about 370 tons of silver to the men who would destroy and plunder all the Jews in the kingdom. This was to be done on the thirteenth day of the month of Adar. The king still did not know that Queen Esther was a Jew.

Upon hearing the proclamation, Mordecai was sickened in himself; and all the Jews began to weep and fast. When Esther's maids saw Mordecai outside the palace gate, they told Queen Esther. She sent Hatach, one of the king's eunuchs, to find out what was going on with him. Mordecai told Hatach everything he knew and gave him a copy of the king's written order to exterminate the Jews. He also told the eunuch to tell Esther to go and beg the king for mercy. Queen Esther knew the rule about approaching the king without being sent for by him—it was a death sentence unless the king extended his gold scepter to that person. She sent a message to Mordecai to tell him her dilemma. After receiving her reply, Mordecai gave her this message:

> Think not with thyself that thou shalt escape in the king's
> house, more than all the Jews. For if thou altogether
> holdest thy peace at this time, then shall there enlargement
> and deliverance arise to the Jews from another place; but
> thou and thy father's house shall be destroyed: and who
> knoweth whether thou art come to the kingdom for such
> a time as this? (Esther 4:13–14)

Knowing that Mordecai was right, Queen Esther devised a plan of her own. She told Mordecai her plan, and told him to tell all the Jews in Shushan to fast for three days. Esther and her and her attendants would do the same. After that, she would approach the king, even if it meant her death. She had not seen the king for thirty days and did not know how he would receive her.

After three days of fasting, she went to see the king. As she was standing outside his inner room, he saw her and extended his rod toward her to give her permission to approach him. He cared for her deeply and asked her what she wanted; and he told her that he would give her up to half of his kingdom. Esther answered the king:

> If I have found favor in the sight of the king, and if it please the king to grant my petition, and to perform my request, let the king and Ha´-man come to the banquet that I shall prepare for them, and I will do tomorrow as the king hath said. (Esther 5:8)

When the king and Haman arrived at the banquet, instead of telling the king about her request, she invited them back for another banquet the second night. Then she promised to tell the king her request. When Haman went home, he began to brag to his family about his new position with the king, his wealth, and the fact that Queen Esther had invited him to dinner two nights in a row with the king. He also talked about the disgust he felt when he would see Mordecai outside the palace gate. His wife suggested that the next day he should ask the king to impale Mordecai on a long pole and hang him seventy-five feet in the air for everyone to see. Haman was delighted with the idea.

However, that same night, the king couldn't sleep and asked his attendants to bring him the written records (the Chronicles), in which was recorded the incident of Mordecai saving the king's life when his two officials had plotted to kill him. As he read the records, he realized that Mordecai had never been rewarded. At about the same time, Haman entered the room to tell the king of his idea for Mordecai's death. Before he could speak, the king asked Haman, "What shall be done unto for the man whom the king delighteth to honor?" (Esther 6:6) Haman, thinking the king was talking about him, answered him in this way:

> For the man whom the king delighteth to honor, Let the royal apparel be brought which the king useth to wear, and the horse that the king rideth upon, and the crown royal which is set upon his head: And let this apparel

and horse be delivered to the hand of one of the king's most noble princes, that they may array the man withal whom the king delighteth to honor, and bring him on horseback through the street of the city, and proclaim before him, Thus shall it be done to the man whom the king delighteth to honor. Then the king said to Ha´-man, Make haste, and take the apparel and the horse, as thou hast said, and do even so to Mor´-de-ca-i the Jew, that sitteth at the king's gate: let nothing fail of all that thou hast spoken. (Esther 6:7–10)

So Haman obeyed the king, and in a grieved state of mind, went home to tell his family what had happened. After hearing what he said, his wife told him, "If Mor´-de-ca-i be of the seed of the Jews, before whom thou hast begun to fall, thou shalt not prevail against him, but shalt surely fall before him" (Esther 6:13).

While Haman was still talking with his family, the king's men came and escorted Haman to Esther's banquet. At the dinner, the king asked Esther what it was she wanted from him; and she told him:

If I have found favor in thy sight, O king, and if it please the king, let my life be given me at my petition, and my people at my request: For we are sold, I and my people, to be destroyed, to be slain, and to perish. But if we had been sold for bondmen and bondwomen, I had held my tongue, although the enemy could not countervail the king's damage. (Esther 7:3–4)

Immediately, the king wanted to know who had done such a terrible thing; and Esther told him it was Haman. Enraged, the king went out to his garden to decide the fate of Haman. In the meantime, Esther had reclined on the couch; and Haman went to her to ask that his life be spared. When the king saw that Haman was on the couch with his wife, he thought Haman was trying to force himself upon her. He knew what he had to do. Haman was escorted out of the king's presence by a eunuch and hung on the same gallows he had made for Mordecai.

Queen Esther was given Haman's estate, and Mordecai was brought into the palace and given the king's signet ring, which had previously been given to Haman. Esther also placed Mordecai in charge of Haman's estate. Once again, Esther pleaded with the king about the lives of all the Jews in his kingdom; and he sent out another decree in all the languages of the people to put a stop to the annihilation of the Jews. The decree declared that the Jews had a right to protect themselves against their enemies—those who would come to kill and plunder them, even if it meant killing their enemies.

The annihilation date (the thirteenth day of Adar) had been set with the first decree. The Jews, however, overpowered every enemy that came to destroy them, and were aided by the leaders and governors because of their fear of Mordecai, who had come into position with the king. On that day they killed five hundred enemies within the fortress at Suza, including Haman's ten sons. The other Jews in the king's provinces killed seventy-five thousand enemies. On the fourteenth day of Adar, the dead bodies of Haman's sons were put on display on the gallows; and the Jews in Suza killed three hundred more men. Nearly seventy-six thousand people who had hated the Jews had been killed. After Mordecai had written down all the events of the two days, he sent out an order for the Jews to annually set aside the fourteenth and fifteenth days of Adar. The year was 473 BC.

> As the days wherein the Jews rested from their enemies, and the month which was turned unto them from sorrow to joy, and from mourning into a good day: that they should make them days of feasting and joy, and of sending portions one to another, and gifts to the poor. (Esther 9:22)

It was a celebration of <u>Purim</u>—taken from the word "pur," which means "the lot" (Esther 9:24), because Haman had cast the lot or the "pur" to destroy the Jews. Mordecai, who had become second in line to the king, and Queen Esther sent out a decree that this celebration always be practiced and remembered among the Jews. It is practiced even unto this day.

Once again, Satan had tried to stop God's plan to send Jesus, the Savior of the world, by putting hatred into the hearts of man for the Jews, God's chosen people; but God was watching. What was meant for the destruction of the Jews, God had turned for good.

## In Conclusion

God gave Babylon to King Cyrus of Persia so that the Judean exiles could go back to Jerusalem to rebuild the temple. It had not yet been a full seventy years, but it would be once the house of God was finished. Led by Sheshbazaar, close to fifty thousand people, loaded down with gold, silver, temple objects, and animals for offerings started their trek to rebuild Jerusalem. They were going home to the city of David.

The first thing to be rebuilt was the altar, so they could offer their sacrifices to the Lord. After that, they would begin to work on the foundation of the temple, God's house. Just like all the years before, the pagan nations (the Gentiles) hated the Jews; and they tried to discourage them from rebuilding their city. So God sent Haggai and Zechariah to prophesy about the future to encourage them to keep going. Now, more than ever, it was crucial for the Jews to regain their identity as a nation. It was important for them to have a central place of worship so other nations would once again know that God had set them apart and that He lived among them. It was almost time for the Messiah to come, and the descendants of this remnant will play a major role in the fulfillment of this amazing prophecy. King Darius ordered the temple to be rebuilt, and it was completed in 515 BC.

Meanwhile in Persia, Haman, a hater of the Jews, tried to plan a revolt to exterminate them; but God had His hand on His people, and Haman's plan backfired upon himself. Queen Esther, after learning from Mordecai about Haman's plan, devised her own plan to save the Jews and risked her life to inform the king. Earlier, the king had made a decree to annhilate the Jews, but after hearing what Queen Esther told him, he made another decree that the Jews had a right to defend themselves. With that decree, the Jews killed seventy-six thousand of their enemies who had come against them; and a new day of celebration was established—the celebration of Purim, which is celebrated even to this day.

God will send three more men of God to help the Jews establish Jerusalem; however, there will be a period of about four hundred years (between the Old and New Testaments) where the world will be turned upside down politically, morally, and spiritually. What kind of an affect will these changes have on the Jews? Will they be able to stand in their rekindled faith and love for God?

## Deeper Insights:

1. When the Jews arrived back in Jerusalem, they wanted to rebuild the altar and restore their worship before doing anything else. Why do you think they felt that way?

2. Why was it important for the Jews to re-establish their city with its temple?

3. What do you think was the real reason the nations in the surrounding areas did not want the Jews to rebuild Jerusalem?

   Read Ezra 4:11–16, which contains the letter of accusations written to King Artaxerxes of Persia. Then read Ezra 4:19–24, which is the king's response.

   Read Ezra 5:8, which contains the letter of accusations written to King Darius. Then read Ezra 6:1–12, which is the king's response.

4. The temple was completed in Jerusalem in about 515 BC, fulfilling the prophecy of the end of a seventy-year exile for the Jews. What did the children of Israel do after the temple was finished? Read Ezra 6:16–22.

5. In Persia, hatred for the Jews began to rear its ugly head. Why did Haman hate Mordecai; and why did he want to exterminate the Jews? Read Esther 3:1–6.

6. Because of Queen Esther's faith and trust in the living God, the evil exterminator Haman was killed, and the Jews were saved.

Read Esther 8:5–8, which tells of Esther's plea to the king to reverse his decree to exterminate the Jews.

Read the king's new decree in Esther 8:11–14.

7. The Jewish community is still celebrating the Festival of Purim today. Read Esther 9:20–32 to see how this festival became an established event.

8. Today, we are seeing a resurgence of anti-semeticism and a hatred for Christians throughout the world.

   Read the following Scriptures to see what Jesus had to say about this kind of hatred: Matthew 10:21–22; Luke 6:22–23; John 3:16–20; 15:18 –25.

9. Can you think of recent times when people have tried to bring harm to or exterminate the Jews?

# CHAPTER 10

## JEWISH REFORMATIONS AND PERSECUTIONS

### Ezra

The stage of favoritism towards the Jews had been set because of the bravery and faith demonstrated by Mordecai and Queen Esther. King Ahasuerus was killed in a palace coup, and his son Artaxerxes began to reign in his place.

Ezra, whose Scriptures we have read in the last chapter, was a Jewish man who still lived in Babylon under the reign of King Artaxerxes in Persia. He was a descendant of Aaron, the chief priest and scribe, and knew the Law of Moses very well—in fact, he had taught it to the Jews in Babylon. King Artaxerxes sent Ezra a letter ordering him to go check on Jerusalem "to inquire concerning Judah and Jerusalem, according to the law of thy God which is in thine hand" (Ezra 7:14).

The king decreed in his letter that Ezra take with him silver and gold from the king, his advisers, and the province of Babylon, along with the freewill offerings from the people and the priests. The silver and gold were to be used first to buy animals and grain for the sacrifices to Ezra's God, and after that, for temple services. Future money would be made available from the royal treasury as needed. He made a decree that the treasurers of Trans-Euphrates were to give Ezra silver, wheat, wine, olive oil, and salt (see Ezra 7:22). He made this decree so that Ezra's God would not be angry with the king and those in his realm. The king gave Ezra this order to establish the law in Judea:

> And thou, Ezra, after the wisdom of thy God, that is in thine hand, set magistrates and judges, which may judge all the people that are beyond the river, all such as know the laws of thy God; and teach ye them that know them not. And whosoever will not do the law of thy God, and the law of the king, let judgment be executed speedily upon him, whether it be unto death, or to banishment, or to confiscation of goods, or to imprisonment. (Ezra 7:25–26)

The king also gave his permission to other Jews who wanted to go with Ezra. In about 457 BC, Ezra gathered together 1,496 men and their families and 258 men to serve in the temple (eighteen from the tribe of Levi). Before they left for Jerusalem, they fasted and prayed for a safe journey from enemies along the way. Ezra consecrated the leading priests and others with them and made them responsible for the money and articles for the temple. After arriving in Jerusalem, they delivered those items to Meremoth, the priest. All the new exiles sacrificed their burnt offerings and delivered the king's orders to the lieutenants and governors of the king in Trans-Euphrates to help the Jews.

## Ezra Learns of Corruption

So much had been accomplished, and the people in Jerusalem were once again being obedient and living under God's blessings, or were they? When Ezra and the new exiles arrived in Jerusalem, Ezra learned from the Israelite leaders that the people had started intermarrying wives from the pagan nations again—women who worshiped idols. What was even worse than that, some of the leaders and officials were the ones who were leading them into it! The Bible says that Ezra was so upset that he tore his clothes and pulled his hair out of his head. Afer all they had been through, and after experiencing God's mercy and love towards them, how could the Jews forget so fast and allow these sins to happen again? Ezra sat in despair all day and prayed to the Lord at the evening sacrifice:

O my God, I am ashamed and blush to lift up my face to thee, my God: for our iniquities are increased over our head, and our trespass is grown up unto the heavens. Since the days of our fathers have we been in a great trespass unto this day; and for our iniquities have we, our kings, and our priests, been delivered into the hand of the kings of the lands, to the sword, to captivity, and to a spoil, and to confusion of face, as it is this day.

And now for a little space grace hath been showed from the LORD our God, to leave us a remnant to escape, and to give us a nail in his holy place, that our God may lighten our eyes, and give us a little reviving in our bondage … And now, O our God … we have forsaken thy commandments. (Ezra 9:6–10)

While Ezra was still praying and weeping, confessing the sins of the people, the Israelites gathered around him and began weeping bitterly; and they made a covenant with God. A list was made of all those who had married pagan wives, and the men confessed their sins before the Lord. Then they sent away their foreign wives and the children that had born to them.

## The Prophet Malachi

Apparently, there were other sins, too. Instead of offering God their best animals for their sacrifices, they began offering blemished animals. The priests became slack by not giving the Israelites truthful instruction in God's ways and were violating the covenant concerning the priesthood. The people started robbing God of his tithes and offerings, and their faith was becoming futile. They were desecrating the Lord's sanctuary. Not only that, but married couples were breaking faith with each other and divorcing. Once again, as the people began to draw away from God, and lose their love for Him, their love for each other began to dissipate.

So God sent Malachi the prophet to point out their sins to them and rebuke them for their unfaithfulness. In the following Scriptures, we see that a list of Jewish names was written down in a book, which would forever be treasured and protected by God.

> A book of remembrance was written before him for them that feared the LORD, and that thought upon his name. And they shall be mine, saith the LORD of hosts, in that day when I make up my jewels; and I will spare them, as a man spareth his own son that serveth him. (Malachi 3:16–17)

> For, behold, the day cometh, that shall burn as an oven; and all the proud, yea, and all that do wickedly, shall be stubble ... But unto you that fear my name shall the Sun of righteousness arise with healing in his wings; and ye shall go forth, and grow up as calves of the stall. And ye shall tread down the wicked; for they shall be ashes under the soles of your feet in the day that I shall do this, saith the LORD of hosts. Remember ye the law of Moses my servant, which I commanded unto him in Hor´-eb for all Israel, with the statutes and judgments. (Malachi 4:1–4)

## Rebuilding the Walls

Nehemiah was a cupbearer to King Artaxerxes in Persia. One day Hanani and some other Jews who were with him came from Jerusalem. Nehemiah asked them how everything was going with the Jews in Jerusalem. They gave Nehemiah a report on their condition:

> The remnant that are left of the captivity there in the province are in great affliction and reproach: the wall of Jerusalem also is broken down, and the gates thereof are burned with fire. And it came to pass, when I heard these

words, that I sat down and wept, and mourned certain days, and fasted, and prayed before the God of heaven. (Nehemiah 1:3–4)

Then Nehemiah, in his sadness for the Jews, prayed and went before the king to ask permission to go to Jerusalem to help rebuild the wall at the place where his fathers had been buried. He also asked that letters be sent to the governors of Trans-Euphrates to grant him a safe journey, and to Asaph, "the keeper of the king's forest" (Nehemiah 2:8), so he would be supplied with timber to rebuild the gates, the city wall, and his own house to live in. Not only did the king grant his request, but also sent his own army officers and soldiers to accompany them.

After they had been in Jerusalem for three days, Nehemiah went out alone at night and inspected the walls and gates of the city. Then he went to the Jews, the priests, the nobles, and leaders told them:

Ye see the distress that we are in how Jerusalem lieth waste, and the gates thereof are burned with fire: come, and let us build up the wall of Jerusalem, that we be no more a reproach. Then I told them of the hand of my God which was good upon me; as also the king's words that he had spoken unto me. And they said, Let us rise up and build. So they strengthened their hands for this good work. (Nehemiah 2:17–18)

The Jews began rebuilding and repairing the walls, towers, and gates, with each group of men taking a separate section. When Sanballat the Horonite and Tobiah the Ammonite heard that the Jews were going ahead with rebuilding and repairing the wall, they began to ridicule them in front of their friends and even the Samarian army. Nehemiah prayed:

Hear, O our God; for we are despised: and turn their reproach upon their own head, and give them for a prey in the land of captivity: And cover not their iniquity, and let not their sin be blotted out from before thee: for

they have provoked thee to anger before the builders.
(Nehemiah 4:4–5)

The Jews continued to build until they had built their wall half as high as it would be when it was finished. The adversaries became more angry and devised a plan to come and fight the Jews. So the Jews prayed and posted guards day and night and prepared to fight for their families and homes. As half of the men worked on the wall, the other half were equipped with weapons; and the officers stood guard behind the workers. As the men worked, they carried their swords at their sides.

As the work was going on, the Jewish nobles and officials were charging high taxes on the fields and vineyards of the Jews in order to pay the king's taxes; and the Jews were losing their land and going hungry. Nehemiah went to the nobles and officials and reprimanded them for exacting usury and making slaves out of their brother Jews. They gave back the money they had taken and did what Nehemiah told them to do. Later on, Nehemiah was appointed governor. He governed the people fairly, even feeding 150 Jews and officials every day at his own table.

When Sanballot, Tobiah, and Geshem heard the wall was being completed, he sent an aide to Nehemiah with a letter accusing him and the Jews of building the wall so they could revolt and make Nehemiah king. Nehemiah did not let fear intimidate him, and the wall was completed within fifty-two days. The enemies knew that God had helped the Jews.

## Nehemiah Calls for Renewal

Nehemiah appointed gatekeepers, singers, and Levites; and he appointed Hananiah as ruler over Jerusalem because he was a faithful, God-fearing man. Nehemiah also found a record of those who had gone into exile. If the names of the priests who were currently serving in the Lord's house were not found in the records, he banned them from the priesthood.

Ezra the priest brought out the book of the Law and read it to all the Jews, with the help of the Levites, to give understanding to the people. They worshiped the Lord, and they wept when they heard the words that were contained in the Law. Nehemiah told the people to go and enjoy food and drink and share with those who had none "for the joy of the LORD is your strength" (Nehemiah 8:10).

Later, the Levites and priests found that it was written in the book of the Law that the Israelites were to live in booths during the feast of the seventh month (Feast of Tabernacles). So they built booths and lived in them while the feast lasted for seven days, and Ezra continued to read out of the book of the Law. During that same month, the Israelites began fasting and confessing their sins, praising the Lord for all that He had done for them from the time of Creation. As they prayed, they recognized that they had once been free when the Lord first placed them in their Promised Land. Now, because of their sins, they had become servants in their land, giving their abundant harvests to a king. They renewed their covenant with the Lord and promised obedience to Him.

The leaders of the Jews went to live in the city of Jerusalem. One out of every ten people were to live there too, so they cast lots to decide who would stay in the city and who would go to live in other cities on their own inherited land that had been given to their forefathers.

After the dedication of the wall, Nehemiah made some reforms based on what was written in the book of the Law.

The Ammonites and Moabites, who had earlier hired Balaam to bring a curse on the Hebrews while they were traveling to their Promised Land (see Numbers 23 and 24), would no longer be able to be a part of the assembly of God.

Nehemiah cleaned out and cleansed a chamber in the temple, replacing the sacred items that belonged there. Earlier, Eliashib the priest had allowed Tobiah, an Ammonite servant, to live in the chamber. Eliashib had taken out the sacred items to be used in the Lord's house and had filled the room with his own things.

Nehemiah assigned a priest, a scribe, and a Levite to be in charge of manning the storehouse and distributing portions to those who were to have them. The people who served in the temple had not been receiving their portions and had gone back to their fields to survive.

Nehemiah also halted buying and selling on the Sabbath. He would shut the gates and lock them the evening of the Sabbath, not opening them until after the Sabbath so the merchants could not enter.

Nehemiah harshly disciplined those who had married women from Ashdod, Ammon, and Moab so they would not allow their children to intermarry with the pagan nations. He reminded them of the sins of King Solomon:

> Did not Solomon king of Israel sin by these things? Yet among many nations was there no king like him, who was beloved of his God, and God made him king over all Israel: nevertheless even him did outlandish women cause to sin. (Nehemiah 13:26)

## Clinging to the Promises

Rebuke and reform had come again—this time by Ezra, Malachi, and Nehemiah. It had become quite apparent that nothing could prevent the human heart from sinning in thought, word, and deed—not miracles, not angels, not prophecies, not discipline, not even the sacrificial system that God had set in place. No matter what God had done, or how close He came to His chosen people, they would soon forget about their relationship with Him. Sin would rear its ugly head and bring about corruption. Only repentant hearts could bring them back to Him.

After all the things the Jews had been through, more trouble was coming for them; but this time, it would be coming from an outside influence. God was preparing to do something new, and He was about to "shake the tree," so to speak. He used the next four hundred years, the time between "*law*" (the Old Testament) and "*grace*" (the New Testament) to prepare their hearts for their coming Messiah. He used the Gentiles, who ruled over them, to test the Jews and dismantle their reliance upon outward rituals and laws that could not change their hearts. As they tired of oppression, unrest, and hopelessness, they longed even more for their coming King, Who would come to help them.

Through God's discipline, He had exposed the sins of the Jews and shattered their hearts. Now He would prepare them to receive mercy and eternal salvation through Jesus—God's Son.

As we have read, the Jews were favored under Persian rule, and they were allowed to worship the living God and practice their religion; however, things were about to change for both the Jews and the Gentiles. The *Holman Bible Atlas*[1] and the *Holy Bible, King James Version,*[2] were used as resources to obtain the information used in the following paraphrase;

## Alexander the Great and Hellenism

In about 333 BC, Alexander the Great conquered Persia and began to expand into the Middle East. This one man was responsible for a huge reformation all across the Near East and West. Everywhere he went, he implemented Greek culture, in an attempt to unify his conquered territories. He planted the seeds for a new period of time that was called the "Hellenistic Period." "Hellas is the Greek word for Greece."[3]

Alexander died at a young age and was not able to fully realize the impact Hellenism would have on the world and the Jews. His vision had been correct— that part of the world did become unified as a result of the Greek culture. Trade between the East and the West flourished, money was standardized, which made trade even easier, and Greek influence began to spread even more. The large cities, such as Alexandria and Antioch, became major centers in this new economic culture. Kings built all kinds of facilities to encourage Greek culture, for both education and entertainment. Greek culture became widespread with its influence touching every sphere of society, such as: religion, moral standards, architecture, people's names, clothing styles, philosophies, entertainment, and economics. This was the new age of mind expansion, poetry, and philosophical thinking. People were enjoying Greek mythology and religion, materialism, and accepted sensual behavior. The spoken language was also affected. The common people of that day used a language called koine Greek. The new language, classical Greek, was more formal and acceptable to the elite.

So what did this new era of change mean for the traditional Jews who lived in the hubbub of Greek culture? Hellenism created a self-gratifying culture that did not tolerate the traditional ways of their religious life. The Jews found themselves being torn between Greek values and lifestyle changes and their own religion. Many of the Greek values were contrary to the Law of Moses, such as worshiping the Greek gods, and giving into sensual behavior. The Jews wanted to prosper like others, but they had to decide at what point they were willing to cross the line of Jewish law and risk compromising their covenant-relationship with God. To avoid that temptation, some of them became even more radical in their Jewish beliefs and practices since it was important for them to not deny the faith of their ancestors. Some Jews tried to combine the two cultural systems, holding to their faith in their traditional religion, but also including some of the humanistic practices. Still, other Jews, for various reasons, succumbed to the Hellenistic culture. It was truly a challenging time for them and a test of their faith! One thing was for sure, Hellenism was here to stay, and it would be the major player that would determine the treatment of the Jews.

## The Reign of the Dynasties

After Alexander's death, the Jews were ruled by three separate dynasties: Ptolemic (Greek), Seleucid (Syrian), and Hasmonean (Greek influence), and by the Roman Empire, each having its own effect on the Jews.

Under the Ptolemic Dynasty, the Jews in Palestine and the city of Alexandria were given relgious freedom. Most of the Jews in Alexandria became fluent in the Greek language and were allowed to translate their

Hebrew scrolls into the Greek language, calling it the Septuagint.

Under the Seleucid Dynasty, favoritism for the Jews began to dissipate. Normally, the Levitical high priests were responsible for overseeing the Jewish community and answered to the government only in certain matters; however, it was during this time that the position of high priest began to become a corrupted political position. It was given to the highest bidder, and the bidder was not required to have a Levitical lineage, which violated the priesthood laws of Moses. Hellenistic influence started to become prevalent during that time because a high priest by the name of Jason catered to the Hellenists, who had helped him win his position. Another corrupt man, Menelaus, outbid Jason and became high priest, which caused a conflict between him and Jason. The Syrian army planned a surprise attack on a Sabbath Day, killing many Jews who were against Menelaus. Jerusalem's walls were destroyed, and a Syrian fortress was set up in the city.

The Hellenists and the new ruler Antiochus hated the Jews and set up laws against their religious practices, militarily enforcing his laws. The Jews who refused to comply with the Hellenistic culture were persecuted, and most of the time, executed for practicing their religion. He set up his own idols in the temple and sacrificed pigs on their altar. These acts of cruelty and blasphemy caused much anger among the Jews, which triggered a revolt against the Syrians and against Jews who were supportive of Hellenism. This revolt was called the Maccabean Revolt, led by a Jewish priest by the name of Mattahias. The revolt was successful until the Syrians came back to Jerusalem on another Sabbath Day, and once again, attacked and killed many Jews.

After the death of Mattahias, his son Judas led his followers on a surprise attack to a Syrian army camp, wiping out that army. Heading onto Jerusalem, the

Maccabees cleaned out the temple of the blasphemous articles that Antiochus had placed in it. They built a new altar and dedicated the temple with a celebration called Hanukkah; however, it wasn't long until the Syrians came back and defeated Jersualem once again. When a new Hellenistic high priest, Alcimus, was installed, he ordered the death of a great number of orthodox Jews. Of course, the Maccabees went to battle with the Syrians again, and Judas was killed. His brother Jonathan, through a set of unusual circumstances, became high priest, ruling over Judea. Upon his death, his brother Simon took his place, and the Hasmonean Dynasty was birthed.

Under this dynasty, for eighty years, the Jews enjoyed peace and independence from the Syrians with a tax-exempt status. During those years, two Jewish sects began to arise—the Pharisees and the Sadducees.

The Pharisees stemmed from the orthodox Jews who had been a part of the Maccabean Revolt. They refused to be Hellenized and were dogmatically committed to the Torah (Jewish Law). The Pharisees were pious, believing their righteousness came by legalistically following the purity laws. Feeling that they were more righteous than the other Jews, they strictly enforced the law on them and added even more laws than were in the Torah. The Pharisees believed in "angelology, demonology, concepts of heaven and hell, and the resurrection."[4] "As interpreters of the law, the scribes provided the Pharisees with authoritative pronouncements upon what the law demanded. The Pharisees regarded this oral tradition to be as fully authoritative as the written law."[5]

The Pharisees were in rivalry with the Sadducees, which were mostly comprised of high priests who came from noble families. They compromised with political leaders to feather their nests and still held their religious and ritualistic position in the temple, overriding the Sanhedrin (the Jewish Council).[6] They followed

Hellenistic ideas to a point, allowing freedom of choice; but they also believed each person should live responsibly toward God. They did not accept the oral tradition of the Pharisees, nor did they believe in resurrection of the dead, demonology, or angels (Mark 12:18; Luke 20:27; Acts 23:8). The Sadducees did not associate with other Jews, but separated themselves from other Jews outside their sect. Due to the conflict over which sect should have political power, hundreds of Pharisees and Sadducees were killed.

## The Roman Empire

In 63 BC, when Pompey besieged Jerusalem, he killed thousands of Jews and took away the independence of the Jewish nation; however, he allowed the Jews to practice their worship in the temple, even though he did not respect their God or the temple.

Some of the traditional orthodox Jews began to form other private sects to separate themselves from the Hellenistic customs that were being practiced by other Jews and to practice the Law of their ancestors. The Zealots was one such group. They had zeal (passion) for the Law and were involved in riots and wars, resisting Roman rule.

The other anti-Hellenistic group of Jews that began to arise was the Essenes, strictly ruled by priests. They lived in various communities out in the dessert near the Dead Sea. Their members committed themselves to a covenant relationship with God and with each other, living very ritualistic lives and adhering closely to the purity laws. They anticipated the Lord's return, as they believed He would come very soon and rid the world of its evil. Historians believe that the Dead Sea scrolls belonged to the Essenes.

**Herod the Great**

In 37 BC, the Roman Senate appointed Herod to be the king of the Jews. There were some affluent Jews, the Herodians, who supported Herod and his rule, but many Jews hated him.

Herod loved to build all kinds of structures that accommodated Hellenism, including a Jewish temple to take the place of the one that Zerubbabel had dedicated after the exile. Even though he did many great things, he raised taxes in order to pay for his projects, which caused him to be even more unpopular.

He became a man of great fear and paranoia, believing that other people were in conspiracy to take his throne. He killed two of his own sons because he became suspicious of them. The prophets had foretold of the coming of a Jewish King, who would have His own throne and who would govern the Jewish nation:

For unto us a child is born, unto us a son is given: and the government shall be upon his shoulder: and his name shall be called Wonderful, Counselor, The Mighty God, The everlasting Father, The Prince of Peace. Of the increase of his government and peace there shall be no end, upon the throne of David, and upon his kingdom, to order it, and to establish it with judgment and with justice from henceforth even forever. The zeal of the LORD of hosts will perform this. (Isaiah 9:6–7)

Herod was aware of these prophecies, and he was terrified of the birth of this King. Before his own death, he would order the brutal murder of all baby boys, two years and under, throughout Bethlehem and the coastal areas to ensure this new King's death. Herod had reason to fear this new King, because He was standing at the door and was about to make His appearance.

# In Conclusion

King Artaxerxes sent Ezra to Jerusalem to make sure that the Law of the living Hebrew God was being taught and followed in Jerusalem. In fact, "death ... banishment ... confiscation of goods, or ... imprisonment" would be waiting for those who would not obey the Law of God and of the king (see Ezra 7:25–26). When Ezra arrived, he found the Jews had already been intermarrying with pagan wives, and he began to intercede in prayer for them. Following on his heels was the prophet Malachi, who God sent to rebuke them for their sins and to try to steer them back on the right track. He prophesied about hope for them, but he also let them know the time was drawing near when God would make Himself known to the Gentiles, as well.

With Nehemiah's arrival, the wall was rebuilt, there was a time of repentance and confession, and reforms were set in place. Even so, sin would keep cropping up in the human heart. Was there no hope for this Jewish nation to remain faithful to God? No, there was not, and that is why Jesus was coming! Without Christ's new everlasting blood covenant of righteousness, there would never be hope for the Jews or the Gentiles, who are all born with the horrible sin nature.

The world was turned upside down with the coming of Alexander the Great and his new humanistic ideology. His ideas and ideals changed the culture of the world the Jews had known. God would use the circumstances that would follow this cultural explosion to prepare the Jews and the Gentiles for the coming Messiah. With the onset of Hellensim, the Jews faced many challenges in their faith in God and the traditional Mosaic Law. Each person had to make a decision as to which "god" they would follow—the God of Abraham, Isaac, and Jacob, or the god of the world.

Just as in the days of old, the Lord raised God-fearing heroes up to fight their causes; but they still suffered much agony from the oppression and hatred of the nations who ruled them. Hatred and murder were always looming in the shadows.

Herod, their Roman king, feared the prophecies in Scripture that told about the coming of a new "King of the Jews." His fear would drive him to murder all male Jewish babies under two years of age to try to prevent His birth. Oh, how the Jews were looking forward to their Messiah, the

King, the One God had promised would come to set up His kingdom. Their anticipation was high, but how long must they wait? Not long! The Messiah was on His way, and nothing and no one would hold Him back. This was the moment Jesus had been waiting for, as well. This was the time for the fulfillment of the prophecies, which were first spoken by God in the Garden of Eden. The Messiah is at the door. Will they know Him? Will they embrace Him?

## Deeper Insights:

1. What conditions did Ezra find when he arrived in Jerusalem? Read Ezra 9:1–2.

2. What did Ezra say was the reason bad things had happened to the Jews? Read Ezra 9:13–15.

3. Read Nehemiah 4:13–23 to see how Nehemiah was able to rebuild the wall while fighting the opposition of their enemies.

4. Read Malachi 3:16–18 to find out about God's "list" of Jewish names.

   Why do you think God's book was written?

   Earlier, God spoke of His "book" when the Israelites had set up the golden calf. Read Exodus 32:31–33.

   The Bible speaks about another book that God is keeping, called the book of life. Read Luke 10:19–20; Hebrews 12:22–23; Revelation 17:8; 20:12–15; Philippians 4:1–3.

   According to these Scriptures, whose names are being written in the book of life? What happens to those whose names are not written in this book?

5. In taking this journey with the Jews, we have seen their sins and shortcomings, and rebellion.

   If you could think of one word that would best describe the God of the Old Testament, what would it be?

6. What were some of the difficulties the Jews faced with the onset of the new Greek culture, which had been established by Alexander the Great?

In our society today, we are plagued with secular humanism, really no different than what the Jews were facing in the "new" Greek society. In what ways can you see Christians compromising their values, their faith, and their walk with God to fit into society and the changing times?

7. After studying about the Jewish nation, and seeing how God chose them and intervened in their lives every step of the way, do you believe we should support Israel today? Why or why not?

The illustration below was drawn by Chris Evans.

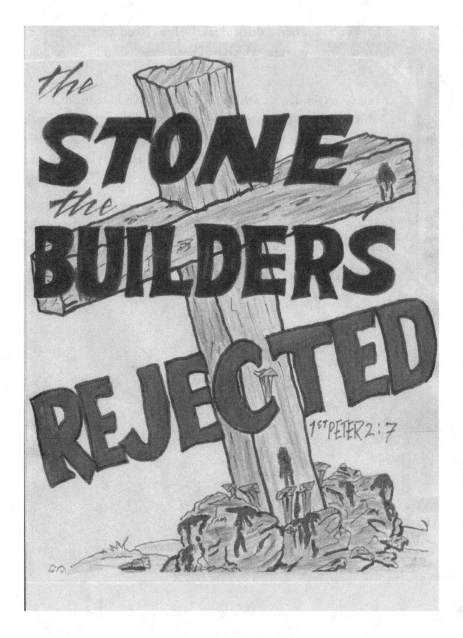

# CHAPTER 11

## GOD COMES DOWN

"When the fullness of the time was come,
God sent forth his Son, made of a woman,
made under the law" (Galatians 4:4).

## Mary and the Angel of the Lord

Mary was a young Jewish girl, probably about thirteen or fourteen, who lived in Nazareth. The Bible says she was a virgin, engaged to be married to a man named Joseph, who was a son of Jacob (Israel) of the house (lineage) of David. One night, God sent Gabriel the angel to speak to Mary:

> Hail, thou art highly favored, the Lord is with thee: blessed art thou among women. And when she saw him, she was troubled at his saying, and cast in her mind what manner of salutation this should be. And the angel said unto her, Fear not, Mary: for thou hast found favor with God. And, behold, thou shalt conceive in thy womb, and bring forth a son, and shalt call his name JESUS. He shall be great, and shall be called the *Son of the Highest*: and the Lord God shall give unto him the throne of his father David: And he shall *reign over the house of Jacob for ever*; and of his kingdom there shall be no end. (Luke 1:28–33; emphasis added)

The Greek word translated *Jesus* is "hilasmŏs´." The meaning of the word is "atonement ... an expiator ... propitiation."[1]

Mary wondered how she could have a child since she was still a virgin and had never been with a man. The angel told her, "The *Holy Ghost* shall come upon thee, and the *power of the Highest* shall <u>overshadow</u> thee: therefore also that holy thing which shall be born of thee shall be called the *Son of God*" (Luke 1:35; emphasis added).

The Greek word translated *overshadow* is "ĕpiskiazō." The meaning of the word is "to cast a shade upon."[2]

"And Mary said, Behold the handmaid of the Lord; be it unto me according to thy word. And the angel departed from her" (Luke 1:38).

## Joseph and the Angel of the Lord

Joseph, a Jewish man, was engaged to Mary.

> Now the birth of Jesus Christ was on this wise: When as his mother Mary was espoused to Joseph, before they came together, she was found with *child of the Holy Ghost*. Then Joseph her husband, being a just man, and not willing to make her a public example, was minded to put her away privily. But while he thought on these things, behold, the angel of the Lord appeared unto him in a dream, saying, Joseph, thou son of David, fear not to take unto thee Mary thy wife: for that which is conceived in her is of the *Holy Ghost*. And she shall bring forth a son, and thou shalt call his name *JESUS*: for he shall *save his people from their sins*.

> Now all this was done, that it might be fulfilled which was spoken of the Lord by the prophet [Isaiah 7:14], saying, Behold, a *virgin shall be with child*, and shall bring forth a son, and they shall call his name <u>Im-man´-u-el</u>, which being interpreted is, *God with us*." (Matthew 1:18–23; emphasis added)

THE KING IS COMING

"Then Joseph being raised from sleep did as the angel of the Lord had bidden him, and took unto him his wife: And knew her not till she had brought forth her firstborn son: and he called his name JESUS" (Matthew 1:24–25).

## Malachi's Prophecy of John the Baptist

Zechariah was a priest in the "priestly division of Abijah: his wife Elizabeth was also a descendant of Aaron" (Luke 1:5, NIV®). "They were both righteous before God, walking in all the commandments and ordinances of the Lord blameless" (Luke 1:6). An angel came to Zechariah while he was burning incense in the temple:

> Fear not, Zech-a-ri´-ah: for thy prayer is heard; and thy wife Elisabeth shall bear thee a son, and thou shalt call his name John. And thou shalt have joy and gladness; and many shall rejoice at his birth. For he shall be great in the sight of the Lord, and shall drink neither wine nor strong drink; and he shall be filled with the Holy Ghost, even from his mother's womb. And many of the children of Israel shall he turn to the Lord their God. And he shall go before him [Jesus] in the spirit and power of Eli´-jah, to turn the hearts of the fathers to the children, and the disobedient to the wisdom of the just; to make ready a people prepared for the Lord. (Luke 1:13-17)

Malachi had prophesied of John in the Scrolls:

> BEHOLD, I will send my messenger, and he shall prepare the way before me: and the Lord, whom ye seek, shall suddenly come to his temple, even the messenger of the covenant [Jesus] whom ye delight in: behold, he shall come, saith the LORD of hosts. (Malachi 3:1)

Zechariah doubted the angel, and the angel muted his speech until after John, his son, was born. Elisabeth would give birth to John, whom Isaiah had prophesied about in Isaiah 40:3: "The voice of him that crieth in the wilderness, Prepare ye the way of the LORD, make straight in the desert a highway for our God."

The Hebrew word translated *LORD* is "Y°hôvâh." The meaning of the word is "(the) self-Existent or Eternal."[3]

## Mary Visits Elisabeth

When the angel had talked to Mary, he had also told her that her elderly cousin Elisabeth was pregnant. That was significant because Elisabeth was barren—that means that God had now opened her womb for a very special purpose, just as He had done for His purposes with other women in the Old Testament.

When Elisabeth was six months pregnant, Mary went to see her in her home in the hills of Judea. When Elisabeth heard Mary's greeting, *"the babe leaped in her womb; and Elisabeth was filled with the Holy Ghost"* (Luke 1:41; emphasis added). By the Holy Spirit, Elisabeth and the baby in her womb both knew that the baby inside of Mary's womb was the Lord. Elisabeth loudly spoke to Mary:

> Blessed art thou among women, and blessed is the fruit of thy womb. And whence is this to me, that the mother of my Lord should come to me? For, lo, as soon as the voice of thy salutation sounded in mine ears, the babe leaped in my womb for joy. And blessed is she that believed: for there shall be a performance of those things which were told her from the Lord. (Luke 1:42-45)

Here the Greek word translated *Lord is* "kuriŏs." The meaning of the word is "from kurŏs (supremacy) … supreme in authority … God … master, Sir."[4]

And Mary said, My soul doth magnify the Lord, and my spirit hath rejoiced in God my Savior. For he hath regarded the low estate of his handmaiden: for, behold, from henceforth all generations shall call me blessed. For he that is mighty hath done to me great things; and holy is his name. And his mercy is on them that fear him from generation to generation. He hath showed strength with his arm; he hath scattered the proud in the imagination of their hearts. (Luke 1:46–51)

"He hath holpen [helped] his servant Israel, in remembrance of his mercy; as he spake to our fathers, to Abraham, and to his seed for ever" (Luke 1:54–55).

## The Birth of John the Baptist

After Elisabeth gave birth to her baby, her neighbors and relatives came for his circumcision, expecting his name to be Zechariah like his father. Elisabeth told them his name would be John. This caused quite a stir because no one in their family had the name of John, so they asked Zechariah. Zechariah, who still could not speak, wrote down the name the baby would be called: "His name is John ... And his mouth was opened immediately, and his tongue loosed, and he spake, and praised God" (Luke 1:63–64).

Zechariah, who was filled with the Holy Ghost, began to prophesy about *Jesus the Lord*, who had come to fulfill the prophecies written in the Scrolls (the Old Testament).

And his father Zech-a-ri´-ah was filled with the Holy Ghost, and prophesied, saying, Blessed be the *Lord God of Israel*; for *he hath visited and redeemed his people*, and hath raised up a horn of salvation for us in the house of his servant David; as he spake by the mouth of his holy prophets, which have been since the world began: that we should be saved from our enemies, and from the hand of all that hate us; to perform the mercy promised to our fathers, and to remember his holy covenant; the oath which he sware to our father Abraham, that he would grant unto us, that we, being delivered out of the hand of our enemies, might serve him without fear, in holiness and righteousness before him, all the days of our life. (Luke 1:68–75; emphasis added)

Zechariah also prayed over his baby son, John, and his "mission" with Jesus Christ:

And thou, child [John], shalt be called the *prophet of the Highest*: for thou shalt go before the face of the Lord to prepare his ways; to give knowledge of salvation unto his people by the *remission of their sins*, through the tender *mercy of our God*; whereby the dayspring from on high hath visited us, and to *give light* to them that sit in darkness and in the shadow of death, to guide our feet into the way of peace. And the child grew, and waxed strong in spirit, and was in the deserts till the day of his showing unto Israel. (Luke 1:76–80; emphasis added)

## The Birth of the Messiah

Daniel, after being exiled into Babylon, had foretold what the angel Gabriel had told him about a specific time for the coming of "Messiah the Prince" (Daniel 9:25). Now that time arrived, shortly after the birth of John.

The Hebrew word translated *Messiah* is "mâshîyach." The meaning of the word is "anointed: usually a consecrated person (as a king, priest, or saint)."[5]

It came to pass in those days, that there went out a decree from Caesar Augustus, that all the world should be taxed. ... And all went to be taxed, every one into his own city. And Joseph also went up from Galilee, out of the city of Nazareth, into Judea, unto the city of David, which is called Bethlehem; (because he was of the house and lineage of David:) To be taxed with Mary his espoused wife, being great with child. And so it was, that, while they were there, the days were accomplished that she should be delivered. And she brought forth her firstborn son, and wrapped him in swaddling clothes, and laid him in a manger; because there was no room for them in the inn. (Luke 2:1–7)

"And the Word [Jesus] was made flesh, and dwelt among us" (John 1:14). Jesus' coming fulfilled the prophecy God had given to Satan after the Fall of man in the Garden of Eden: "And I will put enmity between thee and the woman, and between thy seed and her seed; it shall bruise thy head, and thou shalt bruise His heel" (Genesis 3:15).

The Hebrew word translated *enmity* is "'êybâh." The meaning of the word is "hostility; enmity, hatred."[6]

In this series, we have followed Jesus' ancestral line, which has been recorded in Luke 3:23–38: Christ's genealogy from Jesus Christ to Adam; and Matthew 1:1–16: Christ's genealogy from Abraham to Christ.

# The Angel Prophesies to the Shepherds

There were some shepherds tending their flocks in a field close to the town of Bethlehem, and an angel came to them and prophesied of the Christ: "Fear not: for, behold, I bring you good tidings of great joy, which shall be to all people. For unto you is born this day in the city of David a Savior, which is Christ the Lord" (Luke 2:10–11).

The Greek word translated *Christ* is "Christŏs." The meaning of the word is "anointed, i.e., the Messiah, an epithet of Jesus."[7] Genesis 49:10 prophesies of the coming of "*Shiloh*," which has the meaning, "an epithet of the Messiah."[8]

The angel gave the shepherds a sign to look for so they would know for sure they had found the Christ:

> *Ye shall find the babe wrapped in swaddling clothes, lying in a manger.* And suddenly there was with the angel a multitude of the heavenly host praising God, and saying, Glory to God in the highest, and on earth peace, good will toward men. (Luke 2:12–14; emphasis added)

## Herod the Great

There were some wise men (magi) who came to Jerusalem from the east to find the King of the Jews who had been born. They asked, "Where is he that is born King of the Jews? for we have seen his star in the east, and are come to worship him?" (Matthew 2:2)

Herod, tetrarch of Galilee, heard about this; and he was troubled about another King being worshiped, so he asked the priests and teachers of the Law to tell him what the Scrolls (Scriptures) had to say about the birthplace of Christ. This is the prophecy that had been written in their Scrolls by the prophet Micah in Micah 5:2–3; emphasis added: "But thou *Beth-lehem* Eph´-ra-tah, though thou be little among the thousands *of Judah*, yet out of thee shall he come forth unto me that is to be *ruler in Israel; whose goings forth have been from of old, from everlasting.*"

Jesus would be born fully human in Bethlehem; but He was also fully God, with no beginning or ending.

This upset Herod, so he asked the magi what time the star had appeared to them, and he deceived them.

> [Herod] sent them to Beth-lehem, and said, Go and search diligently for the young child; and when ye have found him, bring me word again, that I may come and worship him also.
>
> When they had heard the king, they departed; and, lo, the star, which they saw in the east, went before them, till it came and stood over where the young child was. When they saw the star, they rejoiced with exceeding great joy. And when they were come into the house, they saw the

young child with Mary his mother, and fell down, and worshiped him: and when they had opened their treasures, they presented unto him gifts; gold, and frankincense, and myrrh. And being warned of God in a dream that they should not return to Herod, they departed into their own country another way. (Matthew 2:8–12)

Here we see Satan's influence on Herod's mind to try to destroy the Savior of the world. Herod was furious when he realized the magi did not return to him. In hopes of killing baby Jesus, he ordered the murder of all baby boys two years old and under. Jeremiah had prophesied of this event: "A voice was heard in Ra′-mah, lamentation, and bitter weeping; Rachel weeping for her children refused to be comforted for her children, because they were not" (Jeremiah 31:15).

The Bible says that nothing happened to baby Jesus because Joseph had received a warning from an angel: "Arise, and take the young child and his mother, and flee into Egypt, and be thou there until I bring thee word: for Herod will seek the young child to destroy him" (Matthew 2:13).

In Matthew 2:15 we find that Joseph and his family stayed in Egypt "until the death of Herod: that it might be fulfilled which was spoken of the Lord by the prophet, saying, Out of Egypt have I called my son." (This had been prophesied in Hosea 11:1.)

Joseph was warned once again not to go back to Judea, because Herod's son Archealaus (Herod the Ethnarch) was reigning. So Joseph took his family into Galilee and settled down and lived in Nazareth, where Jesus "shall be called a Nazarene" (Matthew 2:23). "And the child grew, and waxed strong in spirit, filled with wisdom: and the grace of God was upon him" (Luke 2:40).

# Jesus Is Circumcised

And when eight days were accomplished for the circumcising of the child, his name was called *JESUS*, which was so named of the angel before he was conceived in the womb. And when the days of her

> [Mary's] purification according to the law of Moses were
> accomplished, they brought him to Jerusalem, to present
> him to the Lord; (As it is written in the law of the Lord,
> Every male that openeth the womb shall be called holy
> to the Lord;) [Numbers 3:13] And to offer a sacrifice
> according to that which is said in the law of the Lord, A
> pair of turtledoves, or two young pigeons. (Luke 2:21–24)

Joseph and Mary probably could not afford to bring a lamb for an offering, but they did bring *The Lamb,* Who would become the one-time sacrificial offering for the sins of everyone in the world. The Lord had given Moses instructions about the purification of women after giving birth to their children:

> And when the days of her purifying are fulfilled, for
> a son, or for a daughter, she shall bring a lamb of the
> first year for a burnt offering, and a young pigeon, or
> a turtledove, for a sin offering, unto the door of the
> tabernacle of the congregation, unto the priest. ... And
> if she be not able to bring a lamb, then she shall bring
> two turtles, or two young pigeons; the one for the burnt
> offering, and the other for a sin offering: and the priest
> shall make an atonement for her, and she shall be clean.
> (Leviticus 12:6–8)

## Simeon's Prophecy

Simeon, a man devoted to God who prayed and fasted night and day in the Jewish temple, had been waiting for the "the consolation of Israel" (Luke 2:25).

The Greek word translated *consolation* is "paraklēsis." The meaning of the word is "solace, comfort ... exhortation."[9]

"The Holy Ghost was upon him. And it was revealed unto him by the Holy Ghost, that he should not see death, before he had seen the Lord's Christ" (Luke 2:26).

Simeon came by the Spirit of God into the temple. He took baby Jesus in his arms and said, "Lord, now lettest thou thy servant depart in peace, according to thy word: for mine eyes have seen thy salvation, which thou hast prepared before the face of all people; a light to lighten the Gentiles, and the glory of thy people Israel" (Luke 2:29–32).

The Greek word translated *glory* is "dŏxa." The meaning of the word is "dignity ... honour ... praise ... worship."[10]

This fulfilled the prophecy found in Isaiah:

> I the LORD have called thee [Jesus] in righteousness, and will hold thine hand, and will keep thee, and give thee for a covenant of the people, for a light of the Gentiles; To open the blind eyes, to bring out the prisoners from the prison, and *them that sit in darkness* out of the prison house. (Isaiah 42:6–7; emphasis added)

The Hebrew word translated *Gentiles* is "gôy." The meaning of the word is "a foreign nation ... heathen."[11]

The Hebrew word for *prisoners* is "'âcîyr." The meaning of the word is "bound, i.e. a captive."[12] Jesus will set free the captives from all nations.

Simeon told Mary, "Behold, *this child* is set for the fall and rising again of many in Israel; and for a *sign* which shall be spoken against; (Yea, a sword shall pierce through thy own soul also,) that the thoughts of many hearts may be revealed" (Luke 2:34–35; emphasis added).

This fulfilled the prophecy in Isaiah: "And he shall be for a sanctuary; but for a *stone of stumbling* and for a *rock of offense* to both the houses of Israel, for a gin and for a snare to the inhabitants of Jerusalem" (Isaiah 8:14; emphasis added).

While they were still at the temple, Anna, a widowed prophetess from the Jewish tribe of Asher who lived in the temple, immediately came "and gave thanks likewise unto the Lord, and spake of him to all them that looked for redemption in Jerusalem" (Luke 2:38).

## Jesus Came to Do His Father's Will

The Father, the Son, and the Holy Spirit had been planning and preparing for this big event for a long time. Now Jesus had come to earth to carry out His Father's will.

> Therefore, when Christ came into the world, he said, 'Sacrifice and offering you did not desire, but a body you prepared for me, with burnt offerings and sin offerings you were not pleased.' Then I said, 'Here I am—it is written about me in the scroll—I have come to do your will, my God.' (Hebrews 10:5–7, NIV)

The Bible tells us that when Jesus was twelve years old, He became actively involved in His heavenly Father's will. Joseph, Mary, and Jesus, along with others in a group, went to the Jewish Feast of the Passover in Jerusalem. On their journey home, they discovered that Jesus was not with them, and they went back to try and find Him. They found Him sitting in the temple courts conversing with the teachers, who were amazed at Jesus' knowledge and understanding. When His parents found Him, they wanted to know why He had done this, and He asked them, "How is it that ye sought me? Wist ye not that I must be about my Father's business?" (Luke 2:49)

According to all that was planned, and according to all the Jewish prophecies, Jesus Christ the Messiah had come. Jesus did not come to earth as our Redeemer because it had been prophesied that He would come. The prophecies were spoken because He was already coming. The prophecies had been given by God to let the Jews of the Old Testament know what He was going to do.

## The Ministry of John the Baptist

Jesus lived at home with His family for about thirty years learning the carpentry trade of His earthly father, Joseph, and communing with His heavenly Father. During that time, God had also been preparing John, who lived in the wilderness, to go before Jesus with a message of repentance.

> There was a man sent from God, whose name was John. The same came for a witness, to bear witness of the Light [the Christ], that all men through him might believe. He [John] was not that Light, but was sent to bear witness of that Light. That was the true Light, which lighteth every man that cometh into the world. (John 1:6–9)

While John was in the wilderness, he told the people of Judea, "Repent ye, for the kingdom of heaven is at hand" (Matthew 3:2). This fulfilled Isaiah's prophecy:

> The voice of him that crieth in the wilderness, Prepare ye the way of the LORD, make straight in the desert a highway for our God. Every valley shall be exalted, and every mountain and hill shall be made low: and the crooked shall be made straight, and the rough places plain: And the glory of the LORD shall be revealed, and all flesh shall see it together: for the mouth of the LORD hath spoken it. (Isaiah 40:3–5)

John knew Jesus was the Ancient of Days. In speaking of Jesus, John said, "He that cometh after me is <u>preferred</u> before me: for he was before me" (John 1:15).

The Greek word translated *preferred* is "ginŏmai." The meaning of the word is "to cause to be … generate … to become … come into being."[13]

John said, "And I knew him not: but that he should be made manifest [be made evident] to Israel, therefore am I come baptizing with water" (John 1:31).

John's water baptism was symbolic of being cleansed and coming back to God. John's ministry alerted the people that they needed to repent and be cleansed of their sins through baptism, which prepared their hearts to receive Jesus. This was symbolic of Jesus' death and burial, which was soon to come.

Not everyone came to John to repent. The Jews sent their priests and Levites to ask him who he was. He told them, "I am not the Christ" (John 1:20). When asked if he were Elijah, he denied that and told them, "I am the voice of one crying in the wilderness, Make straight the way of the Lord" (John 1:23). The Pharisees and Sadducees came to harass and discourage him, but John knew their hearts and referred to them as a "generation of vipers" (Matthew 3:7). John told them:

> The axe is laid unto the root of the trees: therefore every tree which bringeth not forth good fruit is hewn down, and cast into the fire. I indeed baptize you with water unto repentance: but he that cometh after me is mightier than I, whose shoes I am not worthy to bear: *he shall baptize you with the Holy Ghost, and with fire:* Whose fan is in his hand, and he will thoroughly purge his floor, and gather his wheat into the garner; but he will burn up the chaff with unquenchable fire. (Matthew 3:10–12; emphasis added)

## Jesus Is Baptized

One day while John was baptizing people in the Jordan River, Jesus came to him to be baptized. John, knowing He was the Christ, said, "Behold the Lamb of God, which taketh away the sin of the world" (John 1:29).

John felt unworthy and said, "I have need to be baptized of thee, and comest thou to me? And Jesus answering, said unto him, Suffer it to be so now: for thus it becometh us to fulfill all righteousness" (Matthew 3:14–15). Then John consented to baptize Jesus. John recorded this amazing event of Jesus' baptism:

> I saw the Spirit descending from heaven like a dove, and it abode upon him. And I knew him not: but he that sent me to baptize with water, the same said unto me, Upon whom thou shalt see the Spirit descending, and remaining on him, the same is he which baptizeth with the Holy

Ghost. And I saw, and bare record that this is the Son of God. (John 1:32–34)

Matthew also recorded the event of Jesus' baptism, in which we see the *Trinity* of God—God in three Persons—the Son, the Holy Spirit, and the Father actively united together.

> And Jesus, when he was baptized, went up straightway out of the water: and, lo, the heavens were opened unto him, and he saw the *Spirit of God* descending like a dove, and lighting upon him: And lo *a voice from heaven, saying, This is my beloved Son*, in whom I am well pleased. (Matthew 3:16–17; emphasis added)

## The Devil Tempts Jesus

After Jesus was baptized and filled with the *Holy Ghost*, the Spirit led Him into the wilderness, "And he was there in the wilderness forty days, tempted of Satan; and was with the wild beasts; and the angels ministered unto him" (Mark 1:12–13).

The Devil was no stranger to Jesus. This was not the first time Jesus had an encounter with him. Jesus, the Creator, had *"created"* this *"anointed cherub"* (Ezekiel 28:14–15) a long time ago, and He knew him very well.

> For by him [Jesus], were all things created, that are in heaven, and that are in earth, visible and invisible, whether they be thrones, or dominions, or principalities, or powers: all things were created by him and for him: And he is before all things, and by him all things consist. (Colossians 1:16–17)

The Devil's pride had caused him to fall, and he had been trying to destroy the works of God ever since. Jesus had come to deal with him once and for all, but being made "in the likeness of men" (Philippians 2:7), Jesus would have no power of His own and would have to totally rely on

His Father's strength and power, which would be given to Him through His obedience. The Devil knew the prophecies written in the Scrolls. He knew he must cause Jesus to sin and fall so that man's redemption and reconciliation to God would not be possible; and he didn't have much time to do it.

The Bible says that while Jesus was in the wilderness for those forty days, He did not eat anything, and He was hungry. So the Devil first tempted Him with food. "And the devil said unto him, If thou be the Son of God, command this stone that it be made bread. And Jesus answered him, saying, It is written, That man shall not live by bread alone, but by every word of God" (Luke 4:3-4).

Jesus had spoken Deuteronomy 8:3, the written Word of God from the Scrolls of the Old Testament. The Devil tempted Jesus a second time:

> And the devil, taking him up into a high mountain, showed unto him all the kingdoms of the world in a moment of time. And the devil said unto him, All this power will I give thee, and the glory of them: for that is delivered unto me; and to whomsoever I will I give it. If thou therefore wilt worship me, all shall be thine. And Jesus answered and said unto him, Get thee behind me, Satan: for it is written, Thou shalt worship the Lord thy God, and him only shalt thou serve. (Luke 4:5-8)

Jesus had spoken Deuteronomy 6:13-14, the written Word of God from the Scrolls of the Old Testament. The Devil tempted Jesus a third time, but this time, the Devil also quoted Scripture to Jesus:

> And he brought him to Jerusalem, and set him on a pinnacle of the temple, and said unto him, If thou be the Son of God, cast thyself down from hence: For it is written, He shall give his angels charge over thee, to keep thee: and in their hands they shall bear thee up, lest at any time thou dash thy foot against a stone [Psalm 91:11–12]. And Jesus answering said unto him, It is said, Thou shalt not tempt the Lord thy God. (Luke 4:9–12)

Jesus had spoken Deuteronomy 6:16, the written Word of God from the Scrolls of the Old Testament. Notice, Jesus didn't spend time arguing with this ancient adversary—He spoke the written Word of God. "And when the devil had ended all the temptation, he departed from him for a season" (Luke 4:13).

Jesus had quoted the Scriptures that had been given to Moses by God for the children of Israel, which was the written Word of God; and in which there is power and authority. Jesus knew Satan was the great deceiver with no truth in him. This is what Jesus had to say about him: "He was a murderer from the beginning, and abode not in the truth, because there is no truth in him. When he speaketh a lie, he speaketh of his own: for he is a liar, and the father of it" (John 8:44).

# In Conclusion

Jesus Christ came to *"bless all nations,"* as had been foretold to Abraham and written in the ancient Scrolls of the Old Testament. The Holy Spirit implanted the divine seed of Jesus into the body of a young Jewish virgin. Jesus, Who came to earth fully God, also became fully man! Through Herod, the Devil who hates God and man tried to destroy baby Jesus; but God was watching and protecting Him.

John the Baptist prepared the way for Jesus' ministry by calling all men to repent of their sins and be baptised with water. God was after the hearts of men, and he was no longer interested in sacrifices and offerings as a means of atonement. "The sacrifices of God are a broken spirit: a broken and a contrite heart, O God, thou wilt not despise" (Psalm 51:17).

After Jesus was baptized and filled with the Holy Spirit, the Spirit led Jesus into the desert to be tempted of the Devil, who tried to make Jesus sin; but Jesus was given strength by the Spirit. Just as Jesus spoke and breathed everything into existence, He spoke the written Word of the Old Testament to overcome the Devil's fiery darts. The prophecy written in Deuteronomy 18 that God had declared through Moses was being fulfilled:

I will raise them up a Prophet from among their brethren,
like unto thee, and will put my words in his mouth; and
he shall speak unto them all that I shall command. And it
shall come to pass, that whosoever will not hearken unto
my words which he shall speak in my name, I will require
it of him. (vv. 18–19)

Jesus was this Prophet. Now, filled with the Spirit, Jesus will begin
His ministry; and He will go first to the Jews, who have waited so long
for God's promises to be fulfilled. What will He have to tell them, and
how will they respond?

## Deeper Insights:

1.  After reading Luke 1:34–35, can you begin to understand how
    Jesus was born fully God and fully man?

    Being an unmarried virgin, how did Mary view this new situation
    in her life? Read Luke 1:46–55.

2.  Mary was pregnant with the Son of God; and her elderly, barren
    cousin, Elisabeth, was pregnant with John, the one who would
    prepare the way for Jesus.

    What happened to Elisabeth when Mary went to see her? Read
    Luke 1:41–45.

    What happened to Zechariah in Luke 1:67?

    What happened to Simeon in Luke 2:25–26?

3.  What kind of baptism did John the Baptist preach to the people
    in order to prepare them for Jesus? Read Matthew 3:11; Mark 1:4;
    Acts 19:4–5.

    John said in John 1:33 that Jesus would baptize the people with
    the Holy Ghost and with fire.

What is the difference between John's baptism with water and Christ's baptism with the Holy Ghost and with fire? Read Acts 2:1–6.

4.  Why do you think Jesus was baptized when He had never sinned and did not need to repent of anything? Read Matthew 3:15 and John 1:29–34. What did John see when he baptized Jesus? Read John 1:32–34.

5.  After Jesus was baptized and filled with the Spirit, the Spirit led Him out into the desert. After Jesus had fasted forty days, the Devil tempted Him. Why do you think God allowed Jesus to be tempted by the Devil when He was weak and hungry?

    Mark 1:12–13 says the angels ministered to Jesus. In what way do you think the angels ministered to Him?

# CHAPTER 12

## JESUS BRINGS SOMETHING NEW

## Jesus' Ministry Begins

After His time of temptation with the Devil, Jesus, Who was about thirty years old, "returned in the power of the Spirit into Galilee" (Luke 4:14) to the Jews who had been waiting for the prophecies about His arrival to be fulfilled. On one particular Sabbath Day while He was attending the Jewish synagogue He grew up in, the Scroll of the prophet was handed to Him; and He read Isaiah 61:1–2 aloud:

> The Spirit of the Lord is upon me, because he hath anointed me to *preach the gospel* [good news] to the poor; he hath sent me to *heal the broken-hearted*, to *preach deliverance* to the captives, and recovering of sight to the blind, to *set at liberty* them that are bruised, *to preach the acceptable year of the Lord.* (Luke 4:18–19; emphasis added)

Jesus had made His mission clear. After Jesus closed the book and sat down, He told them: "This day is this Scripture fulfilled in your ears. And all bare him witness, and wondered at the gracious words which proceeded out of his mouth. And they said, Is not this Joseph's son?" (Luke 4:21–22).

Before we can begin to understand Christ's mission here on earth, we really need to understand that He is God, the Son. God consists of *three* distinct Persons, who are called the "Godhead." Those Persons are *God* the Father, *God* the Son, and *God* the Holy Spirit. These three are "One." References to this are found in Matthew 3:16–17; John 14:26, 15:26; 2

Corinthians 13:14; Galatians 4:4–6; Colossians 2:9; and Deuteronomy 6:4. Jesus is the *"fullness of the Godhead bodily* [in a human body]" (Colossians 2:9; emphasis added). He was not just a man. Whatever God had done in the past, Jesus was there, too. Jesus is referred to as the "Word" in the New Testament: "In the *beginning* was the Word [Jesus] and the Word was with God, and the Word was God" (John 1:1; emphasis added).

Jesus was the Creator—"All things were made by him" (John 1:3). Listen to what the Father said to Jesus in Hebrews 1:8:

> GOD who ... spake in time past unto the fathers by the prophets, Hath in these last days spoken unto us by his Son ... Thy throne, *O God*, is for ever and ever: a scepter of righteousness is the scepter of thy kingdom. Thou hast loved righteousness, and hated iniquity; therefore *God*, even thy God, hath anointed thee with the oil of gladness above thy fellows. And, Thou, Lord, in the beginning hast laid the foundation of the earth; and the heavens are the works of thine hands. (Hebrews 1:1–10)

Now Jesus laid down the glory He had with His Father in heaven to come to earth. He came to fulfill the prophecies which He, His Father, and the Spirit had given to the prophets of old about Him long ago.

Can you even begin to imagine how Jesus must have felt? He had come to earth in human form to walk among His creation to reconcile them to God. He had seen the darkness, suffering, and despair of all their Jewish ancestors through the ages, and He had walked among them, as well; but only a few had recognized Him. Now, He would make Himself known; and He would bring them the kingdom of God that had been talked about in the prophecies.

When Jesus heard that John had been put in prison, He went to "The land of Zeb´-u-lun, and the land of Naph´-tali, by the way of the sea, beyond Jordan, Galilee of the Gentiles; the people which sat in darkness saw great light; and to them which sat in the region and shadow of death light is sprung up" (Matthew 4:15–16). This had been prophesied in Isaiah 9:1–2.

He began to preach, "Repent: for the kingdom of heaven is at hand" (Matthew 4:17).

## Jesus Calls Twelve Disciples

Jesus began to call a group of men to follow Him. They were not fully aware of whom Jesus was, but there was a certain authority in His voice that drew them and compelled them to make a choice. When He called out, "Follow Me," they immediately left family and friends to go with Him. Twelve men became His disciples, who would go out to preach the gospel of salvation and heal the masses of people: Simon (Peter) and his brother Andrew, James, John, Philip, Bartholomew, Levi (Matthew), Thomas, James, Thaddaeus, Simon the Zealot, and Judas Iscariot.

His very presence drew crowds of people to Him. He taught them about His favor that would be shown to certain people, those who are "poor in spirit ... they that mourn ... those who are meek ... they which do hunger and thirst after righteousness ... the merciful ... the pure in heart ... the peacemakers ... they which are persecuted for righteousness' sake" (Matthew 5:3–10).

As Jesus ministered to them, He told them, "The time is fulfilled, and the kingdom of God is at hand: repent ye, and believe the gospel" (Mark 1:15). He didn't speak theories, philosophies, or tickle their ears with things they wanted to hear. In His human form, Jesus spoke the *truth* that He received from His Father. His heart was filled with love and compassion for people, and He talked to them about love, mercy, and issues of the heart—not about following the regulations of the Law.

When Jesus was with people, He knew the condition and thoughts of their hearts and minds. Nothing was hidden from Him in whom the Spirit of God dwelt. He knew those who were thirsting for the "living water" He offered. As He walked among them, He saw those who were blind, deaf, and crippled, those with leprosy, paralysis and fevers, and many other afflictions; and He healed them. Wherever He went, the crowds came to hear what He had to say because His fame quickly spread from town to town. They were desperate to receive His healing and to be set free from spiritual bondage that kept them from God's peace.

He drove out demons that were causing people to have seizures and act like lunatics. By His authority, He commanded the demons to leave. They knew Who He was, and they hated Him, because they were of the Devil. He commanded them, "Hold thy peace, and come out of him" (Mark 1:25), and they did!

When Jesus was walking through the crowds, He knew when someone reached out and touched Him, like the time the woman who had been bleeding for twelve years reached out to touch the hem of His garment: "She said within herself, If I may but touch his garment, I shall be whole. … Jesus turned him about, and when he saw her, he said, Daughter, be of good comfort; thy faith hath made thee whole" (Matthew 9:21–22).

Jesus walked on the water, and by His spoken word, He fed thousands of people with a few loaves of bread and a few fish, calmed the winds and the storms of the sea, and forgave the sins of the people. The books of Matthew, Mark, Luke, and John record numerous accounts of the miracles done by Jesus, including people being raised from the dead.

## Matters of the Heart

Jesus was always looking into the heart of man, because that is where all sin begins. He taught that when sin dwells in our hearts, we are guilty of sin, whether we outwardly express it or not. For example, Jesus equated anger with murder (see Matthew 5:21–22) and lust with adultery (see Matthew 5:27–28). He also taught them the "Golden Rule": "Whatsoever ye would do that men should do to you, do ye even so to them: for this is the law and the prophets" (Matthew 7:12).

He told them to love their enemies and to pray for those who wrongfully use them and persecute them (see Matthew 5:43–44). He told them not to judge others, but to forgive them (see Luke 6:37). "For if ye forgive men their trespasses, your heavenly Father will also forgive you: But if ye forgive not men their trespasses, neither will your Father forgive your trespasses" (Matthew 6:14–15).

God had given the Israelites the Ten Commandments, and Jesus summed all these commandments up into two commandments by quoting these two Old Testament Scriptures:

> Thou shalt love the Lord thy God with all thy heart, and
> with all thy soul, and with all thy mind [see Deuteronomy
> 6:5]. This is the first and great commandment. And the
> second is like unto it, Thou shalt love thy neighbor as
> thyself [see Leviticus 19:18]. On these two commandments
> hang all the law and the prophets. (Matthew 22:37–40)

Jesus was teaching them love, and love is not against the Law. In fact,
love fulfills the Law (see Romans 13:10).

Jesus especially responded to those who had faith in Him—nothing
had more meaning to Him, and He spent much of His time teaching
people how to do that. He loved the little children who were so trusting
and dependent, and told them that they must receive God's kingdom in
the same way, with childlike faith (see Mark 10:14–15).

## Jesus Teaches the People How to Fast and Pray

Jesus loved to be alone with His Father to pray to Him and fellowship with
Him. Being with people and ministering to them often caused Jesus to
tire. He would go away to quiet places and rest with His heavenly Father,
Who would refresh and restore Him mentally, physically, and spiritually.
So He knew the importance of prayer and intimacy with His Father, and
He wanted the people to share time with the Father, too.

> When thou prayest, enter into thy closet, and when thou
> hast shut thy door, pray to thy Father which is in secret;
> and thy Father which seeth in secret shall reward thee
> openly ... your Father knoweth what things ye have need
> of, before ye ask him ... when thou fastest, anoint thine
> head, and wash thy face; That thou appear not unto men
> to fast, but unto thy Father, which is in secret: and thy
> Father, which seeth in secret, shall reward thee openly.
> (Matthew 6:6–18)

Jesus taught them this prayer as an example of how they should come to their Father. It is a prayer which gives God glory as we depend on Him to sustain us, protect us, and forgive us.

> Our Father which art in heaven, Hallowed be thy name. Thy kingdom come. Thy will be done in earth, as it is in heaven. Give us this day our daily bread. And forgive us our debts, as we forgive our debtors. And lead us not into temptation, but deliver us from evil: For thine is the kingdom, and the power, and the glory, for ever. Amen. (Matthew 6:9–13)

## Jesus Declares His Deity

When Moses had been on the mountain, he had encountered the presence of God in the burning bush; and God had called Himself "I AM." Here, the Hebrew words translated "I am" are "hâyâh." The meaning of the words is "to exist."[1]

"I am the God of thy father, the God of Abraham, the God of Isaac, and the God of Jacob" (Exodus 3:6).

Jesus referred to Himself as "I am" many times as He gave people hope. In the cases below, the Greek words translated "I am" are "ĕimi." The meaning of the words is "I exist (used only when emphatic) ... am, have been."[2]

> "I am the way, the truth, and the life: no man cometh unto the Father, but by me" (John 14:6).

> "I am the resurrection, and the life: he that believeth on me, though he were dead, yet shall he live. And whosoever liveth and believeth in me shall never die" (John 11:25–26).

"I am the light of the world: he that followeth me shall not walk in darkness, but shall have the light of life" (John 8:12).

"I am the good Shepherd: the good Shepherd giveth his life for the sheep" (John 10:11).

"I am the door: by me if any man enter in, he shall be saved, and shall go in and out, and find pasture" (John 10:9).

In the days of Moses, God had fed the Israelites manna, the "bread of heaven" (Psalm 105:40) in the desert. Jesus is now telling the Jews that He is the Living Bread Who has come down from heaven to give them eternal life:

He that believeth on me hath everlasting life. I am that bread of life. Your fathers did eat manna in the wilderness, and are dead. This is the bread which cometh down from heaven, that a man may eat thereof, and not die. I am the living bread which came down from heaven: if any may eat of this bread, he shall live for ever: and the bread that I will give is my flesh, which I will give for the life of the world. (John 6:47-51)

Jesus was constantly inviting the people to come to Him and give Him their burdens and cares.

Come unto me, all ye that labor and are heavy laden, and I will give you rest. Take my yoke upon you, and learn of me; for I am meek and lowly in heart: and ye shall find rest unto your souls. For my yoke is easy, and my burden is light. (Matthew 11:28–30)

In John 8:56–58, Jesus makes bold statements declaring His deity. When speaking to a Samaritan woman who told Him, "I know that Mes-si´-ah cometh, which is called Christ: when he is come, he will tell us all things," Jesus told her, "I that speak unto thee am he" (John 4:25–26). One day, Jesus told the Jews:

> Your father Abraham rejoiced to see my day: and he saw it, and was glad. Then said the Jews unto him, Thou art not yet fifty years old, and hast Thou seen Abraham? Jesus said unto them, Verily, verily, I say unto you, Before Abraham was, I am. (John 8:56–58)

Jesus told the multitudes and His disciples to not exalt any man into positions that belong to God alone, such as rabbi, father, master: "Be not ye called Rabbi: for one is your Master, even Christ ... And call no man your father upon the earth: for one is your Father, which is in heaven. ... Neither be ye called masters, for one is your Master, even Christ" (Matthew 23:8–9).

# Jesus Exposes the Sins of the Jewish Leaders of the Law

The Pharisees and teachers of the Law were missing the point. For example, they paid their tithes, but they neglected "judgment, mercy, and faith" (Matthew 23:23). They loved to be exalted for their self-righteous acts, but were oftentimes cruel and oppressive to the people. They even twisted the Scriptures for their own agenda. They would often be found in the crowds of people, trying to trap Jesus with His own words to try to find flaw with His teachings. They also questioned the proof of His authority because He cast out demons, forgave sins, and even raised the dead. It was just another area in which the Devil was controlling the hearts and minds of men to try to ruin Jesus' message for people to be saved. They called Him names, such as "blasphemer" (Matthew 9:1–3) and "Be-el'ze-bub, the prince of the devils" (Matthew 12:24). Jesus loved the sinners and often ate and drank with them and the tax collectors. The Pharisees ridiculed Him and called Him a drunkard and a glutton. He told them: "They that be whole need not a physician, but they that are sick. But go ye and learn what that meaneth, I will have mercy, and not sacrifice: for

I am not come to call the righteous, but sinners to repentance" (Matthew 9:12–13).

One day, Jesus told Nicodemus, a Jewish leader, "Except a man be born again, he cannot see the kingdom of God" (John 3:3). Nicodemus didn't understand how a man could re-enter his mother's womb and be "born again." Jesus told him about something new—not religion, and not the Law; but being reborn by the Spirit of God: "Except a man be born of water and of the Spirit, he cannot enter into the kingdom of God" (John 3:5).

When the leaders criticized Jesus for healing and helping people on the Sabbath, He told them that He was Lord of the Sabbath (see Mark 2:27–28). When they ridiculed Jesus' disciples, who broke the tradition of the Law by not washing their hands before they ate, Jesus told them that evil comes from the heart: "For out of the heart proceed evil thoughts, murders, adulteries, fornications, thefts, false witness, blasphemies: These are the things which defile a man: but to eat with unwashen hands defileth not a man" (Matthew 15:19–20).

The Pharisees looked good on the outside, but Jesus could see inside of their evil hearts. He told the people not to do what the Pharisees do. All the good that they do, they do to look good to others; and they love to be treated as though they are superior to others. "They make broad their phylacteries" (Matthew 23:5).

"In the NT it [a phylactery] denotes a prayer fillet…a small strip of parchment, with portions of the Law written on it; it was fastened by a leather strap either to the forehead or to the left arm over against the heart, to remind the wearer of the duty of keeping the commandments of God in the head and in the heart…The Pharisees broadened their 'phylacteries' to render conspicuous their superior eagerness to be mindful of God's Law."[3]

He told them: "Search the Scriptures; for in them ye think ye have eternal life: and they are they which testify of me. And ye will not come to me, that ye might have life" (John 5:39–40). "The publicans and the harlots go into the kingdom of God before you. For John came unto you in the way of righteousness, and ye believed him not: but the publicans and the harlots believed him" (Matthew 21:31–32).

When Jesus spoke His truth to them, they felt His finger pointing at them; but they did not want to repent. Jesus was drawing the Jewish people away from them with His ministry of grace and miracles. He was drawing them away with His love and hope. They had high positions of authority over the Jews, and they had comfort and wealth because they had feathered their own nests with the Roman government. They would do whatever they had to do to discredit Jesus and bring Him down.

## Herod Kills John the Baptist

As time went on, Herod ordered John the Baptist's head to be cut off. John's disciples buried John, and then they told Jesus what had happened. When Jesus heard, He was sorrowful at the news of John's death and went away in a boat to be by Himself; but wherever Jesus went, the crowds followed. His compassion for them would not allow Him to keep to Himself very long. So on that sorrowful day, He began to heal them and fed over five thousand people with five loaves of bread and two fish (see Matthew 14:13–21).

Feeling fearful, Herod began to spread lies in order to discredit Jesus and His miracles. He began to announce that Jesus was really John the Baptist who had come back from the dead, and that was why He was able to do these miracles. One day, Jesus asked His disciples:

> Whom do men say that I the Son of man am? And they said, Some say that thou art John the Baptist: some, Eli´-jah; and others, Jeremiah, or one of the prophets. He saith unto them, But whom say ye that I am? And Simon Peter answered and said, Thou art the Christ, the Son of the living God. And Jesus answered and said unto him, Blessed art thou, Simon Bar-jo´-na: for flesh and blood hath not revealed it unto thee, but my Father which is in heaven. And I say also unto thee, That thou art Peter, and upon this rock I will build my church; and the gates of hell shall not prevail against it. (Matthew 16:13–18)

The Greek word translated *Peter* is "Petros." The meaning of the word is "individual stone."[4]

187

The Greek word translated *rock* is "petra." The meaning of the word is "large rock formation, in contrast to individual stones … with a focus that this is a suitable, solid foundation."[5]

There are different schools of thought about Jesus' statement, "upon this rock I will build my church." Did Christ mean He would build His Church upon the confessions of those who believed He was "the Christ, the Son of the living God," as Peter had confessed; or that He would build His Church upon Peter, whose faith recognized Christ as the Messiah; or was Jesus saying He would build His Church upon Himself, the foundational Rock? Jesus had declared Himself throughout the New Testament to be the "Stone" and the "Rock." After Christ was resurrected, Peter did play a major role in preaching to the Jews; and later, he played a major role in evangelizing the Gentiles, building the Church of Christ. No matter how we choose to interpret the verse above, this we know: Christ is the solid Rock, the foundation upon which the living stones (believers in Christ) are set upon to buld the temple, the Church of Christ.

> As you come to him, the living Stone—rejected by humans but chosen by God and precious to him— you also, like living stones, are being built into a spiritual house to be a holy priesthood, offering spiritual sacrifices acceptable to God through Jesus Christ. (1 Peter 2:4–5, NIV®)

## The Transfiguration

Just six days later, Jesus took three of His disciples, Peter, James, and John way up on a mountain.

> And he was <u>transfigured</u> before them. And his <u>raiment</u> became shining, exceeding white as snow; so as no fuller [bleach] on earth can white them. And there appeared unto them Eli´-jah with Moses: and they were talking with Jesus. And Peter answered and said to Jesus, Master, it is good for us to be here: and let us make three <u>tabernacles</u>;

one for thee, and one for Moses, and one for Eli´-jah. (Mark 9:1–5)

The Greek word translated *transfigured* is "mĕtamŏrphŏō." The meaning of the word is "change ... transform."[6]

The Greek word translated *raiment* is "himatiŏn." The meaning of the word is "clothes."[7]

The Greek word translated *tabernacles* is "skēnē." The meaning of the word is "tent or cloth hut ... habitation."[8]

In Leviticus 23:40–43 and Nehemiah 8:14, we find that the Lord had required the Israelites to celebrate the Feast of Tabernacles. After they had gathered their fruits, they built booths to live in for seven days. This was done to remember that the Lord had made them live in tents when He had brought them out of Egypt. The Transfiguration was significant, but why?

First of all, we see Jesus there, glowing and brilliant as God the Son. We see Moses, the Lawgiver, who according to Deuteronomy 34, died in Moab. Then we see Elijah the prophet who never died, but was taken up into heaven (see 2 Kings 2:1–15). Just prior to this event, Peter had declared to Jesus, "Thou art the Christ, the Son of the living God," and now we see Peter coming up with the idea that they needed to set up booths, which God had required of the Israelites under the Law. A cloud came over them, and God the Father spoke to them from the cloud, "This is my beloved Son: hear him."

God did not acknowledge Moses or Elijah, but He declared that Jesus is His Son and that they needed to listen to Him. Hebrews 3:3–5 tells us this:

> Consider the Apostle and High Priest of our profession, Christ Jesus; Who was faithful to him that appointed him, as also Moses was faithful in all his house. For this *man* was counted worthy of more glory than Moses, inasmuch as he who hath builded the house hath more honor than the house. For every house is builded by some man; but he that built all things is God. And Moses verily was faithful in all his house, as a servant, for a testimony of

those things which were to be spoken after; But Christ as
a son over his own house.

God was doing something new and different. The Bible says that after
hearing God's voice, the disciples were very afraid.

"And Jesus came and touched them, and said, Arise, and be not afraid.
And when they had lifted up their eyes, they saw no man, save Jesus only"
(Matthew 17:6–8). When they looked up and saw only Jesus standing
there, He told them, "Tell the vision to no man, until the Son of man
be risen again from the dead" (Matthew 17:9). He had just given them a
prophecy of His death and resurrection, and they will soon see it fulfilled.

## Jesus Sends His Disciples Out

After being taught by Him, He sent His disciples out with His power to
preach repentance to the Jews first, not the Gentiles at this time. They
were to deliver the "good news" that Christ is the Messiah they had been
waiting for, as had been prophesied in their Scrolls. He told the disciples
not to go to the Gentiles or the Samaritans.

> Go rather to the lost sheep of the house of Israel. And as
> ye go, preach, saying, The kingdom of heaven is at hand.
> Heal the sick, cleanse the lepers, raise the dead, cast out
> devils: freely ye have received, freely give. Provide neither
> gold, nor silver, nor brass in your purses, Nor scrip for
> your journey, neither two coats, neither shoes, nor yet
> staves: for the workman is worthy of his meat. (Matthew
> 10:6–10)

> Behold, I send you forth as sheep in the midst of wolves:
> be ye therefore wise as serpents, and harmless as doves.
> But beware of men: for they will deliver you up to the
> councils, and they will scourge you in their synagogues;
> And ye shall be brought before governors and kings for
> my sake, for a testimony against them and the Gentiles.

But when they deliver you up, take no thought how or what ye shall speak: for it shall be given you in that same hour what ye shall speak. For it is not ye that speak, but the Spirit of your Father which speaketh in you. (Matthew 10:16–20)

Jesus says in John 7:7 that the world hated Him, "because I testify of it, that the works thereof are evil." God's truth exposes sin and offends people if their hearts are not where they should be. Jesus told them:

If I had not done among them the works which none other man did, they had not had sin: but now have they both seen and hated both me and my Father. But this cometh to pass, that the word might be fulfilled that is written in their law, They hated me without a cause. (John 15:24–25)

Jesus told His disciples that they would also be hated, persecuted, and killed. He told them not to fear this, but to always fear God.

Fear them not therefore: for there is nothing covered, that shall not be revealed; and hid, that shall not be known. What I tell you in darkness, that speak ye in light: and what ye hear in the ear, that preach ye upon the housetops. And fear not them which kill the body, but are not able to kill the soul: but rather fear him which is able to destroy both soul and body in hell. (Matthew 10:26–28)

Whosoever therefore shall confess me before men, him will I confess also before my Father which is in heaven. But whosoever shall deny me before men, him will I also deny before my Father which is in heaven. Think not that I am come to send peace on earth: I came not to send peace, but a sword. For I am come to set a man at variance against his father, and the daughter against her mother, and the daughter-in-law against her mother-in-law. And

> a man's foes shall be they of his own household. He that
> loveth father or mother more than me is not worthy of
> me: and he that loveth son or daughter more than me
> is not worthy of me. And he that taketh not his cross,
> and followeth after me, is not worthy of me. (Matthew
> 10:32–38)

As the disciples walked with Jesus, they learned to be like Him; and they loved Him, knowing He was Christ their Lord. When He knew the disciples were ready, He sent them out to teach the same message that He had been teaching and to do what He had been doing. They were to be disciples who imitated their Master.

Jesus also selected seventy other men besides the original Twelve to go out together, two by two, ahead of Him (see Luke 10:1). All of His chosen were to go out, not armed with weapons, but armed with the truth that Jesus is the Son of God, to teach the love of Christ, and to tell them of the need to repent of their sins so they could be forgiven.

"[He] gave them power against unclean spirits, to cast them out, and to heal all manner of sickness and all manner of disease" (Matthew 10:1). Jesus told them: "Go ye therefore, and teach all nations, baptizing them in the *name* [not names] of the Father, and of the Son, and of the Holy Ghost" (Matthew 28:19; emphasis added).

> Into whatsoever city ye enter, and they receive you not, go
> your ways out into the streets of the same, and say, Even
> the very dust of your city, which cleaveth on us, we do
> wipe off against you: notwithstanding be ye sure of this,
> that the kingdom of God is come nigh unto you. (Luke
> 10:10–11)

[Jesus told them]

> I beheld Satan as lightning fall from heaven. Behold, I give
> unto you power to tread on serpents and scorpions, and
> over all the power of the enemy: and nothing shall by any
> means hurt you. Notwithstanding in this rejoice not, that

the spirits are subject unto you; but rather rejoice, because your names are written in heaven. (Luke 10:18–20)

Blessed are the eyes which see the things ye see: For I tell you, that many prophets and kings have desired to see those things which ye see, and have not seen them; and to hear those things which ye hear, and have not heard them. (Luke 10:23–24)

# In Conclusion

Jesus is God the Son, and He has a great passion for His creation. He came to earth to bring a new everlasting covenant of grace to His people, which would include the Gentiles.

As Jesus began His ministry of truth and grace, He called twelve men to follow Him and become His disciples. Later, He called more to go out and preach the kingdom of God. He ordained them and gave them His power over the demonic and His power to heal the sick; and He taught them how to live in faith and love. He declared Himself to be the Son of God, receiving all power and wisdom from His Father.

As He walked among the people, He felt great love and compassion for them and performed miracles to make them whole again. He loved being with them. He mingled with the sinners because He came to save them; however, He rebuked the self-righteous hearts of the scribes, Sadducees, and Pharisees who lived hypocritical lives to make themselves look better than everyone else; and He rebuked them for oppressing the poor.

Jesus obeyed the Jewish laws and traditions, and He celebrated the Jewish feasts; however, He came to abolish the use of laws and rituals as a way to bring reconciliation and right standing with God. Those external things could only make men clean on the outside. He summed up the Law into two commandments: Love God and love others.

In the Transfiguration, the disciples saw that Jesus' deity and His authority were established over the Law and the prophets. Then He sent them out to do as their Master had done and to speak what the Father would give them to speak.

Jesus would continue to teach the people and be with them, but He knew His time on earth would soon end. He must prepare them for what was about to happen. The Jewish leaders would be on the lookout for a time to trap Jesus and bring Him to His death. How will He spend His last days before He must face that hour? We are going on that journey with Jesus as He makes His preparations to do what He came to do—redeem His creation.

## Deeper Insights:

1. When the Messiah (Christ) came to earth, He was on a mission.

   Read the following Scriptures and list the things Jesus came to do:

   Matthew 26:26–28; Luke 4:17–19; Romans 16:20; 2 Corinthians 5:21; Ephesians 2:11–13; Hebrews 1:3, 2:14–18, 8:1–6; 1 Peter 1:18–20; 1 John 3:8

2. To see how Jesus recruited His disciples, read Matthew 4:18–22.

   Why do you think they would leave everything to follow Jesus?

3. We are not to have the "godliness" of the hypocritical Pharisees. Read the following Scriptures to see what we should and should not have manifesting in our lives, if Christ is our Master:

   Romans 12:9–21, 14:13, 17–21; 1 Corinthians 9:24–27; Ephesians 4:1–3; 1 Thessalonians 4:11–12; 1 Timothy 5:22; Titus 2:11–15; Hebrews 13:15–17

4. Jesus stressed that we need to forgive others.

   Read the following Scriptures to see what Jesus said about forgiveness.

   Matthew 18:21–22; Mark 11:25–26; Luke 6:37; Luke 17:3–4; Ephesians 4:32

5. Why was Jesus more concerned about changing the hearts of man than seeing them obey the Law?

Read the following Scriptures to see why our hearts need to be purified in Christ:

Matthew 12:34–36, 15:19

6. Why do you think Jesus told His disciples to go to the Jews first? Read Acts 28:26–28.

7. Why did some of the Jews hate Jesus and His Father?

Read John 3:19–20, 15:24–25.

Read the following Scriptures to better understand why many people hate followers of Jesus today:

Matthew 24:9; John 15:18–21; 1 John 3:11–13

8. In Matthew 10:28, Jesus tells us to fear God. Why should we fear God?

Read Psalm 19:9–12; Proverbs 1:7, 8:13, 14:27; and Revelation 15:3-4.

# CHAPTER 13

## THE FINAL DAYS BEFORE JESUS' DEATH

## The King of the Jews Enters Jerusalem

On numerous occasions, Jesus had prophesied to His disciples of His upcoming death and resurrection. By telling them before it happened, they would remember His prophecies and believe after it happened. When Jesus and his disciples were on their way to Jerusalem for the Passover, He told them what kind of death He would suffer:

> Behold, we go up to Jerusalem; and the Son of man shall be betrayed unto the chief priests and unto the scribes, and they shall condemn him to death, And shall deliver him to the Gentiles to mock, and to scourge, and to *crucify* him: and the third day he shall rise again. (Matthew 20:18–19; emphasis added)

In preparation of His arrival into Jerusalem, Jesus sent two of His disciples to a certain place to find and bring an ass for Him to ride upon. When Jesus entered the city on the ass, the crowds of Jews spread palm branches on the road before Him. They were yelling and shouting:

> Hosanna to the Son of David: Blessed is he that cometh in the name of the Lord; Hosanna in the highest. And when he was come into Jerusalem, all the city was moved, saying, Who is this? And the multitude said, This is Jesus the prophet of Nazareth of Galilee. (Matthew 21:9–11)

The Greek word translated *hosanna* is "hōsanna." The meaning of the word is "oh save ... an exclamation of adoration."[1]

Most of the Jews were thinking that Jesus was the King Who had come to set up His earthly kingdom and deliver them from Roman oppression.

When Jesus went to the temple in Jerusalem, He saw corruption. Instead of people worshiping God, there were buyers and sellers in the temple area. In His righteous anger, He turned over all their tables and quoted their own law to them:

> It is written, My house shall be called the house of prayer; but ye have made it a den of thieves. The blind and the lame came to him in the temple; and he healed them. And when the chief priests and scribes saw the wonderful things that he did, and the children crying in the temple, and saying, Ho-san´-na to the son of David; they were sore displeased And said unto him, Hearest thou what these say? And Jesus saith unto them, Yea; have ye never read, Out of the mouth of babes and sucklings thou hast perfected praise? (Matthew 21:13–16)

While Jesus was teaching in the temple, the Jewish leaders came in and were listening to Him, questioning His authority to do and say these things. At one point, He asked them this question: "Did ye never read in the Scriptures, the *stone* which the builders rejected, the same is become the head of the corner: this is the Lord's doing, and it is marvelous in our eyes?" (Matthew 21:42) This had been prophesied in Psalm 118:22–23.

> Therefore say I unto you, The kingdom of God shall be taken from you, and given to a nation bringing forth the fruits thereof. And whosoever shall fall on this stone shall be broken: but on whomsoever it shall fall, it will grind him to powder. (Matthew 21:43–44)

Jesus was referring to Himself as the *"Stone."* Now He would be bringing the "kingdom of God" to the Gentiles, who had never been included in the covenant with the Jews. Isaiah had also prophesied of this cornerstone that was coming: "Behold, I lay in Zion for a foundation a stone, a tried stone, a precious corner stone, a sure foundation" (Isaiah 28:16).

The things Jesus told the leaders made them angry, and they were determined to have Jesus arrested; but they would have to wait. The crowds of Jews that had come for the Passover feast were excited about their new King who they believed would set them free politically and nationally. They knew if they caused the Jews to be angry, it could start a huge riot.

## Judas Plots to Betray Jesus

At the beginning of His ministry, when Jesus had selected Judas as His disciple, He already knew that Judas had unbelief and would betray Him. Jesus had told His disciples: "Have not I chosen you twelve, and one of you is a devil? He spake of Judas Iscariot the son of Simon: for he it was that should betray him, being one of the twelve" (John 6:70–71).

Now it was time for that betrayal to begin.

> Then entered Satan into Judas surnamed Iscariot, being of the number of the twelve. And he went his way, and communed with the chief priests and captains, how he might betray him unto them. And they were glad, and covenanted to give him money. And he promised, and sought opportunity to betray him unto them in the absence of the multitude. (Luke 22:3–6)

The leaders agreed to give Judas thirty pieces of silver to hand Jesus over to them, which had been prophesied in Zechariah 11:12.

# The Lord's Supper (the Passover Meal)

On the day the Passover was killed, Jesus instructed two of His disciples to go to Jerusalem to find and secure a certain upper room that would be prepared for them. He told them to make the room ready for their Passover meal. Later, when Jesus and the disciples were seated in the upper room for the Passover meal, He exposed His betrayer. He told them:

> He that dippeth his hand with me in the dish, the same shall betray me. The Son of man goeth as it is written of him: but woe unto that man by whom the Son of man is betrayed! It had been good for that man if he had not been born. Then Judas, which betrayed him, answered and said, Master, is it I? He said unto him, Thou hast said. (Matthew 26:23–25)

Jesus established the first "holy Communion" as a memorial of what He was about to do.

> And as they were eating, Jesus took bread, and blessed it, and brake it, and gave it to the disciples, and said, Take, eat: this is *my body*. And he took the cup, and gave thanks, and gave it to them, saying, Drink ye all of it; For this is *my blood* of the new testament, which is shed for many for the remission of sins. (Matthew 26:26–28; emphasis added)

What did Jesus mean "this is my blood of the new testament…for the remission of sins"? The Greek word translated *testament* is "diathēkē." The meaning of the word is "covenant."[2] The Greek word translated *remission* is "aphĕsis." The meaning of the word is "freedom … pardon … deliverance, forgiveness, liberty."[3]

Jesus was going to become our "mercy seat," our "atonement cover," as had been foreshadowed in the most holy place with the ark of the covenant on the Day of Atonement. Jesus would do this by pouring out His own blood to pardon all sin and set the captives free. There would be no more need to make atonement through the blood of animals. In fact, Christ was bringing an end to the Law to be used for reconciliation between God and man. It would be an eternal covenant of grace, by the Spirit of God. The remnant of Jews in the Old Testament days who had believed in the promise of the Messiah would be included in this new covenant, along with everyone who would now believe in the Christ who did come.

The Greek word translated *grace* is "charis." The meaning of the word is "acceptable, benefit, favour, gift ... joy, liberality, pleasure, thankworthy."[4]

Jesus was giving the disciples and all who would ever believe something tangible (the bread and the cup) to remember what He was about to do. Jesus told them, "this do in remembrance of me" (Luke 22:19).

After their Passover meal, Jesus became a Servant to them. He took off His clothes, wrapped a towel around His body, and began washing His disciples' feet with water from a basin. "Peter saith unto him, Thou shalt never wash my feet. Jesus answered him, If I wash thee not, thou hast no part with me" (John 13:8).

> So after he had washed their feet, and had taken his garments, and was set down again, he said unto them, Know ye what I have done to you? Ye call me Master and Lord: and ye say well; for so I am. If I then, your Lord and Master, have washed your feet; ye also ought to wash one another's feet. For I have given you an example, that ye should do as I have done to you. Verily, verily, I say unto you, The servant is not greater than his lord; neither he that is sent greater than he that sent him. (John 13:12–16)

## Jesus Gives Assurance to His Disciples

This would be Jesus' last night with His disciples before His death, and He wanted to prepare them for what was coming and to assure them of their relationship with Him and His Father. He told them, "A new commandment I give unto you: That ye love one another; as I have loved you, that ye also love one another. By this shall all men know that ye are my disciples, if ye have love one to another" (John 13:34–35).

Even though He was going to leave them and go back to His Father, He wanted them to know He was not going to leave them as orphans. He will send *God's Spirit* to live in them. He told them:

> If ye love me, keep my commandments. And I will pray the Father, and he shall give you another *Comforter*, that he may abide with you for ever; Even the *Spirit of truth*; whom the world cannot receive, because it seeth him not, neither knoweth him: but ye know him; for he dwelleth with you, and shall be in you. I will not leave you comfortless: I will come to you. (John 14:15–18; emphasis added)

Here Jesus identifies Himself as the Spirit of God as well: "I will come to you." How can that be? Remember the triune "Godhead." "But ye are not in the flesh, but in the Spirit, if so be that the Spirit of God dwell in you. Now if any man have not the *Spirit of Christ*, he is none of his" (Romans 8:9; emphasis added).

> The Comforter, which is the Holy Ghost, whom the Father will send in my name, he shall teach you all things, and bring all things to your remembrance, whatsoever I have said unto you. Peace I leave with you, my peace I give unto you; not as the world giveth, give I unto you. Let not your heart be troubled, neither let it be afraid. (John 14:26–27)

> It is expedient for you that I go away: for if I go not away, the Comforter will not come unto you; but if I depart, I will send him unto you. And when he is come, he will reprove the world of sin, and of righteousness, and of judgment. (John 16:7–8)

# The Garden of Gethsemane

> And when they had sung a hymn, they went out into the mount of Olives. And Jesus saith unto them, All ye shall be offended because of me this night: for it is written, I will smite the shepherd, and the sheep shall be scattered. But after that I am risen, I will go before you into Galilee. (Mark 14:26–28)

Peter promised Jesus that He would never be offended because of Jesus, but Jesus knew different. He told Peter, "This day, even in this night, before the cock crow twice, thou shalt deny me thrice" (Mark 14:30).

Jesus and His disciples then went to a nearby garden in a place called Gethsemane. Jesus told them to wait for Him while Peter, James, and John went with Him to pray; but as they went along, Jesus became deeply sorrowful and told them to stay and watch with Him.

Even though Jesus was fully God, He was also fully human. He felt agony and sorrow knowing what He was about to go through. As He went a little farther, He fell down with His face on the ground and prayed: "O my Father, if it be possible, let this cup pass from me: nevertheless not as I will, but as thou wilt" (Matthew 26:39).

The disciples who had waited for Jesus fell asleep. When Jesus returned to them, He reprimanded them and told them: "Watch and pray, that ye enter not into temptation: the spirit indeed is willing, but the flesh is weak" (Matthew 26:41). Again, He went away and prayed: "O my Father, if this cup may not pass away from me, except I drink it, thy will be done" (Matthew 26:42).

When Jesus returned to His disciples, they were asleep again, so He left them and went back and prayed the same prayer again to His Father. At the beginning of "our" time, Satan had brought temptation into the world to entice God's creation to sin; and he started in the Garden of Eden. Now in the Garden of Gethsemane, he was tempting Jesus to sin by giving up and not going through with His death that would save so many from their sins. Satan wanted Jesus to fail so he would not be able to die for us and redeem us; however, even in Jesus' great sorrow and emotional trauma, He did not surrender to the Devil's temptation to change His mind and give up. Eternal salvation for His creation was hanging in the balance. Instead, in His hour of weakness, He cried out to His Father for help and His will to be done; and His Father helped Him: "And there appeared an angel unto him from heaven, strengthening him. And being in an agony he prayed more earnestly: and his sweat was as it were great drops of blood falling down to the ground" (Luke 22:43–44).

Some time that night, we find that Jesus began to pray, first for Himself, then for others:

> [Jesus] lifted up his eyes to heaven, and said, Father, the hour is come; glorify thy Son, that thy Son also may glorify thee: As thou hast given him power over all flesh, that he should give eternal life to as many as thou hast given him. And this is life eternal, that they might know thee the only true God, and Jesus Christ, whom thou hast sent. I have glorified thee on the earth: I have finished the work which thou gavest me to do. And now, O Father, glorify thou me with thine own self with the glory which I had with thee *before the world was.* (John 17:1–5; emphasis added)

Jesus prayed for His disciples:

> I came out from thee, and they have believed that thou didst send me. I pray for them: I pray not for the world, but for them which thou hast given me, for they are thine. And all mine are thine, and thine are mine; and I am glorified in them. ... While I was with them in the world, I kept them in thy name: those that thou gavest me I have kept, and none of them is lost, but the son of perdition [Judas Iscariot]; that the Scripture might be fulfilled. ... I have given them thy word; and the world hath hated them, because they are not of the world, even as I am not of the world. I pray not that thou shouldest take them out of the world, but that thou shouldest keep them from the evil. They are not of the world, even as I

am not of the world. Sanctify them through thy truth: thy word is truth. (John 17:8–17)

Jesus prayed for the people of all nations, even those who *would believe* in the future, who had not yet born at that time.

> Neither pray I for these alone, but for them also which *shall believe on me* through their word; That they all may be one; as thou, Father, art in me, and I in thee, that they also may be one in us: that the world may believe that thou hast sent me. ... And I have declared unto them thy name, and will declare it: that the love wherewith thou hast loved me may be in them, and I in them. (John 17:20–26; emphasis added)

When He went back to the disciples the last time, He told them, "Sleep on now, and take your rest: behold, the hour is at hand, and the Son of man is betrayed into the hands of sinners. Rise, let us be going: behold, he is at hand that doth betray me" (Matthew 26:45–46).

## Jesus Is Betrayed and Arrested

"Judas then, having received a band of men and officers from the chief priests and Pharisees, cometh thither with lanterns and torches and weapons" (John 18:3).

The Greek word translated *band* is "spĕira." The meaning of the word is "a mass of men (a Roman military cohort)."[5] It is possible then that there could have been as many as 600 men in the band.

Judas had told them, "*Whomsoever I shall kiss*, that same is he; hold him fast. And forthwith he came to Jesus, and said, Hail, master; and kissed him. And Jesus said unto him, Friend, wherefore art thou come?" (Matthew 26:48–50; emphasis added)

> Jesus therefore, knowing all things that should come upon him, went forth, and said unto them, Whom seek

ye? They answered him, Jesus of Nazareth. Jesus saith unto them, I am he. And Judas also, which betrayed him, stood with them. As soon then as he had said unto them, I am he, they went backward, and fell to the ground. Then asked he them again, Whom seek ye: And they said, Jesus of Nazareth. Jesus answered, I have told you that I am he: if therefore ye seek me, let these go their way: That the saying might be fulfilled, which he spake, Of them which thou gavest me have I lost none. (John 18:4–9)

So Jesus was arrested. One of the men standing with Jesus became upset and took his sword and cut off the ear of the high priest's servant. Jesus could have called for the help of more than seventy-two thousand angels, but He did not. Jesus told the man:

Put up again thy sword into his place: for all they that take the sword shall perish with the sword. Thinkest thou that I cannot now pray to my Father, and he shall presently give me more than twelve legions of angels. But how then shall the Scriptures be fulfilled, that thus it must be? (Matthew 26:52–54)

After Jesus reattached the servant's ear to his head, He spoke to the crowd:

Are ye come out as against a thief with swords and staves for to take me? I sat daily with you teaching in the temple, and ye laid no hold on me. But all this was done, that the Scriptures of the prophets might be fulfilled. Then all the *disciples forsook him, and fled.* (Matthew 26:55–56; emphasis added)

Jesus had prophesied they would scatter in Matthew 26:31–32.

# Jesus' Trial

Caiaphas was high priest that year, and Jesus was taken to Annas, Caiaphas' father-in law. After Annas questioned Jesus, he sent Him to Caiaphas. Peter had been following Jesus from a distance to see what would happen to Him. When Jesus was presented to Caiaphas, Peter went and sat with the officers who were there so that he would know what was going to take place.

> Now the chief priests, and elders, and all the council, sought *false* witness against Jesus, to put him to death...At the last came two false witnesses, And said, This fellow said, I am able to destroy the temple of God, and to build it in three days. (Matthew 26:59–61)

Jesus kept silent. He had not been talking about the Jewish temple building, but about His own body, which the Spirit of God would raise three days after His death. The high priest asked Jesus if He was "the Christ, the Son of God," and Jesus replied, "Thou hast said: nevertheless I say unto you, Hereafter shall ye see the Son of man sitting on the right hand of power, and coming in the clouds of heaven" (Matthew 26:63–64).

Caiaphas the high priest accused Jesus of blasphemy, which was a death penalty according to Jewish law (see Leviticus 24:16.) So they all agreed that He should be put to death. The leaders began to spit on Him and hit Him and mock Him, which had been prophesied in Isaiah 50:6: "I gave my back to the smiters, and my cheeks to them that plucked off the hair: I hid not my face from shame and spitting."

While Peter was sitting in the courtyard, one of Caiaphas' servant girls accused him of having been with Jesus. Peter denied the accusation and went outside the gate, where another servant girl also accused him of having been with Jesus. Again, Peter denied knowing Jesus. Later, a bystander recognized him as a Galilean because of the way he spoke; and he also accused him of being with Jesus. Peter "began to curse and to swear, saying, I know not the man. And immediately the cock crew" (Matthew 26:74). "And the Lord turned, and looked upon Peter. And Peter remembered the word of the Lord, how he had said unto him, Before the cock crow, thou shalt deny me thrice. And Peter went out, and wept bitterly" (Luke 22:61–62).

> And the men that held Jesus mocked him, and smote him. And when they had blindfolded him, they struck him on the face, and asked him, saying, Prophesy, who is it that smote thee? And many other things blasphemously spake they against him. (Luke 22:63–65)

The next morning, they asked Jesus again if He was the Son of God; and Jesus replied, "Ye say that I am" (Luke 22:70), confirming to the elders, scribes, and chief priests that Jesus must die.

When Judas realized that his action of betrayal had brought a death sentence to Jesus, he was sick inside himself. He went to the Jewish leaders to return the silver, admitting he had sinned and betrayed innocent blood. The leaders said to him:

> What is that to us? see thou to that. And he cast down the pieces of silver in the temple, and departed, and went and hanged himself. And the chief priests took the silver pieces, and said, It is not lawful for to put them into the treasury, because it is the price of blood. And they took counsel, and bought with them the potter's field, to bury strangers in. (Matthew 27:4–7)

This had been prophesied in Zechariah 11:13.
Acts 1:18–20 tells us what happened when Judas hanged himself:

> Now this man purchased a field with the reward of iniquity; and falling headlong, he burst asunder in the midst, and all his bowels gushed out. And it was known unto all the dwellers at Jerusalem; insomuch as that field is called in their proper tongue, A-cel´-da-ma, that is to say, The field of blood. For it is written in the book of Psalm [69:25], Let his habitation be desolate, and let no man dwell therein: and, His bishopric let another take.

They bound Jesus and took Him to Pilate, the Roman governor. Jewish leaders accused Him of "perverting the nation, and forbidding to give tribute to Caesar, saying that he himself is Christ a King" (Luke 23:2). Jesus would not respond to any of the accusations against Him, which had been prophesied in Isaiah 53:7: "He was oppressed and he was afflicted, yet he opened not his mouth: he is brought as a lamb to the slaughter, and as a sheep before her shearers is dumb [silent], so he openeth not his mouth."

Pilate told the Jews to take Jesus and judge Him by their own laws. They told him, "It is not lawful for us to put any man to death" (John 18:31).

The Jews' refusal to kill Jesus would bring the Roman style of execution—crucifixion upon Jesus, which He had prophesied would happen to Him in Matthew 20:18–19.

When Pilate asked Jesus if He was the King of the Jews, Jesus responded by asking him: "Sayest thou this thing of thyself, or did others tell it thee of me? Pilate answered, Am I a Jew? Thine own nation and the chief priests have delivered thee unto me: what hast thou done?" (John 18:34–35) Jesus told Pilate:

> My kingdom is not of this world: if my kingdom were of this world, then would my servants fight, that I should not be delivered to the Jews: but now is my kingdom not from hence. Pilate therefore said unto him, Art thou a king then? Jesus answered, Thou sayest that I am a king. To this end was I born, and for this cause came I into the world, that I should bear witness unto the truth. Every one that is of the truth heareth my voice. Pilate saith unto him, What is truth? And when he had said this, he went out again unto the Jews, and saith unto them, I find in him no fault at all. (John 18:36–38)

When Pilate announced that he could not find any fault with Jesus, the Jews accused Jesus of causing riots and trouble from Galilee to Jerusalem. When Pilate learned that Jesus was from Galilee, he sent Him to Herod, who was over that jurisdiction. Herod had heard about Jesus and His miracles, and He was hoping Jesus would perform for Him; however, when he questioned Him, Jesus would not answer him. The Jewish leaders continued to accuse Him, and Herod's soldiers made fun of Him, dressing Him in a beautiful robe. Then Herod sent Jesus, still bound, back to Pilate. Pilate did not believe that Jesus was guilty of doing anything wrong. So he called the chief priests and rulers to come to him, and he told them he found no fault in Jesus. He would punish Him and let Him go.

## The Crowds Demand Crucifixion

There was a custom in place during the time of the Passover, by which the Roman governor would release a prisoner. Pilate sat down on the judgment seat, and his wife sent him this message:

> Have thou nothing to do with that just man: for I have suffered many things this day in a dream because of him. But the chief priests and elders persuaded the multitude that they should ask Bar-ab´-bas, and destroy Jesus. (Matthew 27:19–20)

Pilate knew the chief priests had caused this because of envy. He asked them if he should release Jesus, the Christ, or Barabbas. The crowds continued to cry out to Pilate to release Barabbas (see Luke 23:18–21). Pilate asked the Jews, "What will ye then that I shall do unto him whom ye call the King of the Jews? And they cried out again, Crucify him" (Mark 15:12–13).

Then Pilate asked the emotionally charged crowd, "Why, what evil hath he done? And they cried out the more exceedingly, Crucify him" (Mark 15:14).

> When Pilate saw that he could prevail nothing, but that rather a tumult was made, he took water, and washed his hands before the multitude, saying, I am innocent of the blood of this just person: see ye to it. Then answered all the people, and said, His blood be on us, and on our children. (Matthew 27:24–25)

They did not realize that what they had said was already in God's plan; however, God's intent was not to punish them, but to save them by His blood.

Pilate released Barabbas, who was guilty of sedition and murder; but he sentenced Jesus, an innocent man, who was guilty of no wrong or sin to be scourged with "Roman scourges, barbed with lumps of lead and pieces of bone."[6]

## Jesus Is Tortured

"And so Pilate, willing to content the people, released Bar-ab´-bas unto them, and delivered Jesus, when he had *scourged* him, to be crucified" (Mark 15:15; emphasis added).

According to Jewish law in Deuteronomy 25:2–3, it was permissible for a wicked man to receive up to forty stripes. The movie, *The Passion of the Christ*, gives a vivid portrayal of what Jesus' body would have looked like. Isaiah had prophesied of His horrific condition: "His visage was so marred more than any man, and his form more than the sons of men" (Isaiah 52:14).

> Then the soldiers of the governor took Jesus into the common hall, and gathered unto him the whole band of soldiers. And they *stripped* him, and put on him a scarlet robe. And when they had plaited a *crown of thorns*, they put it upon his head, and a reed in his right hand: and they bowed the knee before him, and *mocked him*, saying, Hail, King of the Jews! And they *spit* upon him, and took the reed, and *smote him* on the head. And after that they had mocked him, they took the robe off from him, and put his own raiment on him, and led him away to crucify him. (Matthew 27:27–31; emphasis added)

> Then came Jesus forth, wearing the crown of thorns, and the purple robe. And Pilate saith unto them, Behold the man! When the chief priests therefore and officers saw

him, they cried out, saying, Crucify him, crucify him. Pilate saith unto them, Take ye him, and crucify him: for I find no fault in him. The Jews answered him, We have a law, and by our law he ought to die, because he made himself the Son of God. When Pilate therefore heard that saying, he was the more afraid. (John 19:5–8)

Pilate spoke to Jesus:

Speakest thou not unto me? Knowest thou not that I have power to crucify thee, and have power to release thee? Jesus answered, Thou couldest have no power at all against me, except it were given thee from above: therefore he that delivered me unto thee hath the greater sin. (John 19:10–11)

More than ever, Pilate tried to find a way to release Jesus; but the Jews cried out to Pilate, telling him he would not be Caesar's friend, but would be against him if he released Jesus.

It was the preparation of the Passover, and about the sixth hour: and he saith unto the Jews, Behold your King! But they cried out, Away with him, away with him, crucify him. Pilate saith unto them, Shall I crucify your King? The chief prests answered, We have no king but Caesar. … Then delivered he him therefore unto them to be crucified. And they took Jesus, and led him away. (John 19:14–16)

Jesus had called Himself the "Stone," and He was rejected by His own people, the Jews. Isaiah had prophesied of Jesus' rejection:

He is despised and rejected of men; a man of sorrows, and acquainted with grief: and we hid as it were our faces from him; he was despised, and we esteemed him not. Surely he hath borne our griefs, and carried our sorrows: yet we did

> esteem him stricken, smitten of God, and afflicted. But
> he was wounded for our transgressions, he was bruised
> for our iniquities: the chastisement of our <u>peace</u> was upon
> him; and with his stripes we are healed. (Isaiah 53:3–5)

The Hebrew word translated *griefs* is "chŏlîy." The meaning of the word is "malady, anxiety, calamity, disease … sick(ness)."[7]

The Hebrew word translated *sorrows* is "mak'ôbâh." The meaning of the word is "anguish … affliction, grief, pain."[8]

The Hebrew word translated *peace* is "shalom." The meaning of the word is "safe, well, happy, friendly … welfare, i.e. health, prosperity."[9]

# In Conclusion

Jesus, knowing that His time with His disciples was coming to an end, began to prophesy to them about His soon-coming death and resurrection.

Judas Iscariot, one of the Twelve Disciples, plotted with the scribes and Pharisees to trap Jesus and to be paid thirty pieces of silver for his betrayal. Jesus, Who knows everything, also knew about this. He exposed Judas' betrayal at the Passover meal. After their meal, Jesus taught them to become servants when He washed and dried His disciples' feet. He did this to show them they must humble themselves and become servants to others.

Jesus established the memorial of "holy Communion" when He prophesied, once again, of His death and resurrection. He took bread, which represented His body, and wine, which represented His blood, to show them He was establishing a New Covenant for the remission of sins. He set up this sacrament for them so they would remember Him when He was gone, but He would not leave them like orphans. He told them He would also send them the Holy Spirit of God to dwell in them.

Jesus and the disciples went up on the Mount of Olives to pray. While Jesus wrestled with and agonized over the "cup" that was before Him, He asked His Father to remove it, if possible. His human side was tempted to not go through with His death; however, He counted the cost of what would be lost if He didn't die for humanity, and He submitted to His

Father's will. After asking His Father to help Him, the angels came and ministered to Him and gave Him strength.

Just as Judas had planned, he betrayed Jesus; and He was handed over to the Roman soldiers. A long night ensued as Jesus endured His trial, accusations, and torture; but He would not defend Himself, and He wouldn't give in.

Pilate, who believed Jesus was innocent, gave Jesus over to be crucified because of the outcry of the Jews. Will Jesus die? Yes, we know that, because history documents His death, and the Bible tells us He did. We are now going to follow Jesus to His death, even though it is hard to read about it. We are going to visit His crucifixion site to try to learn and appreciate, in part, what He went through for each of us. In that process, we will begin to understand, in a small way, the significance of the Crucifixion and what He accomplished for us because of it. We will begin to understand the value God has placed upon us. Hope will come through His death.

# Deeper Insights:

1. Jesus told His disciples several times that He was going to die and be raised in three days. Why do you think it was important for them to know what was going to happen to Jesus ahead of time?

2. Jesus is called the "Stone," which causes people to stumble and offends them. Read Romans 9:30–33. Why, in Matthew 21:42–44, did Jesus tell the Jewish leaders that the kingdom of God would be taken away from the Jews and given to the Gentiles?

3. Read Matthew 26:26–29, which gives the account of the Passover meal with Jesus and His disciples. In these passages, Jesus foretold of His death.

   Why did Jesus tell the disciples to continue to take the bread and the wine?

4. At the Lord's Supper, why did Jesus wash the disciples' feet? Read John 13:12–16 and Luke 22:25–27.

5. Who did Jesus promise He would send to His disciples after His ascension into heaven? Read John 14:15–21, 26.

How would the Holy Spirit help them? Read the following Scriptures and identify what it says about Him: Luke 1:35; John 14:16, 16:13; Acts 2:17–18, 9:31; Romans 8:9–16, 26–27, 14:17, 15:15–16; 1 Corinthians 2:10–16, 12:3–11; Galatians 5:22–23; Ephesians 1:12–14, 16–18.

6. Scripture tells us Satan entered into Judas. Read Luke 22:3–6; John 13:2, 27; John 17:12.

Judas, who had been a disciple of Jesus, betrayed Him. This question often arises: If Judas had asked Jesus to forgive him, which he did not, would he have received that forgiveness?

There are Scriptures that tell us about the true character of Judas. Read John 6:70–71 and John 12:1–8.

7. In the hour of Jesus' temptation to quit, what did He say and what happened that gave Him the strength to carry on? Read Luke 22:42

The Bible says that Jesus could have prayed, and His Father would have sent him "twelve legions of angels" to stop His suffering and death. Why didn't He call for the angels? Read Matthew 26:52–54.

# CHAPTER 14

## JESUS IS CRUCIFIED AND BURIED

## The Long Walk to Golgatha

Crucifixion (death on a wooden cross), was not a death penalty that was practiced in the Hebrew Law set up by Moses. Stoning and burning appear to have been the forms of punishment they used for the death penalty for capital offenses. In the Old Testament, after someone was put to death for a crime deserving the death penalty, their dead body might have been hung on a tree to serve as a warning to others.

Crucifixion was, however, practiced among the Romans for the worst and lowest criminals. The Jewish leaders who incited the crowds demanded the Romans give Jesus a death of crucifixion. He was falsely accused, but He would be hung upon a wooden cross, as He had prophesied He would, becoming *accursed for us*. "Christ hath redeemed us from the curse of the law, being made a curse for us: for it is written, Cursed is every one that hangeth on a tree" (Galatians 3:13).

The Roman soldiers were leading Jesus away to the outside of the city to be crucified by them—the Gentiles. Unbeknown to His crucifiers, they were actually leading Jesus to His death on a cross as the sacrificial Lamb. In the Old Testament days, the "Altar of Burnt Offering" and the sacrifices were symbolic of Jesus' death. By sacrificing His own life, He would become a "sin offering" to bring atonement for all people. Why did His Father send Jesus to His death? "For God so loved the world that he gave his only begotten Son, that whosoever believeth in him should not perish, but have everlasting life" (John 3:16).

Under the Mosaic Law, animals were designated to be scapegoats, which carried away the sins of the Israelites to a place outside the city. They, too, led Jesus out of the city of Jerusalem to "a place called Gol'-go-tha, that is to say, the Place of the Skull" (Matthew 27:33). He became the scapegoat, who carried our sins on His body outside the city to the site of His crucifixion.

> For the bodies of those beasts, whose blood is brought into the sanctuary by the high priest for sin, are burned without [outside] the camp. Wherefore Jesus also, that he might sanctify the people with his own blood, suffered without the gate. (Hebrews 13:11–12)

They placed the heavy crossbeam upon Jesus so He could carry it to His own death. He carried it until He was at a point of complete exhaustion and no longer had the strength to carry it. From that time on, Simon, a man from Cyrene, was forced to carry it for Him. Jesus was not physically alone, because a crowd consisting of mockers, haters, thrill seekers, bystanders, and those who loved Him, followed Him to His death. The women who knew Jesus were there, too, wailing and lamenting over His suffering; however, this was a journey that no matter how many were with Him, Jesus would walk alone.

## The Crucifixion

The New Bible Dictionary gives us an idea, according to tradition, of what happened to Jesus after He was taken to the place of crucifixion:

"The condemned man was stripped naked, laid on the ground with the cross-beam under his shoulders, and his arms or his hands tied or nailed (Jn 20:25) to it. This cross-bar was then lifted and secured to the upright post, so that the victim's feet, which were then tied or nailed, were just clear of the ground, not high up as so often depicted. The main weight of the body was usually borne by a projecting peg, astride which the victim sat. There the condemned man was left to die of hunger and exhaustion."[1]

The Scriptures say in John 20:25 that Jesus' hands and feet were nailed, as prophesied in Psalm 22:16: "For dogs have compassed me: the assembly of the wicked have inclosed me: they pierced my hands and my feet."

Above His head was placed an inscription which had been written by Pilate, that read, "JESUS OF NAZARETH THE KING OF THE JEWS" (John 19:19; emphasis preserved). They offered Him wine mixed with myrrh, a form of anesthesia; but Jesus did not take it from them. There were two men being crucified at the same time as Jesus. Jesus was placed between these two robbers, fulfilling the prophecy in Isaiah 53:12: "and he was numbered with the transgressors." It was 9:00 in the morning, and His crucifixion had begun. Jesus prayed to His Father about those who were crucifying him, "Father, forgive them; for they know not what they do" (Luke 23:34).

> Then the soldiers, when they had crucified Jesus, took his garments, and made four parts, to every soldier a part; and also his coat: now the coat was without seam, woven from the top throughout. They said therefore among themselves, Let us not rend [tear] it, but cast lots for it, whose it shall be. (John 19:23–24)

This had been prophesied in Psalm 22:18: "They part my garments among them, and cast lots upon my vesture."

As Jesus hung on that cross in humiliation and pain, people mocked Him and made fun of Him, just as it had been prophesied in the Book of Psalms:

> I am a worm, and no man; a reproach of men, and despised of the people. All they that see me laugh me to scorn: they shoot out the lip, they shake the head, saying, He trusted on the LORD that he would deliver him: let him deliver him, seeing he delighted in him. (Psalm 22:6–8)

People passed by Jesus saying, "Thou that destroyest the temple, and buildest it in three days, save thyself. If thou be the Son of God, come down from the cross" (Matthew 27:40). The chief priests, scribes, and elders said of Him:

> He saved others; himself he cannot save. If he be the King of Israel, let him now come down from the cross, and we will believe him. He trusted in God; let him deliver him now, if he will have him: for he said, I am the Son of God. (Matthew 27:42–43)

The soldiers mocked Him as well: "If thou be the King of the Jews, save thyself" (Luke 23:37).

> And one of the malefactors [criminals] which were hanged railed on him, saying, If thou be Christ, save thyself and us. But the other answering rebuked him, saying, Dost not thou fear God, seeing thou art in the same condemnation? And we indeed justly; for we receive the due reward of our deeds: but this man hath done nothing amiss. And he said unto Jesus, Lord, remember me when thou comest into thy kingdom. And Jesus said unto him. Verily I say unto thee, Today shalt thou be with me in paradise. (Luke 23:39–43)

The Greek word translated *paradise* is "paradĕisŏs." The meaning of the word is "of Oriental ... a park ... an Eden (a place of future happiness)."[2]

## The Last Hours of Jesus' Life

This prophetic psalm gives a picture of the last part of Jesus' life on the cross as He was speaking to His Father:

> Thou art he that took me out of the womb: thou didst make me hope when I was upon my mother's breasts. I was cast upon thee from the womb: thou art my God

from my mother's belly. Be not far from me; for trouble is near; for there is none to help. Many bulls have compassed me: strong bulls of Bashan have beset me round. They gaped upon me with their mouths, as a ravening and a roaring lion.

I am poured out like water, and all my bones are out of joint: my heart is like wax; it is melted in the midst of my bowels. My strength is dried up like a potsherd; and my tongue cleaveth to my jaws; and thou hast brought me into the dust of death. For dogs have compassed me: the assembly of the wicked have inclosed me: they pierced my hands and my feet. I may tell [count] all my bones: they look and stare upon me. (Psalm 22:9–17)

At noon, darkness came over all the land and lasted for three hours until 3:00, at which time "Jesus cried with a loud voice, saying, E´-li, E´-li, la´-ma sa-bach´-tha-ni? That is to say, My God, my God, why hast thou forsaken me?" (Matthew 27:46)

Why did Jesus feel forsaken by His Father? The prophet Isaiah had prophesied about this: "All we like sheep have gone astray; we have turned every one to his own way; and the LORD hath laid on him the iniquity of us all" (Isaiah 53:12).

Christ was suffering physically, but He was also suffering mentally, emotionally, and spiritually because our sins were upon Him. His Father had sent Him to earth for this very reason, and He had willingly *obeyed*. Earlier, Jesus spoke these words to His Father, which had also been prophesied in Psalm 40:6–7:

Sacrifice and offering thou wouldest not, but a body hast thou prepared me: in burnt offerings and sacrifices for sin thou hast had no pleasure. Then said I, Lo, I come (in the volume of the book it is written of me) *to do thy will, O God.* (Hebrews 10:5–7; emphasis added)

He was innocent, but now He was bearing our sin and shame. Jesus was now feeling abandoned and rejected by His Father, something He had never known before. God the Father is holy and could not look upon our sins that Jesus was bearing, and He turned away from Jesus until He succumbed to His death. When speaking of the Lord, Habakkuk in the Old Testament had said, "Thou art of purer eyes than to behold evil, and canst not look on iniquity" (Habakkuk 1:13).

In those hours of torment, Jesus felt utterly alone and brokenhearted; and He felt forsaken. He could have called the angels to stop everything, and He could have retaliated; but He didn't. He had come for this reason: "to put away sin by the sacrifice of himself" (Hebrews 9:26). He came to make "intercession for the transgressors" (Isaiah 53:12)—intercession for all of us!

The Mosaic system of offerings had been set up as a foreshadow of what Jesus was now doing on that cross. He was offering Himself for our sins. He was doing away with the Law that had been used to bring reconciliation and atonement. It had been established to show the Israelites that they were sinners who needed forgiveness for their sins. Now, through the eternal Spirit, all the sins of the entire world—past, present, and future, were being transferred onto Him. He was paying for our sins once and for all with His own human body and blood, which became a substitute for the whole human race.

During the last moments of His life, Jesus remembered His mother, who had made the choice to obey His Father to carry the Son of God in her womb:

> Now there stood by the cross of Jesus his mother, and his mother's sister, Mary the wife of Cle´-o-phas, and Mary Mag´-da-lene. When Jesus therefore saw his mother, and the disciple standing by, whom he loved, he saith unto his mother, Woman, behold thy son! Then saith he to the disciple, Behold thy mother! And from that hour that disciple took her unto his own home.
>
> After this, Jesus knowing that all things were now accomplished, that the Scripture [Psalm 69:21] might be

fulfilled, saith, I thirst. Now there was set a vessel full
of vinegar: and they filled a sponge with vinegar, and
put it upon hyssop, and put it to his mouth. When Jesus
therefore had received the vinegar, he said, It is finished:
and he bowed his head, and gave up the ghost. (John
19:25–30)

The following verse records this last moment of Jesus this way in
the Book of Luke: "And when Jesus had cried with a loud voice, he said,
Father, into thy hands I commend my spirit: and having said thus, he gave
up the ghost" (Luke 23:46).

"Being found in fashion as a man, he humbled himself, and became
obedient unto death, even the death of the cross" (Philippians 2:8). Jesus,
the Lion of the tribe of Judah, became the sacrificial Lamb.

Certain amazing events took place at the moment of Jesus' death:
"The veil of the temple was rent [torn] in twain from the top to the
bottom" (Matthew 27:51).

The curtain that had torn in two "from the top to the bottom" was
the curtain that hung in the temple between the holy place and the most
holy place. This was significant because the curtain had been a barrier
between the people and God. Only the Jewish high priest could enter into
God's presence in the most holy place, and only on the Day of Atonement.
When Jesus died, the curtain was split from top to bottom, signifying the
barrier was now gone for all people. Jesus' body became the veil, opening
the way for us to go directly to God. We can now stand in the presence
of the Father in heaven, completely forgiven and accepted through the
blood of Jesus Christ.

"The earth did quake, and the rocks rent [broke apart]; And the
graves were opened and many bodies of the saints which slept arose, And
came out of the graves after his resurrection" (Matthew 27:51). "Now
when the centurion, and they that were with him, watching Jesus, saw the
earthquake, and those things that were done, they feared greatly, saying,
Truly this was the Son of God" (Matthew 27:54).

When Jesus was dying, He said, "It is finished," and it was! The *new
everlasting blood covenant* had begun for the forgiveness of sins, just as Jesus
had prophesied to His disciples at the Passover meal: "This is my blood

221

of the new testament, which is shed for many for the remission of sins" (Matthew 26:28).

## Jesus' Burial

> The Jews therefore, because it was the preparation, that the bodies should not remain upon the cross on the sabbath day, (for that sabbath day was a high [special] day,) besought Pilate that their legs might be broken, and that they might be taken away. (John 19:31)

Apparently, it was customary to break the legs of those being crucified to hasten their death. With broken legs, they would not be able to use their legs to push themselves up in order to breathe.

> Then came the soldiers, and brake the legs of the first, and of the other which was crucified with him. But when they came to Jesus, and saw that he was dead already, they brake not his legs: But one of the soldiers with a spear pierced his side, and forthwith came there out blood and water. And he that saw it bare record, and his record is true: and he knoweth that he saith true, that ye might believe. For these things were done, that the Scripture should be fulfilled, A bone of him shall not be broken. And again another Scripture saith, They shall look on him whom they pierced. (John 19:32–37)

This had been prophesied in Zechararriah 12:10.

Numbers 9:12 says that the bones of the sacrificial lambs that the Israelites prepared for their Passover meal were not to be broken. This had been a shadow of the forthcoming death of Jesus, the sacrificial Lamb of God.

Joseph, a wealthy man from Arimathea, asked Pilate if he could have Jesus' body so that he could prepare it for burial; and Pilate granted him permission.

And there came also Nic-o-de´-mus, which at the first
came to Jesus by night, and brought a mixture of myrrh
and aloes, about a hundred pound weight. Then took they
the body of Jesus, and wound it in linen clothes with the
spices, as the manner of the Jews is to bury. Now in the
place where he was crucified there was a garden; and in
the garden a new sepulcher, wherein was never man yet
laid. There laid they Jesus therefore because of the Jews'
preparation day; for the sepulcher was nigh at hand. (John
19:39–42)

The Jewish leaders began to worry because Jesus had said He would
rise again after three days. They expressed their concern to Pilate, and
he gave an order for the tomb to be sealed with a stone and a guard be
stationed there to watch it.

Jesus was dead and buried, but why? Was He really just an ordinary man
as many had said? After ministering for just three short years, Jesus, the
so-called King of the Jews, had been persecuted, tortured, and crucified at
the age of thirty-three. Jesus had declared Himself to be the Messiah, and
He had told His disciples that this was going to happen. He was "the *stone*
the builders rejected" (1 Peter 2:7, NIV®; emphasis added). Most of the
Jews did not believe in Him or recognize Him as the Messiah, the Christ.
Isaiah had prophesied about this in Isaiah 53:1: "Who hath believed our
report? and to whom is the arm [Jesus] of the LORD revealed?"

## Jesus' Death Affects Everyone

Everyone was affected by Jesus' death, each in his own way. What a
disappointment for the Jews who had been counting on Jesus to deliver
them from the Roman government. They had been waiting for a mighty
king who would stand up and deliver them; but this man, well, He hadn't
been much of a political leader, but He did talk about the kingdom of God.
He had been more interested in being a servant to the people than their
King. He couldn't have been the King from the lineage of David whom
God had promised their forefathers.

Then there were those who had lost someone they dearly loved—Jesus' family members, disciples, and other close friends. The disciples were disappointed because Jesus had said He was the Son of God, and if so, He wasn't supposed to die, even though He had told them He would. They must have felt confused and alone, having no leader, teacher, or friend. What were they supposed to do now?

The new believers—those who had been healed and delivered of demons—people who now had hope renewed, were disappointed. They were wondering what had all of this been about? Had He been a false leader or an imposter? He did die the death of a criminal.

The Jewish leaders were glad the Roman soldiers had killed Jesus. He was out of the way now, and things could go on as before. They may have been thinking that Jesus had been such a troublemaker anyway, pointing His finger at them, making them feel bad with His accusations. After all, He had equated himself with God. If Jesus had really been the Son of God, He would not have allowed anyone to kill Him.

## In Conclusion

Many people have asked the question, "Who killed Jesus, the Jews or the Romans?" We know that the Jews demanded His crucifixion, and we know that the Romans carried out their request, making them both responsible. This is what Isaiah had prophesied so very long ago:

> He was taken from prison and from judgment: and who shall declare his generation? For he was cut off out of the land of the living: for the transgression of my people was he stricken. And he made his grave with the wicked, and with the rich in his death; because he had done no violence, neither was any deceit in his mouth. (Isaiah 53:8–9)

Jesus died because of our sins. It was our sins and His love for us that held Him to that cross, not the nails, the Jewish leaders, or the Roman soldiers. He could have changed that situation with a thought or a whisper to His Father. He went as a lamb led to slaughter, because He knew that the fate of every person who had ever been born, or would ever be born, rested on His death and the shedding of His blood. He was God the Son, and He knew that what He did that day would determine what would happen for the rest of eternity.

He carried our sins to the Cross of humiliation, and suffered a death designed for an accursed person, the lowest of criminals. He hung there, hour after hour, bearing our sins, sicknesses, and infirmities in His pain-filled body. Emotionally, Jesus was broken, feeling forsaken by His Father. He had to endure it, because it was the only way to destroy the power of the Devil over death and bring freedom to us.

Jesus was the suffering Servant. The Bible says that He was hated and rejected by men, and during His life, He experienced sorrow and grief. His was a death of humiliation because, according to the Law, anyone who hung on a tree was accursed by God; and crucifixion by the Romans was executed only to the worst of the worst. He had told His disciples He was going to die and be raised again, but now, it was hard for them to remember, let alone accept, what He had said.

As Jesus was suffering on the cross, he didn't try to retaliate while they mocked Him—He prayed and asked His Father to forgive them. In His last breath, when He knew that everything had been accomplished, he said, "It is finished." And it was! The earth shook, and the curtain that was hanging in the temple between the holy place and the most holy place was torn from the top to the bottom. Jesus had paid the death penalty once and for all for the sins of all humanity, and His Father's wrath was satisfied. Jesus' body became our veil. Now we can go directly through Jesus, our Mediator, to stand in the presence of the Father in heaven, completely forgiven and accepted if we know Christ. We are no longer under the curse of the Law.

To all who looked on, Jesus was dead; however, He had prophesied that after three days, He would rise from the dead. Will His prophecies come true? If so, how will He do that?

LOUISE A. FUGATE

## Deeper Insights:

1. Jesus is known as the "suffering Servant." Read (Isaiah 53:3–5).

   Why do you suppose God allowed Him to suffer so much as a man here on earth?

   Read Hebrews 2:9–10, 17–18, 4:14–16, 5:7–9; and 1 Peter 2:19–24.

   According to the Bible, is it normal for believers in Christ to suffer? Read Matthew 5:10–12; Romans 8:16–28; and 2 Corinthians 1:3–10.

   Why does God allow suffering for believers in Christ? Read James 1:1–4; 1 Peter 1:6–9; 3:13–22, and 4:12–19.

2. Why did Jesus feel forsaken by His Father while He was dying on the cross?

3. After Jesus died, a soldier pierced His side, probably to verify that Jesus was dead; and blood and water flowed out (see John 19:34–35).

   Why might the fact that blood and water flowed from Jesus' side be important for us to know? Read 1 John 5:6–9.

4. What happened on the ninth hour of Jesus' crucifixion? Read Luke 23:44–46.

5. How did the curtain in the temple typify Jesus' body as the veil? Read Hebrews 9:6–14.

   What changed? Read Hebrews 10:19–22.

# CHAPTER 15

## THE RESURRECTION AND ASCENSION OF JESUS

## Jesus Descends Into Hell

While Jesus the man had physically died, He was busy dealing with the Devil—the evil one who had been deceiving the lives of His people since Creation. Once and for all, Jesus had stripped him of his power. The Bible says that after Jesus' death, He "descended first into the <u>lower</u> parts of the earth" (Ephesians 4:9), to preach to the dead the "good news" about what He had done.

In Greek the word translated *lower* is "katōtĕrŏs." The meaning of the word is "inferior (locally, of Hades)."[1]

The Hebrew word translated *Hades* is "shᵉʾôl." The meaning of the word is "the world of the dead (as if a subterranean retreat) ... grave, hell, pit."[2]

> For Christ also hath once suffered for sins, the just for the unjust, that he might bring us to God, being put to death in the flesh, but quickened by the Spirit: By which also he went and preached unto the <u>spirits</u> in <u>prison</u>; Which sometime were disobedient, when once the long-suffering of God waited in the days of Noah, while the ark was a preparing, wherein few, that is, eight souls were saved by water. (1 Peter 3:18–20)

Here the Greek word translated *spirits,* is "pnĕuma." The meaning of the word is, "rational soul ... vital principle, mental disposition ... ghost, life ... mind."[3]

The Greek word translated *prison,* is "phulakē." The meaning of the word is "a guarding ... cage, hold ... ward, watch."[4]

> Who shall give account to him that is ready to judge the quick and the dead. For for this cause was the gospel preached also to them that are <u>dead</u>, that they might be judged according to men in the flesh, but live according to God in the spirit. (1 Peter 4:5–6)

The Greek word translated *dead,* is "nĕkrŏs." The meaning of the word is "a corpse."[5]

Jesus said, "For as Jonah was three days and three nights in the whale's belly; so shall the Son of man be three days and three nights in the <u>heart</u> of the earth" (Matthew 12:40).

The Greek word translated *heart* is "kardia" and, in this case, means "middle."[6]

With the information we have here, we can conclude that after Christ died, He went to a place where the spirits of men (those who had already died in the past) were being held in confinement in the middle of the earth. Why was Jesus there? He went to preach the gospel, the "good news," to them—Jesus had died to pay for their sins and set them free. Though their flesh was dead, they were now spiritually alive in Christ and able to say, "Death is swallowed up in victory. O death, where is thy sting? O grave, where is thy victory?" (1 Corinthians 15:55). Only God knows to whom Jesus preached and what happened while He was there.

## God Raises Jesus From the Dead

King David had prophesied that Jesus would not stay in the grave: "For thou wilt not leave my <u>soul</u> in <u>hell</u>; neither wilt thou suffer thine Holy One to see <u>corruption</u>" (Psalm 16:10).

In this context, the Hebrew word translated *soul* is "nephesh." The meaning of the word is "body...dead...ghost."[7]

In this context, the Hebrew word translated *hell,* is "sh°ôl." The meaning of the word is "hades or the world of the dead (as if a subterranean retreat), including its accessories and inmates ... grave ... pit."[8]

The Hebrew word translated *corruption* is "shachath." The meaning of the word is "destruction."[9]

God the Father would not leave Jesus' dead body in the grave to decay. Here we see David's prophetic words ring out again: "But God will redeem my soul from the power of the grave: for he shall receive me" (Psalm 49:15).

Mary Magdalene was the woman from whom Jesus had cast out seven demons, and she loved Him deeply. She and another Mary had gone to the place of the tomb to see where Jesus was buried and then went home to prepare for the Sabbath, which was the next day. The day after the Sabbath, the two of them came back carrying their spices to prepare Jesus' body for burial, wondering who would roll the stone away from the tomb for them (see Mark 16:2–8). When they arrived, they had quite a surprise.

> They found the stone rolled away from the sepulcher. And they entered in, and found not the body of the Lord Jesus ... two men stood by them in shining garments: And as they were afraid, and bowed down their faces to the earth, they said unto them, Why seek ye the living among the dead? He is not here, but is risen: remember how he spake unto you when he was yet in Galilee, Saying, The Son of man must be delivered into the hands of sinful men, and be crucified, and the third day rise again. And they remembered his words. (Luke 24:2–8)

The angel also told the women to go and tell Jesus' disciples that He had risen from the dead, and they could see Him in Galilee. When the women told them, Peter and another disciple went to the tomb to see for themselves. They saw "the linen clothes lie, And the napkin, that was about his head, not lying with the linen clothes, but wrapped together in a place by itself" (John 20:6–7). After they saw that Jesus was missing, they went home, "For as yet they did not understand the Scripture, that He must rise again from the dead" (John 20:9).

It was evident that no one had gone into the sepulcher and robbed Jesus' body. Even if they had managed to roll the stone away from the entrance, the robbers probably would not have taken the time to fold His linen clothes and head wrap. So what could have happened? The Bible gives this explanation:

> Behold, there was a great earthquake: for the angel of the Lord descended from heaven and came and rolled back the stone from the door, and sat upon it. His countenance was like lightning, and his raiment white as snow; and for fear of him the keepers did shake, and became like dead men. (Matthew 28:2–4)

Jesus' body was not there because on the third day after His death, God had raised Him from the dead. He sent an angel who rolled away the stone that had sealed the tomb.

The Spirit of God had brought Him up out of hell, the world of the dead, and resurrected His body from the grave. "For though he was crucified through weakness, yet he liveth by the power of God" (2 Corinthians 13:4).

Peter told the men of Judea, "This Jesus hath God raised up, whereof we all are witnesses" (Acts 2:32). Later, Paul would write to the church at Corinth about Jesus' resurrection:

> But now is Christ risen from the dead, and become the first fruits of them that slept. For since by man [Adam] came death, by man [Jesus] came also the resurrection of the dead. For as in Adam all die, even so in Christ shall all be made alive. (1 Corinthians 15:20–22)

The Greek word translated *firstfruits* is "apareche'." The meaning of the word is "a beginning of sacrifice, i.e. the (Jewish) firstfruits."[10]

After Jesus was resurrected, many other people were also resurrected out of their graves: "And the graves were opened; and many bodies of the saints which slept arose, And came out of the graves after his resurrection, and went into the holy city, and appeared unto many" (Matthew 27:52–53).

The guards who had been watching the tomb went and told the chief priests and elders all that had happened, and they bribed the soldiers with money, telling them to spread the word that Jesus' disciples had come at night and stolen His body.

## Jesus Is Seen by Many for Forty Days

After Simon Peter and the other disciple had gone home, Mary Magdalene, who had been weeping, looked into the sepulcher and saw two angels— one sitting where Jesus' feet had been, and one sitting where His head had been. The angel asked her why she was crying, and she told him it was because Jesus was missing and she didn't know where He had been taken. When she had finished speaking to the angel, she turned back around; and there was a man standing there, and she thought he was the gardener. He asked her, "Woman, why weepest thou? whom seekest thou?" (John 20:15) Thinking the man had taken Jesus, she asked him where he had taken Him, because she wanted to go get His body. The man was Jesus, and He spoke to her:

"Jesus saith unto her, Mary. She turned herself, and saith unto him, Rab-bo´-ni; which is to say, Master" (John 20:16). He told her, "Touch me not; for I am not yet ascended to my Father: but go to my brethren, and say unto them, I ascend unto my Father, and your Father; and to my God, and your God" (John 20:17).

Later, two of Jesus' disciples were walking to the village of Emmaus, discussing what had happened to Jesus. Jesus appeared unto them and began to walk with them, but the Bible says they were not able to recognize Him. They told Jesus all that had happened and how Jesus was supposed to have been the One Who had come to redeem Israel, but now He was dead. Then Jesus began to tell them what the Scriptures said about Him, and He did something to remind them of Who He was:

> He sat at meat with them, he took bread, and blessed it,
> and brake, and gave to them. And their eyes were opened,

and they knew him; and he vanished out of their sight. And they said one to another, Did not our heart burn within us, while he talked with us by the way, and while he opened to us the Scriptures? (Luke 24:30–32)

The two men went back to Jerusalem and while they were telling the disciples that they had seen Jesus, Jesus came and "stood in the midst of them, and saith unto them, Peace be unto you" (Luke 24:36). The disciples were terrified and thought that they had been looking at a spirit.

Jesus asked them, "Why are ye troubled? And why do thoughts arise in your hearts? Behold my hands and my feet, that it is I myself: handle me, and see; for a spirit hath not flesh and bones, as ye see me have" (Luke 24:38–39).

"Then said Jesus to them again, Peace be unto you: as my Father has sent me, even so send I you. And when he had said this, he *breathed on them*, and saith unto them, *Receive ye the Holy Ghost*" (John 20:21–22; emphasis added).

Jesus also asked them for some meat to show them He could eat. They gave Him some fish and honeycomb, and He ate it. He told them:

These are the words which I spake unto you, while I was yet with you, that all things must be fulfilled, which were written in the law of Moses, and in the prophets, and in the psalms, concerning me. Then opened he their understanding, that they might understand the Scriptures, And said unto them, Thus it is written, and thus it behooved Christ to suffer, and to rise from the dead the third day. And that repentance and remission of sins should be preached in his name among all nations, beginning at Jerusalem. And ye are witnesses of these things. (Luke 24:44–48)

Thomas, one of the disciples, was not there when Jesus was talking to them. Later, when they told Thomas, he did not believe them, and he told them:

Except I shall see in his hands the print of the nails, and put my finger into the print of the nails, and thrust my hand into his side, I will not believe. And after eight days again his disciples were within, and Thomas with them: then came Jesus, the doors being shut, and stood in the midst, and said, Peace be unto you. Then saith he to Thomas, Reach hither thy finger, and behold my hands; and reach hither thy hand, and thrust it into my side: and be not faithless, but believing. And Thomas answered and said unto him, my Lord and my God. Jesus saith unto him, Thomas, because thou hast seen me, thou hast believed: blessed are they that have not seen, and yet have believed.

And many other signs truly did Jesus in the presence of his disciples, which are not written in this book: But these are written, that ye might believe that Jesus is the Christ, the Son of God; and that believing ye might have life through his name. (John 20:25–31)

One morning, Jesus went to seven of His disciples who were fishing in their boats, but catching nothing. These seven disciples were: "Simon Peter, and Thomas called Did´-y-mus, and Na-than´-a-el of Cana in Galilee, and the sons of Zeb´-e-dee. And two other of his disciples" (John 21:2).

Jesus was standing on the shore, and His disciples did not recognize Him. He told them: "Cast the net on the right side of the ship, and ye shall find. They cast therefore, and now they were not able to draw it for the multitude of fishes" (John 21:6). When they did as He told them, their nets were overflowing. One of the disciples said to Simon Peter, "It is the Lord" (John 21:7).

The night before Jesus had been crucified, for fear of being persecuted or even brought to death, Peter had hid in the shadows and had denied Jesus three times before the cock had crowed, just as Jesus had said he would. His sorrow was great! Peter had been in anguish ever since. When he heard Jesus was on the shore, he wrapped his coat around his body and jumped into the sea because he was naked. Jesus told the disciples, who were in the boat with bulging nets full of fish, to bring their fish and come on shore to eat. They came, and after they had all eaten, Jesus spoke to Peter.

> Simon, son of Jonah, lovest thou me more than these? He saith unto him, Yea, Lord; thou knowest that I love thee. He saith unto him, *Feed my lambs.* He saith to him again the second time, Simon, son of Jonah, *lovest thou me?* He saith unto him, Yea, Lord; thou knowest that I love thee. He saith unto him, *Feed my sheep.* He saith unto him the third time, Simon, son of Jonah, lovest thou me? Peter was grieved because he said unto him the third time, Lovest thou me? And he said unto him, Lord, thou knowest all things; thou knowest that I love thee. Jesus saith unto him, *Feed my sheep.* (John 21:15–17; emphasis added)

Later on, the eleven disciples (Judas was dead) met Jesus on a mountain in Galilee, where Jesus had told them to go.

> And when they saw him, they worshiped him: but some doubted. And Jesus came and spake unto them saying, All power is given unto me in heaven and in earth. Go ye therefore, and teach all nations, baptizing them in the *name* [not names] of the Father, and of the Son, and of the Holy Ghost: Teaching them to observe all things whatsoever I have commanded you: and, lo, I am with you always, even unto the end of the world. A´-men. (Matthew 28:17–20)

1 Corinthians 15:6–7 also gives accounts of Christ's appearances to over five hundred people.

Before Jesus ascended, He told them to wait in Jerusalem until the coming of the Holy Ghost:

[Jesus] showed himself alive after his passion by many infallible proofs, being seen of them forty days, and speaking of the things pertaining to the kingdom of God: And, being assembled together with them, commanded them that they should not depart from Jerusalem, but wait for the *promise of the Father*, which, saith he, ye have heard of me. For John truly baptized with water; but *ye shall be baptized with the Holy Ghost* not many days hence. (Acts 1:3–5; emphasis added)

"Ye shall receive power, after that the Holy Ghost is come upon you: and ye shall be witnesses unto me both in Jerusalem, and in all Judea, and in Sa-mar´-i-a, and unto the uttermost part of the earth" (Acts 1:8).

## Jesus Ascends Up Into Heaven

And, behold, I send the promise of my Father upon you: but tarry ye in the city of Jerusalem, until ye be endued with power from on high. And he led them out as far as to Bethany, and he lifted up his hands, and blessed them. (Luke 24:49–50)

And when he had spoken these things, while they beheld, he was taken up; and a cloud received him out of their sight. And while they looked steadfastly toward heaven as he went up, behold, two men stood by them in white apparel; Which also said, Ye men of Galilee, why stand ye gazing up into heaven? This same Jesus, which is taken up from you into heaven, shall so come in like manner as ye have seen him go into heaven. (Acts 1:9–11)

This fulfilled the prophecy in Psalm 68:18: "Thou has ascended on high, thou hast led captivity captive: thou hast received gifts for men; yea, for the rebellious also, that the LORD God might dwell among them."

> "Now that he ascended, what is it but that he also descended first into the lower parts of the earth? He that descended is the same also that ascended up far above all heavens, that he might fill all things" (Ephesians 4:9–10).

"And without controversy great is the mystery of godliness: God was manifest in the flesh, justified in the Spirit, seen of angels, preached unto the Gentiles, believed on in the world, received up into glory" (1 Timothy 3:16).

> He [Jesus] was in the world, and the world was made by him, and the world knew him not. He came unto his own, and his own received him not. But as many as received him, to them gave he power to become the sons of God, even to them that believe on his name: Which were born, not of blood, nor of the will of the flesh, nor of the will of man, but of God. And the Word was made flesh, and dwelt among us, (and we beheld his glory, the glory as of the only begotten of the Father), full of grace and truth. (John 1:10–14)

Jesus says, "I am he that liveth, and was dead; and, behold, I am alive for evermore, A′-men; and have the keys of hell and of death" (Revelation 1:18).

## In Conclusion

When Jesus was in hell, He preached the "good news" of salvation to those who had already died, and He took the keys to "hell and death," stripping the Devil of his power. After the Spirit of God raised Jesus from the grave, many came up out of their graves and were seen by the people; but Jesus was the "first fruits" of those who slept, having been the first to be resurrected from the dead. When Jesus was resurrected, there was an earthquake; and an angel rolled away the stone that had sealed His tomb—Jesus wasn't there any longer. After His resurrection, many people were raised from the dead and appeared to others.

Jesus appeared as flesh and bone to many people over a period of forty days. With His disciples gathered around Him, Jesus told them to wait in Jerusalem until the Holy Ghost, the Spirit of God, would come upon them and baptize them with His power. Then God raised Jesus up in a cloud and ushered Him into the throne room of heaven, where He now sits on the right hand of God, the Father, interceding for us.

Jesus has left the earth to go up to heaven, but He has left the disciples with a promise that He will send the Comforter, the Holy Ghost to them. They are to wait in Jerusalem until that happens. Who is the Holy Ghost, and what will He do? Let's join the disciples, and many others, as they wait for what Jesus has promised them.

## Deeper Insights:

1.  Read 1 Peter 4:5–6. Why did Jesus descend into the middle of the earth to speak to the dead?

    What do you think He told them?

2.  Jesus was raised from the dead by the Spirit of God—He "became the first fruits of them that slept" (1 Corinthians 15:20–23).

    What does Scripture say will happen to believers after we die? Read John 6:40 and 1 Corinthians 15:35–54.

    When, we die as believers in Christ, our bodies are resurrected, what will they be like? Read Philippians 3:21 and 1 John 3:2.

3.  After Jesus' resurrection, many people were raised from their graves and walked about, being seen by many (Matthew 27:52–53). Why do you think this happened? What does the Bible call these people? (They are not called zombies.)

4.  There were many eye witnesses who saw Jesus after He was resurrected. Read the following Biblical accounts: Matthew 28:7–10, 16–20; Luke 24:13–31, 34–48; John 20:11–20, 24–29, 21:1–23; Acts 1:1–3, 9–11, 7:55, 9:3–6; 1 Corinthians 15:6–9.

5. Read John 20:17, 24–29. Why do you think Jesus told Mary not to touch Him and yet told His disciples and Thomas to touch Him?

What did Jesus want Thomas to do with His side?

What does this say to you about Jesus' resurrected body? Read Luke 24:36–43. How do you think Jesus was able to walk through walls?

6. Before Jesus parted from the earth in a cloud, ascending to heaven, what did He tell His disciples to preach? Read Luke 24:44–48.

What did Jesus tell them to stay in Jerusalem and wait for? Read Luke 24:49. In what manner will Jesus return to take with Him those who put their trust in Him as their Savior? Read Acts 1:11.

# CHAPTER 16

## THE HOLY SPIRIT, GOD IN US

### Who Is the Holy Spirit?

One day, when Jesus had been talking with a Samaritan woman at a well, He told her:

> The hour cometh, and now is, when the true worshipers shall worship the Father in spirit and in truth: for the Father seeketh such to worship Him. God is a Spirit: and they that worship him must worship him in spirit and in truth. (John 4:23)

With our sin nature, we cannot worship God in spirit and in truth. We must have the Holy Spirit, the Spirit of Christ, in us to do that. "Now if any man have not the Spirit of Christ, he is none of his" (Romans 8:9).

The Holy Spirit is not a force, and He is not an "it." The Bible, in many Scriptures, clearly refers to the Holy Spirit as "He" and "Him." He is the *third person* in the Trinity—God the Father; God the Son; and *God the Holy Spirit*.

When God created us, He gave us our spirit (breath of life). At death, the breath of life leaves our body. Where did our spirit come from? It came from God: "The LORD God formed man of the dust of the ground, and breathed into his nostrils the breath of life; and man became a living soul" (Genesis 2:7).

Job also makes this declaration in Job 33:4: "The Spirit of God hath made me, and the breath of the Almighty hath given me life."

When Eve, and then Adam, sinned in the Garden of Eden, all humans from that time on inherited the sin nature; and we have been spiritually dead and spiritually separated from God. There was no hope of that changing until Christ came. It is through faith in Christ that we receive the Spirit of God. Then we are no longer "children of the flesh," but we become "children of the promise...children of God" (Romans 9:8). As His children, we can "worship the Father in spirit and in truth." Galatians 4:6–7 says: "Because ye are sons, God hath sent forth the Spirit of his Son into your hearts, crying, Abba, Father. Wherefore thou art no more a servant, but a son; and if a son, then an heir of God through Christ."

*Abba* is "is an Aramaic word...and is the word framed by the lips of infants, and betokens unreasoning trust; 'father' expresses an intelligent apprehension of the relationship. The two together express the love and intelligent confidence of the child."[1]

When we receive Christ, we are spiritually "born again." We are reconciled, reunited, reconnected, and energized with His power, much like a light bulb when the electricity is turned on. We are made alive in Christ—we are transformed; however, we must continuously renew our minds with prayer and reading God's Word.

## The Baptism With the Holy Ghost

Jesus had told the disciples to wait in Jerusalem for the Holy Ghost to come upon them. So eleven disciples went to an upper room in Jerusalem to wait. Jesus' mother, brothers, and the women joined them there along with others—about one hundred and twenty altogether. While they were waiting, the men cast lots to replace Judas' position, which had been prophesied in Psalm 109:8: "Let another take his office." The lot fell to Matthias, who became the twelfth disciple.

> AND when the day of Pentecost was fully come, they were all with one accord in one place. And suddenly there came a sound from heaven as of a rushing mighty wind, and it filled all the house where they were sitting. And there appeared unto them cloven tongues like as of fire,

and it sat upon each of them. And they were all filled with the Holy Ghost, and began to speak with other tongues, as the Spirit gave them utterance.

And there were dwelling at Jerusalem Jews, devout men, out of every nation under heaven. Now when this was noised abroad, the multitude came together, and were confounded, because that every man hear them speak in his own language. (Acts 2:1–6)

The people thought that the disciples were drunk, but Peter told them that they were not and that this had been prophesied by the prophet Joel:

And it shall come to pass in the last days, saith God, I will pour out of my Spirit upon all flesh: and your sons and your daughters shall prophesy, and your young men shall see visions, and your old men shall dream dreams: and on my servants and on my handmaidens I will pour out in those days of my Spirit; and they shall prophesy. (Acts 2:17–18)

That day, Peter told the Jews:

Therefore let all the house of Israel know assuredly, that God hath made that same Jesus, whom ye have crucified, both Lord and Christ. Now when they heard this, they were pricked in their heart, and said unto Peter and to the rest of the apostles, Men and brethren, what shall we do? Then Peter said unto them, Repent, and be baptized every one of you in the name of Jesus Christ for the remisson of sins, and ye shall receive the gift of the Holy Ghost. For the promise is unto you, and to your children, and to all that are afar off, even as many as the Lord our God shall call. (Acts 2:36–39)

## The Holy Spirit Gives Gifts

Without the Holy Spirit, we have no power. Without Him, we cannot come to Christ. Just as the golden candlestick in the first Tabernacle, with its stand and branches, was filled with oil to bring light into the holy place, the Holy Spirit fills all believers in Christ with His divine oil and brings light into us—we become God's temple on earth.

He gives us His *fruit*, which is a *sign* that we have the Holy Spirit living in us. We can choose to express this fruit in our lives and enjoy God's peace (walk in the Spirit), or we can choose to walk according to our sin nature (walk in the flesh) and forfeit that peace. It is our choice.

> The fruit of the Spirit is love, joy, peace, long-suffering, gentleness, goodness, faith, meekness, temperance: against such there is no law. And they that are Christ's have crucified the flesh with the affections and lusts. If we live in the Spirit, let us also walk in the Spirit. (Galatians 5:22–25)

He gives spiritual gifts, too: "Word of wisdom. ... word of knowledge ... faith ... the gifts of healing ... working of miracles ... prophecy ... discerning of spirits ... tongues ... interpretation of tongues" (1 Corinthians 12:8–10). In chapter 13, we find that the Bible says that love must accompany all the gifts of the Holy Spirit, or they profit nothing. "And now abideth faith, hope, charity, these three; but the greatest of these is charity" (1 Corinthians 13:13).

The Greek word translated *charity* is "agapē." The meaning of the word is "love, i.e. affection or benevolence."[2]

## The Holy Spirit Convicts

God looks into our hearts and knows who we are and why we act the way we do. He knows all about our sins, our weaknesses and failures, our sorrows and losses, our disappointments, and our addictions—all of our pain. The following Scriptures tell us that *God knows all about us*:

O LORD, thou has searched me, and known me. Thou knowest my downsitting and mine uprising; thou understandest my thought afar off. Thou compassest my path and my lying down, and art acquainted with all my ways. For there is not a word in my tongue, but, lo, O LORD, thou knowest it altogether. (Psalm 139:1–4)

Eye hath not seen, nor ear heard, neither have entered into the heart of man, the things which God hath prepared for them that love him. But God hath revealed them unto us by his Spirit: for the Spirit searcheth all things, yea, the deep things of God. (1 Corinthians 2:9–10)

"The Comforter ... will <u>reprove</u> the world of sin, and of righteousness, and of Judgment" (John 16:7–8).

The Greek word translated *reprove* is "ĕlĕgehō." The meaning of the word is "to confute, admonish ... convict, convince, tell a fault, rebuke."[3]

The conviction of the Holy Spirit draws us to godly sorrow and repentance. Confessing our sins to Jesus to receive His forgiveness brings healing and wholeness to us, mentally, physically, and spiritually. "And if any man sin, we have an advocate with the Father, Jesus Christ the righteous: And he is the <u>propitiation</u> for our sins" (1 John 2:1–2).

The Greek word translated *propitiation* is "hilasmŏs." The meaning of the word is "atonement."[4]

Here is a small poem written by an unknown source to help us keep our sin in check:

> "Whatever dims thy sense of truth,
> Or stains thy purity,
> Though light as breath of summer air,
> Count it as sin to thee."

It is refreshing to know that God knows everything about us and still wants to have a relationship with us. We don't have to lie to Him or pretend. He wants our honesty so He can give us His forgiveness.

## The Holy Spirit Is Our Intercessor

> The Spirit also helpeth our <u>infirmities</u>: for we know not what we should pray for as we ought: but the Spirit itself maketh <u>intercession</u> for us with groanings which cannot be uttered. And he that searcheth the hearts knoweth what is the mind of the Spirit, because he maketh <u>intercession</u> for the saints according to the will of God. (Romans 8:26–27)

The Greek word translated *infirmities* is "astheĕnĕia." The meaning of the word is "feebleness (of body or mind) … frailty … sickness … weakness."[5]

The first Greek word translated *intercession* in the above Scripture is "hupĕrĕntugehanō." The meaning of the word is "to incercede in behalf of."[6]

The second Greek word translated *intercession* in the above Scripture is "ĕntugehanō." The meaning of this word is "to confer with … to entreat (in favor or against) deal with."[7]

## The Holy Spirit Gives Us Power

There are times in our lives when circumstances tend to dictate how we think, sometimes distorting the truth. Satan, who is always seeking to destroy God's creation, can come in like a flood bringing his fiery darts of temptation to doubt and fear our heavenly Father. During those times we can pray to receive power to discern the truth between the lies of Satan and the reality of God. God has given us His *spiritual armor*, and He tells us how to use it:

> Put on *the whole armor of God*, that ye may be able to stand against the wiles of the devil. For we wrestle not against flesh and blood, but against principalities, against powers, against the rulers of the darkness of this world, against spiritual wickedness in high places.

Wherefore take unto you the whole armor of God, that ye may be able to stand in the evil day, and having done all, to stand. Stand therefore, having your loins girt about with truth, and having on the breastplate of righteousness; And your feet shod with the preparation of the gospel of peace.

Above all, taking the shield of faith, wherewith ye shall be able to quench all the fiery darts of the wicked. And the take the helmet of salvation, and the sword of the Spirit, which is the word of God: Praying always with all prayer and supplication in the Spirit, and watching thereunto with all perseverance and supplication for all saints. (Ephesians 6:11–18; emphasis added)

Believers in Christ have been given His power to overcome the Devil. *"Submit yourselves therefore to God. Resist the devil,* and he will flee from you" (James 4:7; emphasis added).

## The Holy Spirit Seals Us

"Now he which stablisheth us with you in Christ, and hath anointed us, is God; Who hath also *sealed* us, and given the earnest of the Spirit in our hearts" (2 Corinthians 1:21-22; emphasis added).

"When you believed, you were marked in him with a seal, the promised Holy Spirit, who is a deposit guaranteeing our inheritance until the redemption of those who are God's possession." (Ephesians 1:13–14, NIV®)

"And grieve not the Holy Spirit of God, whereby ye are *sealed* unto the day of redemption" (Ephesians 4:30; emphasis added).

The Holy Spirit is everything we need. He has promised to never leave or forsake us (see Hebrews 13:5). He is our Transformer, our Lifeline, our Sanctifier, and our Sustainer. He brings healing, peace, renewal, refreshment, conviction, forgiveness, and all His other gifts. He is our

Breath of Life, and He will raise us up out of our graves to meet Christ in the air to be with Him forever.

## Preparing to Die So We Can Live

Maybe you have been considering asking Jesus to be your Lord and Savior, or maybe you have never considered it at all. Maybe you knew Jesus before, but you have walked away from Him. For just a moment, let's talk about the serious reasons why making a decision for Christ, or returning to Him, should be a consideration. Here is the plain and simple truth:

Everyone is a sinner. Good people *and* evil people are all born into sin. Even if this were not the case, having one thought, doing one thing, or speaking one word that violates God's holiness qualifies us as sinners. All unrighteousness is sin.

"For whosoever shall keep the whole law, and yet offend in one point, he is guilty of all" (James 2:10).

"To him that knoweth to do good, and doeth it not, to him it is sin" (James 4:17).

"Whatsoever is not of faith is sin" (Romans 14:23).

"For all have sinned, and come short of the glory of God" (Romans 3:23).

No matter how good we are within ourselves, "The Scripture hath concluded all under sin" (Galatians 3:22). God is so serious about this that He says, "He that committeth sin is of the devil; for the devil sinneth from the beginning" (1 John 3:8). That's why Jesus came—to bring us back to God!

Preparing to die is preparing for our eternal future. At the moment we take our last breath, all decisions have been made that will be made about our eternity. The Bible says in several places that when we become believers in Christ, He writes our names in His book, called the book of life. At the end of time, there will be a day of judgment for the dead. Revelation tells us what will happen to those whose names have not been written in the book of life:

"And death and hell were cast into the lake of fire. This is the second death. And whosoever was not found written in the book of life was cast into the lake of fire" (Revelation 20:14–15).

Earthly time as we know it seems to be picking up speed toward the end of *something*, and more and more movies and narratives are being made to remind us that the earth just might be coming to an end. They are right—it is, but it will be in God's plan and His timing. There are no certainties about how many years, days, hours, or even minutes we each have left on this earth. The young and the old are taken, the good and the bad are taken, and those who are saved, and those who are not, are taken in death. Our bodies will die and rot in the grave, but our souls and spirits will live forever.

Those who accept the free gift of salvation will receive Christ's righteousness and become alive in Christ. They will be raised up from their grave to spend eternity forever with the Father, the Son, and the Holy Spirit in heaven. Just think about it, everyone we ever loved, who knew Jesus, will be in heaven with us—we will be with each other again—forever.

"But if the Spirit of him that raised up Jesus from the dead dwell in you, he that raised up Christ from the dead shall also quicken your mortal bodies by his Spirit that dwelleth in you" (Romans 8:11).

We need to know, however, that there really is a literal hell, which is reserved for those who have not received Christ's forgiveness before their death on earth; and it is a place of eternal punishment. Jesus gives a parable in Luke 16 that tells of a beggar and a rich man who both died. The beggar was carried by the angels to Abraham's bosom and was comforted. The rich man went to <u>hell</u> and was tormented. There was a "great gulf" fixed between the two places, which no one could pass over, but the rich man could see Lazarus comforted in Abraham's bosom.

In this context, the Greek word translated "*hell*" is "Tartarŏs." The meaning of the word is "the deepest abyss of hades … to incarcerate in eternal torment, cast down (to hell)."[8]

"God spared not the angels that sinned, but cast them down to hell, and delivered them into chains of darkness, to be reserved unto judgment" (2 Peter 2:4).

If God did not spare His angels that sinned, He will not spare us if we reject His free gift of salvation through Christ. At the end of time, God will throw death and hell into the lake of fire (see Revelation 20:14–15). The Bible speaks of this place as "the vengeance of eternal fire" (Jude 7); "unquenchable fire" (Matthew 3:12); "everlasting fire" (Matthew 18:8, 25:41); "burning with brimstone" (Revelation 19:20).

"The Lord knoweth how ... to reserve the unjust unto the day of judgment to be punished" (2 Peter 2:9).

"These shall go away into everlasting punishment: but the righteous into life eternal" (Matthew 25:46).

When we put our faith in Christ, we will not see this hell of punishment when we die; but we will "fall asleep in Christ" (1 Corinthians 15:18). We have the promise that our bodies will be resurrected out of our graves, and we will spend eternity in heaven with God.

God is love and full of mercy, there is no doubt about that; but He is also just and holy. If we reject the free gift of salvation from the One Who paid the price, who is going to help us? There is nothing more God can do for us—we will then have to pay the death penalty ourselves. There will be no friends, family, pastors, or lawyers—no one to help us when we stand all alone before God, still covered in our own sinful unrighteousness. We will bow to Him, because the Bible says in Isaiah 45:23, "Unto me every knee shall bow." As we receive our death sentence, knowing we will be eternally punished and separated from the very One Who tried to save us, we will know it is by our own doing. God will pay each one the wages of spiritual death He has promised to those who reject Him.

"For the wages of sin is death; but the gift of God is eternal life through Jesus Christ our Lord" (Romans 6:23).

The following scenario helps demonstrate how easy Christ has made it for us.

Let's pretend you have wrecked your boat out at sea. Your boat has gone down, and you have nothing to hang on to. You are just treading water for as long as you can. All of a sudden, someone in another boat comes along and offers to throw you a life preserver to save you and bring you into the safety of their boat. What will happen if you tell them, "No thank you, I'm good, I will figure out what to do by myself"? You can only tread water so long, and eventually, you are going to get tired and drown! Christ is your life preserver!

## How to Become a Christian (a Believer in Christ)

We don't need to change our lives before we come to Jesus. He wants us to come just as we are, with all of our baggage. By His indwelling Spirit, He will change us and show us how to live. Jesus said, "The Comforter… he shall teach you all things, and bring all things to your remembrance, whatsoever I have said unto you" (John 14:26).

In Him, we become pure before God, and our sins are not counted against us.

"Come now, and let us reason together, saith the LORD: though your sins be as scarlet, they shall be as white as snow; though they be red like crimson, they shall be as wool" (Isaiah 1:18).

Jesus said, "Verily, verily, I say unto thee, Except a man be born again, he cannot see the kingdom of God" (John 3:3). We are not talking about a man going back into his mother's womb—we are talking about being spiritually born again. How can we do that? "Godly sorrow worketh repentance to salvation" (2 Corinthians 7:10).

When we realize that we have sinned against a holy God, Who loves us enough to die for us, we can come to Christ and ask for His forgiveness. Coming to Christ is as easy as a heartfelt prayer. If you have never asked Jesus to be your Lord and Savior, and you feel the Spirit of God tugging at your heart to do so at this time, tell Him now. Praying is just talking to God from your heart. No formal written prayers, rituals, or formulas are required. What is important is that you seek God's forgiveness from your heart and tell Him so. He will do the rest. Remember, God knows you, so you can't tell Him anything He doesn't already know about you. "For whosoever shall call upon the name of the Lord shall be saved" (Romans 10:13).

Since this is such a serious eternal matter, this next section has been provided to help anyone who desires to become a believer in Christ (a Christian), and for those who want to come back to Him. Written below are some suggested prayers that may help you find the words to talk to God, or use your own; but let your words be said from your heart.

## Acknowledge Christ

"Jesus, I believe you are the Christ, the Son of the Living God. I believe You suffered and died, and have poured out Your blood to pay for my sins. I believe that the Spirit of God raised You from the dead, and You are now alive in heaven with God the Father."

## Confess to Jesus

"I know that I am a sinner, and the penalty for my sins is death. I cannot be good enough to save myself from Your judgment."

## Ask Jesus to Forgive Your Sins

"Forgive me, Jesus, for all the sins I have ever committed and wash them away. Save me and give me a pure heart. I ask You to become my personal Savior. Teach me to love You, and fill me with Your Holy Spirit so that I may live for You."

## Tell someone

Find a Christian friend or family member, a pastor, or even a Christian program on the Internet about your decision to accept Christ. "For with the heart, man believeth unto righteousness, and with the mouth confession is made unto salvation" (Romans 10:10).

## Be Baptized

Baptism signifies the death of our old sin nature and being resurrected as a new creation in Christ. Call or find a pastor of a Christian church, or ask another believer in Christ to baptize you with water in the name of the Father, the Son, and the Holy Spirit. John the Baptist baptized Jesus, and Jesus commanded us to be baptized as well. (It is important to be baptized, but we must remember the thief on the cross. He was unable to be baptized with water, yet Jesus said he would be with Him in paradise. It is not about legalism, but believing in, and trusting Christ to save us from our sins.)

"He that believeth and is baptized shall be saved; but he that believeth not shall be damned" (Mark 16:16).

"Therefore we are buried with him by baptism into death: that like as Christ was raised up from the dead by the glory of the Father, even so we also should walk in newness of life" (Romans 6:4).

Jesus said, "I am the resurrection, and the life: he that believeth in me, though he were dead, yet shall he live: And whosoever liveth and believeth in me shall never die" (John 11:25–26).

## In Conclusion

God is a Spirit, and we cannot worship Him in "spirit and in truth" (John 4:23) until we come to repentance and receive Christ as our Lord and Savior and are "born again." When we do, we receive the Holy Spirit. Jesus promised that after He left to go to heaven, He would send the Holy Spirit to us.

The Holy Spirit is our helper. He gives us gifts, convicts us of our sins, intercedes for us, empowers us, comforts us, heals us, and seals us to be kept for God. These are just a few of the ways He works in our lives. He also gives us the breath of life, and He will raise us up from the grave to meet Jesus in the clouds to be with Him forever.

Everyone is a sinner and needs Christ's forgiveness because "the wages of sin is death; but the gift of God is eternal life through Jesus Christ our Lord" (Romans 6:23).

Jesus fulfilled the Law and the prophets in the Old Testament by His death, resurrection, and ascension into heaven. Now let's find out how he fulfilled them and what it means for us today.

## Deeper Insights:

1. Jesus promised He would send the Holy Spirit to us after He left the earth.

   Why was the Holy Spirit not given until after Jesus ascended up to heaven? Read John 7:38–39?

   What is the gift of the Holy Spirit contingent upon? Read Acts 2:38.

2. After reading Acts 2:1–6, 38–39, and 19:1–6, do you think the baptism of the Holy Ghost is for us today?

3. Why is it we cannot worship God in "spirit and in truth" if we do not have the Holy Spirit? Read John 3:3, 5–6 and Ephesians 2:1–6.

4. Read the following Scriptures to better understand some of the ministries of the Holy Spirit in believers of Christ: John 14:16–26; 16:13; Acts 2:1–4; Romans 8:11, 16; 14:17; 15:16; 2 Thessalonians 2:13; and 1 John 2:20, 27; 4:1–6.

5. Read 1 Corinthians 12, which talks about the spiritual gifts from the Holy Spirit.

6. Read 1 Corinthians 13, which talks about love.

   What name is mentioned for the Spirit of God in Romans 8:9?

# CHAPTER 17

## JESUS FULFILLED THE LAW AND THE PROPHETS

### God Gave His Promises Before He Gave the Law

In this two-part series, we have studied that humanity has had a sin problem since Adam and Eve chose to disobey God in the Garden of Eden and that through their disobedience, spiritual death came to them, separating them from God. All of humanity has inherited the sin nature that came to our first parents. Without the Spirit of God people are spiritually dead with no hope after death, but God had a plan to help us come back to Him. This plan would be played out over thousands of years through a tiny Hebrew nation. That Hebrew nation of people, which began with Abraham, would become the ancestors of the promised Savior of the world.

Abraham's faith was *"counted to him for righteousness"* because "he *believed* in the LORD" (Genesis 15:6). He didn't come from a Jewish family. He was a Gentile, whose family members were idol worshipers in a pagan nation. God called Abraham out from among them and gave him a promised son named Isaac and promises of a specified land, many children, and an everlasting covenant with God for the descendants that would come through Isaac. Later, God changed Abraham's name to Israel, and his sons became known as the twelve tribes of Israel—the Israelites. Later they would become known as the Jewish nation.

It was to these Israelites that God gave a covenant of Law through Moses which taught them about His holiness, teaching them what was right and what was wrong. He set them aside to live holy as He is holy, and

He would always save a remnant of the faithful ones to usher in Jesus the Messiah, Who would "bless all nations," including the Gentiles.

Interestingly, God give Abraham His promises 430 years before He established the Law. Abraham wasn't even circumcised (a sign that he was in covenant with God), until *after* God gave him the promises (see Genesis 17:1–14). Clearly the promises of God were not dependent upon the Law, but on God's faithfulness as a promise keeper.

## The Law Was Weak

Under the covenant of Law, God established a way for the Israelites to become reconciled to Him through the sacrificial system. He told them: "For the life of the flesh is in the blood: and I have given it to you upon the altar to make an atonement for your souls: for it is the blood that maketh an atonement for the soul" (Leviticus 17:11).

In Hebrew the word translated *atonement* is "kâphar." The meaning of the word is "to cover ... cancel ... cleanse ... forgive, be merciful ... pardon ... purge ... reconcile."[1]

Their unblemished animals were sacrificed and literally became a substitute for them, making atonement for their sins; however, in God's long-range plan, this covenant of Law through Moses was meant to be temporary, lasting only "till the seed [Christ] should come to whom the promise was made" (Galatians 3:19). God set it up as a foreshadow of the sacrifice of Christ—it pointed to His coming, but it was never to be used after His own sacrificial death and resurrection.

Atonement under the Law did not make the people righteous in God's eyes, because it could not *take away* their sins. Not only that, they had to perform the sacrifices over and over again.

> For the law having a shadow of good things to come, and not the very image of the things, can never ... make the comers thereunto perfect. ... there is a *remembrance* again made of sins every year. For it is *not possible* that the blood of bulls and of goats should take away sins. (Hebrews 10:1–4; emphasis added)

They were reconciled to God, but their guilt remained.

> This is an illustration for the present time, indicating that the gifts and sacrifices being offered were not able to clear the conscience of the worshiper. They are only a matter of food and drink and various ceremonial washings— external regulations applying *until the time of the new order.* (Hebrews 9:9–10, NIV®; emphasis added).

The Jews could not keep every single law perfectly. When they sinned, a curse came upon them for their disobedience, which God had written into the Law for those who disobeyed His commands (see Deuteronomy 27:11–26). The Jewish people could not go directly to God. The high priest made intercession for them, but there was no personal relationship between God and the people; and Gentiles (those who were not Jews) were excluded from the everlasting covenant with God. Only Abraham, Isaac, Jacob, and their descendents were included.

The Tabernacle (temple) was made with human materials and was temporary, not eternal. The old must be done away with so the new could be established.

## Jesus Came to Fulfill, Not Destroy

Jesus did not come to abolish the Law which showed God's holiness; but he abolished the Law as a means of making atonement for our sins and reconciling us to God. "For Christ is the end of the law for righteousness to every one that believeth" (Romans 10:4).

Jesus said, "Think not that I am come to destroy the law, or the prophets: I am not come to destroy, but to <u>fulfill</u>" (Matthew 5:17).

The Greek word translated *fulfill* is "plēröö." The meaning of the word is "satisfy, execute ... finish ... verify ... accomplish ... complete, end, (be, make) full."[2]

"For verily I [Jesus] say unto you, Till heaven and earth pass, one jot or one tittle shall in no wise pass from the law, till all be <u>fulfilled</u>" (Matthew 5:18).

The Greek word translated *fulfilled* in this Scripture is "ginŏmai." The meaning of the word is "to cause to be … to become, to (come into being)."[3]

So if the Law was weak, why did God establish it in the first place? If God had not established His Law, how would we know what is right or wrong, or that we need forgiveness? This is what Paul told the early Jewish Christians:

"The law was our schoolmaster to bring us unto Christ, that we might be justified by faith. But after that faith is come, we are no longer under a schoolmaster. For ye are all the children of God by faith in Christ Jesus" (Galatians 3:24–26).

## Jesus Brought a New Covenant of Grace

When the time was right, God sent His Son Jesus down to earth to bring a New Covenant of grace, because "We are all as an unclean thing, and all our righteousnesses are as filthy rags; and we all do fade as a leaf; and our iniquities, like the wind, have taken us away" (Isaiah 64:6).

> [Christ] being found in fashion as a man … humbled himself, and became obedient unto death, even the death of the cross. Wherefore God also hath highly exalted him, and given him a name which is above every name: That at the name of Jesus every knee should bow, of things in heaven, and things in earth, and things under the earth; And that every tongue should confess that Jesus Christ is Lord, to the glory of God the Father. (Philippians 2:8–11)

Jesus willingly laid down His crown in heaven and came to earth to be born as a human to a young Jewish woman named Mary from the tribe of Judah. Jesus is the Lion from the tribe of Judah, which is the tribe of kings. He came as a suffering Servant to give up His life and shed His blood to redeem the souls of all people to spiritually reconcile them back to God. God had given the Jews a promise of a *New Covenant*.

Behold the days come, saith the Lord, when I will make
a *new covenant* with the house of Israel and with the house
of Judah: not according to the covenant that I made
with their fathers ... For this is the covenant that I will
make ... I will put my laws into their mind, and write
them in their hearts: and I will be to them a God, and
they shall be to me a people ... For I will be merciful to
their unrighteousness, and their sins and iniquities will I
remember no more. (Hebrews 8:8–12; emphasis added)

Christ made a New Covenant of grace for the Jews and the Gentiles.
How? "Christ ... hath loved us, and hath given *himself for us an offering and
a sacrifice* to God for a sweet-smelling savor" (Ephesians 5:2; emphasis
added).

When Jesus died, He became the curse for us—eliminating the curse
of death that God had placed upon us through the Law. He blotted "out
the handwriting of ordinances that was against us, which was contrary
to us, and took it out of the way, nailing it to his cross" (Colossians 2:14).

For what the law could not do, in that it was weak through
the flesh, God sending his own Son in the likeness of
sinful flesh, and for sin, condemned sin in the flesh: That
the righteousness of the law might be fulfilled in us, who
walk not after the flesh, but after the Spirit. (Romans
8:3–4)

This is God's gift to us. We can't earn it, buy it, beg for it, or steal it.
"For by grace are ye saved *through faith*; and that not of yourselves: it is the
gift of God, not of works, lest any man should boast" (Ephesians 2:8–9;
emphasis added).

The Greek word translated *grace* is "charis." The meaning of the
word is "the divine influence upon the heart, and its reflection in the
life ... acceptable ... favour, gift ... pleasure.[4] Just as Abraham's faith was
"counted to him for righteousness," we can see in the following Scriptures
that all who have faith in Christ are called Abraham's children; and by that
faith, they receive the same *"righteousness of faith."*

> He [Abraham] received the sign of circumcision, a seal of the righteousness of the faith which he had yet being uncircumcised: that he might be the father of all them that *believe*, though they be not circumcised [Gentiles]; that righteousness might be imputed upon them also: And the father of circumcision to them who are not of the circumcision [Jews] only, but who also walk in the steps of that *faith* of our father Abraham, which he had being yet uncircumcised. For the promise, that he should be the heir of the world, was *not* to Abraham, or to his seed, *through the law*, but *through the righteousness of faith*. (Romans 4:11–13; emphasis added)

With Jesus as our Redeemer, we do not have to fear death, condemnation, or judgment, ever! The Devil has lost his power over those who belong to Christ.

> Forasmuch then as the children are partakers of flesh and blood, he [Jesus] also himself likewise took part of the same; that through death he might destroy him that had the power of death, that is, the devil; And deliver them who through fear of death were all their lifetime subject to bondage. (Hebrews 2:14–15)

> [God the Spirit] *raised him* [Jesus] *from the dead*, and *set him at his own right hand in the heavenly places*, Far above all principality, and power, and might, and dominion, and every name that is named, not only in this world, but also in that which is to come: And hath *put all things under his feet*, and gave him to be the *head over all things to the church*, Which is his body, the fullness of him that filleth all in all. (Ephesians 1:20–23; emphasis added)

Under the covenant of grace, God's law is written in the hearts and minds of all believers. We live by the Spirit, not by the written code. Jesus gave us *two laws* to live by, which summed up the entire Law. Can we live by them perfectly? Probably not, but we should seek to do these two things; and if we fail, we can ask Jesus to forgive us, and we can start again. Jesus said:

> Thou shalt *love the Lord thy God* with all thy heart, and with all thy soul, and with all thy mind. This is the first and great commandment. And the second is like unto it, Thou shalt *love thy neighbor* as thyself. On these two commandments hang all the law and the prophets. (Matthew 22:37–40)

## God's Wrath Was Satisfied

The Bible says that when Jesus died, *God's wrath over sin was satisfied.* Listen to what Isaiah prophesied about the Father, which was fulfilled after Jesus had suffered and breathed His last breath:

> It pleased the LORD to bruise him; he hath put him to grief: when thou shalt make his soul an offering for sin, he shall see his <u>seed</u>, he shall prolong his days, and the pleasure of the LORD shall prosper in his hand. He shall see of the travail of his soul, and shall be satisfied: by his knowledge shall my righteous servant <u>justify</u> many; for he shall bear their iniquities. Therefore will I divide him a portion with the great, and he shall divide the spoil with the strong; because he hath poured out his soul unto death: and he was numbered with the transgressors; and he bare the sin of many, and made intercession for the transgressors. (Isaiah 53:10–12)

Here the Hebrew word translated *seed* is "zera." The meaning of the word is "fruit ... child."[5]

The Hebrew word translated *justify* is "tsâdaq." The meaning of the word is "to be, make right...(in a moral or forensic sense) ... cleanse, clear self ... be, turn to righteous (ness)."[6]

The Hebrew word translated *intercession* is "pâga'." The meaning of the word is "come betwixt, cause to entreat, fall (upon)."[7]

There would never be a need for another sacrifice to make atonement for man to reconcile him to God. In fact, it would not be possible for any other gods, sacrifices, self-effort, or laws, to pay for our sins and reconcile us to God.

## The Children of Abraham

> Know ye therefore that they which are *of faith*, the same are the *children of Abraham*. And the Scripture, foreseeing that God would justify the heathen through faith, preached before the *gospel* unto Abraham, saying, *In thee shall all nations be blessed*. So then they which be of faith are blessed with faithful Abraham. (Galatians 3:7–9; emphasis added)

> Christ hath redeemed us from the curse of the law, being made a curse for us ... That the blessing of Abraham might come on the *Gentiles* through Jesus Christ; that we might receive the *promise of the Spirit through faith*. (Galatians 3:13–14; emphasis added)

Even though the promises of an everlasting covenant were first given to the Hebrew nation, God had told them many times in their prophecies that they would inherit the Gentiles. He told them: "For thou shalt break forth on the right hand and on the left; and thy seed shall inherit the Gentiles" (Isaiah 54:3).

"Therefore it is of *faith*, that it might be by *grace*; to the end of the promise might be sure to all the seed; not to that only which is of the law [the Jews], but to that also which is of the *faith* of Abraham; who is the father of us all" (Romans 4:16).

So what is faith? "Now faith is the substance of things hoped for, the evidence of things not seen" (Hebrews 11:1). This is the "word of faith ... That if thou shalt confess with thy mouth the Lord Jesus, and shalt believe in thine heart that God hath raised Him from the dead, thou shalt be saved" (Romans 10:8–9).

## Circumcision by the Spirit

> For he is not a Jew, which is one outwardly; neither is that circumcision, which is outward in the flesh: But he is a Jew, which is one inwardly; and circumcision is that of the heart, in the spirit, and not in the letter; whose praise is not of men, but of God. (Romans 2:28–29)

Now, those who have faith through Christ are *circumcised* in their hearts, and circumcision of the flesh is no longer required, as it was in the Law. "For we are the circumcision, which worship God in the spirit, and rejoice in Christ Jesus, and have no confidence in the flesh" (Philippians 3:3).

"There is no difference between the Jew and the Greek: for the same Lord over all is rich unto all that call upon him. For whosoever shall call upon the name of the Lord shall be saved" (Romans 10:12–13).

Here the Greek word translated *Lord* is "kuriŏs." The meaning of the word is "supreme in authority ... controller ... God ... master, Sir."[8]

In speaking to the Gentiles about the Jews, Paul wrote, "*Through their fall* salvation is come unto the Gentiles, for to provoke them to jealousy" (Romans 11:11; emphasis added). Here, Paul is talking about the *unbelief* of the Jews toward Christ. They did not believe He was their Messiah.

> Behold I lay in Zion a chief *corner stone*, elect, precious: and he that believeth on him shall not be confounded [ashamed]. Unto you therefore which believe he is precious: but unto them which be disobedient, the stone

> which the builders disallowed, the same is made the head
> of the corner, and a stone of stumbling, and a rock of
> offense. (1 Peter 2:6–8)

## The Gentiles and the Olive Tree

Jesus says in John 4:22, "salvation is of the Jews." "Is he the God of the Jews only? is he not also of the Gentiles [non-Jews]? Yes, of the Gentiles also" (Romans 3:29).

Symbolically, the root of the natural olive tree represents Christ. The Jews are of the natural olive tree, and the Gentiles are of a wild olive tree. The unbelief of the Jews brought about the death of Christ through the hands of the Gentiles. Christ's death brought about salvation for everyone who believes, including the Gentiles, allowing them to be grafted in to the covenant. Just because the Jews had unbelief does not mean that God favors the Gentile believers over the Jews. Gentiles are all pagans before they are reborn by the Spirit of God. It is only through Christ that they receive mercy and obtain circumcised hearts. Gentiles must be careful not to fall because of unbelief as well. Paul warned the Gentiles:

> If some of the branches have been broken off, and you,
> though a wild olive shoot, have been grafted in among the
> others and now share in the nourishing sap from the olive
> root, do not consider yourself superior to those other
> branches. If you do, consider this: You do not support
> the root, but the root supports you. You will say then,
> 'Branches were broken off so that I could be grafted in.'
> Granted. But they were broken off because of unbelief,
> and you stand by faith. Do not be arrogant, but tremble.
> For if God did not spare the natural branches, he will not
> spare you either. (Romans 11:17–21, NIV®)

"For if thou wert cut out of the olive tree which is wild by nature, and wert grafted contrary to nature into a good olive tree: how much more shall these, which be the natural branches, be grafted into their own olive tree?" (Romans 11:24)

When Paul was writing to the Gentiles, he told them this:

> Wherefore remember, that ye being in time past Gentiles in the flesh, who are called Uncircumcision by that which is called the Circumcision [Jews] in the flesh made by hands; That at that time ye were without Christ, being aliens from the commonwealth of Israel, and strangers from the covenants of promise, having no hope, and without God in the world: But now in Christ Jesus ye who sometimes were far off are made nigh by the blood of Christ. (Ephesians 2:11–13)

> But ye are a chosen generation, a royal priesthood, a holy nation, a peculiar people; that ye should show forth the praises of him who hath called you out of the darkness into his marvelous light: Which in time past were not a people, but are now the people of God: which had not obtained mercy, but now have obtained mercy. (1 Peter 2:9–10)

## The Chief Cornerstone

The foundation of the Old Testament was the Law and the Prophets, given to the Jews who had faith in the promise of the coming Messiah (Christ). The foundation of the New Testament was the apostles, given to everyone who has faith in the Messiah (Christ), who did come. By His death and resurrection, Jesus has united the two foundations together, with Himself being the "chief cornerstone." Simply put:

> For he is our peace, who hath made both one, and hath broken down the middle wall of partition between us; Having abolished in his flesh the enmity, even the law of commandments contained in ordinances; for to make in

> himself of twain [two] one new man, so making peace;
> And that he might reconcile both unto God in one body
> by the cross, having slain the enmity, thereby: And came
> and preached peace to you which were afar off, and to
> them that were nigh. For through him we both have
> access by one Spirit unto the Father. (Ephesians 2:14–18)

Jesus also included those people of faith from the Old Testament days who died before He came. After His death, Jesus descended into hell, the grave, to preach the "good news of the gospel" to them "that by means of death, for the redemption of the transgressions that were under the first testament, they which are called might receive the promise of eternal inheritance" (Hebrews 9:15).

Even though they were physically dead, they became spiritually alive. Now, Jews and Gentiles who believe in the Christ, Who did come, receive His Holy Spirit; and we are made spiritually alive as well. So it is that both Jews and Gentiles are made alive by the Spirit because of what Christ has done for us.

> For through him [Jesus] we both have access by one Spirit
> unto the Father. ... And are built upon the foundation of
> the apostles and prophets, Jesus Christ himself being the
> chief corner stone; In whom all the building fitly framed
> together growth unto a *holy temple* in the Lord: In whom ye
> also are builded together for a habitation of God through
> the Spirit. (Ephesians 2:18–22)

The Spirit of God has made known to the apostles and prophets "The mystery of Christ" so "that the Gentiles should be fellow heirs, and of the same body, and partakers of his promise in Christ by the gospel." (Ephesians 3:6)

Jesus is building a "holy temple" on the two foundations that He established. He is the cornerstone that joins the two foundations, and we are the stones that He is using to build the temple. How is that possible?

In the Old Covenant of Law, God lived in a tent to be close to the Israelites and to confer with Moses. Then He gave Moses a blueprint to build a portable Tabernacle so He could live among His people while they traveled. Later, Solomon built God a beautiful temple where the Jews could go to a central place to worship Him. Now, in the New Covenant of grace through Christ, God's Spirit lives in each person who comes to Christ and repents, receiving His forgiveness.

The Greek word translated *repent* is "mĕtanŏĕō." The meaning of the word is "to think differently."[9]

Our body then becomes God's temple here on earth. "Know ye not that ye are the temple of God, and that the Spirit of God dwelleth in you?" (1 Corinthians 3:16)

"Ye also, as lively [living] stones, are built up a spiritual house, a holy priesthood, to offer up spiritual sacrifices, acceptable to God by Jesus Christ" (1 Peter 2:5).

## Jesus Has Become Our High Priest

When Jesus became our High Priest, He was different from the human high priests that were under the Law. We are no longer required to go through a human priest to make intercession for us. In fact, we can now have a personal relationship with the Father through Jesus, the heavenly High Priest.

"Others became priests without any oath, but he became a priest with an oath when God said to him, 'The Lord has sworn and will not change his mind: *'You are a priest forever'*" (Hebrews 7:20–21, NIV®).

"For the law appoints as high priests men in all their weakness; but the oath, which came after the law, appointed the Son, who has been made perfect forever" (Hebrews 7:28, NIV®).

Unlike the other high priests, he does not need to offer sacrifices day after day, first for his own sins, and then for the sins of the people. He sacrificed for their sins *once and for all* when he offered himself (see Hebrews 7:27; emphasis added).

"Neither by the blood of goats and calves, but *by his own blood* he entered in once into the holy place, having obtained eternal redemption for us" (Hebrews 9:12; emphasis added).

"For Christ is not entered into the holy places made with hands, which are the figures of the true; but into heaven itself, now to appear in the presence of God for us" (Hebrews 9:24).

Human priests died, and other priests took their place, "but this man [Jesus], because he continueth ever, hath an unchangeable priesthood. Wherefore he is able also to save them to the uttermost that come unto God by him, seeing *he ever liveth* to make intercession for them. (Hebrews 7:23–25; emphasis added)

> Seeing then that we have *a great high priest, that is passed into the heavens, Jesus the Son of God,* let us hold fast our profession. For we have not a high priest which cannot be touched with the feeling of our infirmities; but was in all points tempted like as we are, yet *without sin.* Let us therefore *come boldly unto the throne of grace,* that we may *obtain mercy, and find grace* to help in time of need. (Hebrews 4:14–16; emphasis added)

"Which hope [Jesus] we have as an anchor of the soul, both sure and steadfast, and which entereth into that within the veil" (Hebrews 6:19).

## The King Is Coming Again

Before Jesus left the earth to return to heaven to be with His Father, He gave this promise:

> In my Father's house are many mansions: if it were not so, I would have told you. I go to prepare a place for you. And if I go and prepare a place for you, I will *come again, and receive you unto myself;* that where I am, there ye may be also. (John 14:2–3; emphasis added)

King Jesus is coming back in the clouds to take His believers to be with Him forever. The Spirit of God will resurrect our bodies up out of our graves, just as He did for Jesus and for many who were resurrected out of their graves after Jesus was resurrected (see Matthew 27:52–53). Our bodies will literally be "raptured" into the clouds to meet Jesus in the air—first the believers in Christ who have died, and then the believers in Christ who are living. The word, "rapture," is not actually written in Scripture, but is a term we use to describe the following event:

> For the Lord himself shall descend from heaven with a shout, with the voice of the archangel, and with the trump of God: and the dead in Christ shall rise first: Then we which are alive and remain shall be *caught up* together with them *in the clouds*, to meet the Lord in the air: and so shall we ever be with the Lord. (1 Thessalonians 4:16–17; emphasis added)

Are you ready to meet King Jesus? It may seem like we have all the time in the world to make a decision about Him. The truth is, as we stand on the earth right now with the breath of life within us, we have an opportunity to determine what our future will be. Right now, we have a choice. Once we pass through the threshold of death, we no longer have the option of choosing anything after that. Our destiny will have been set into motion, and we will have chosen where we will spend eternity. Either we will be accepted by the Father and spend eternity with Him in heaven, because our sins have been forgiven through the blood of Jesus Christ; or we will be rejected by Him and be cast into the lake of fire, eternally separated from Him and our loved ones who have accepted Christ.

The timing of our death is an uncertain thing, but that doesn't mean it is not going to happen. We listen to the news and attend enough funerals to realize that death seems to come in an untimely manner, but it comes to everyone. The Bible says, "it is appointed unto men once to die, but after this the judgment" (Hebrews 9:27–28). The Bible tells us about these judgments. For the Christians, "we must all appear before the judgment seat of Christ; that every one may receive the things done in his body, according to that he hath done, whether it be good or bad" (2 Corinthians 5:10).

The Greek word translated *judgment* is "bēma." The meaning of the word is "a Tribunal ... set foot on, throne."[10]

Our salvation is not what will be in question here, because our sins were judged and paid for when Christ died on the cross for us. We are no longer under the curse of the Law.

"For he hath made him [Jesus] to be *sin for us*, who knew no sin; that we might be made the righteousness of God in him" (2 Corinthians 5:21; emphasis added).

> Every man's work shall be made manifest: for the day shall declare it, because it shall be revealed by fire; and the fire shall try every man's work of what sort it is. If any man's work abide which he hath built thereupon, he shall receive a reward. If any man's work shall be burned, he shall suffer loss: but he himself shall be saved; yet so as by fire. (1 Corinthians 3:13–15)

For the unsaved, there will be a "great white throne judgment." "Whosoever was not found written in the book of life was cast into the lake of fire." (Revelation 20:11–15) God, being just and fair, will show them that their names are not written in the book of life; and they will have no excuse:

> For the invisible things of him from the creation of the world are clearly seen, being understood by the the things that are made, even his eternal power and Godhead; so that they are without excuse: Because that, when they knew God, they glorified him not as God, neither were thankful; but became vain in their imaginations, and their foolish heart was darkened. (Romans 1:20–21)

> "How shall we escape, if we neglect so great salvation?" (Hebrews 2:3)

> When Jesus came to earth to die, He came as a suffering Servant. When He returns to earth He will come as our Judge and King. He will come to destroy Babylon (see Revelation 17), which "represents the archenemy of

Christ and of His church,"11 and He will defeat Satan and his armies (see Revelation 19). Jesus will fulfill the remainder of the prophecies and reign as King forever on David's throne! John recorded the following prophecy in Revelation about the great and glorious day of the coming of our Lord Jesus Christ, the King of Kings!

And I saw heaven opened, and behold a white horse; and he that sat upon him was called Faithful and True, and in righteousness he doth judge and make war. His eyes were as a flame of fire, and on his head were many crowns; and he had a name written, that no man knew, but he himself. And he was clothed with a vesture dipped in blood: and his name is called The Word of God. And the *armies* which were in heaven followed him upon white horses, *clothed in fine linen, white and clean.* And out of his mouth goeth a sharp sword, that with it he should smite the nations: and he shall rule them with a rod of iron: and he treadeth the winepress of the fierceness and wrath of Almighty God. And he hath on his vesture and on his thigh a name written, KING OF KINGS, AND LORD OF LORDS. (Revelation 19:11–16; emphasis added)

"Now unto the King eternal, immortal, invisible, the only wise God, be honor and glory for ever and ever" (1 Timothy 2:17).

Jesus gave everything He had to save us. Now that we have become more aware of all that Jesus Christ has done for us to set us free and bring us eternal life in heaven with Him, what will we do about it? We can choose to accept Him as our Savior, or we can choose to reject Him.

Jesus is seeking us out and calling for us to come to Him: "And the Spirit and the bride say, Come. And let him that heareth say, Come. And let him that is athirst come. And whosoever will, let him take the water of life freely" (Revelation 22:17).

You are the one Jesus is calling. You are the one to whom He is saying, "Follow Me." He knows you by name, and He is watching you and waiting for you to answer Him.

Thank You, heavenly Father, for Your passionate heart of love that keeps pursuing us and calling to us to come to You. Thank You that You are faithful to us, and we can depend on Your promises. I pray that You will use this personal study to bless each person who reads it. For each one who is still making a decision about You, help them to recognize their need for a Savior and bow their hearts at Your feet, for it is there that we receive forgiveness and newness of life. I ask these things in Jesus' Name, the Name above all names.

# RESOURCES

## Chapter 1

1. J.I. Packer and D.J. Wiseman, *NEW BIBLE DICTIONARY, THIRD* EDITION (Leicester, England and Downers Grove: Inter-varsity Press, Reprinted 2006) p. 1156

## Chapter 2

1. J.I. Packer and D.J. Wiseman, *NEW BIBLE DICTIONARY, THIRD* EDITION (Leicester, England and Downers Grove: Inter-varsity Press, Reprinted 2006) p. 651-652

## Chapter 3

1. James Strong, S.T.D., LL.D., A CONCISE DICTIONARY OF THE WORDS IN THE HEBREW BIBLE in *STRONG'S EXHAUSTIVE CONCORDANCE OF THE BIBLE* (Nashville: Royal Publishers, Inc.), p. 18, #842
2. IBID p. 9, #155

## Chapter 4

1. James Strong, S.T.D., LL.D., A CONCISE DICTIONARY OF THE WORDS IN THE HEBREW BIBLE in *STRONG'S EXHAUSTIVE CONCORDANCE OF THE BIBLE* (Nashville: Royal Publishers, Inc.), p. 15, #669
2. IBID p. 17, #781

## Chapter 5

1.  James Strong, S.T.D., LL.D., A CONCISE DICTIONARY OF THE WORDS IN THE HEBREW BIBLE in *STRONG'S EXHAUSTIVE CONCORDANCE OF THE BIBLE* (Nashville: Royal Publishers, Inc.), p. 78, #5180
2.  IBID p. 36, #2220
3.  IBID p. 36, #2232
4.  IBID p. 121, #8267
5.  J.I. Packer and D.J. Wiseman, *NEW BIBLE DICTIONARY, THIRD* EDITION (Leicester, England and Downers Grove: Inter-varsity Press, Reprinted 2006) p. 826
6.  BIBLICAL CYCLOPEDIC INDEX, Carchemish, in the *HOLY BIBLE, KING JAMES VERSION, PTL COUNSELLORS EDITION*, (Nashville: Thomas Nelson, Inc., Publishers, 1975), p. 76

## Chapter 6 N/A

## Chapter 7

1.  THE *HOLY BIBLE, KING JAMES VERSION, PTL COUNSELLORS EDITION*, (Nashville: Thomas Nelson, Inc., Publishers, 1975), p. 739
2.  Pat and David Alexander, Rapid Factfinder in *ZONDERVAN HANDBOOK TO THE BIBLE* (Grand Rapids: Zondervan Publishing House, 1999), p. 464
3.  BIBLICAL CYCLOPEDIC INDEX, Edomites, in the *HOLY BIBLE, KING JAMES VERSION, PTL COUNSELLORS EDITION*, (Nashville: Thomas Nelson, Inc., Publishers, 1975), p. 104
4.  Pat and David Alexander, Rapid Factfinder in *ZONDERVAN HANDBOOK TO THE BIBLE* (Grand Rapids: Zondervan Publishing House, 1999), p. 468

## Chapter 8

1.  Thomas V. Brisco, *HOLMAN BIBLE ATLAS*, a Complete guide to the Expansive Geography of Biblical History (Nashville: Broadman & Holman Publishers, 1998), p.161, paragraphs 1-2
2.  Pat and David Alexander, Rapid Factfinder in *ZONDERVAN HANDBOOK TO THE BIBLE* (Grand Rapids: Zondervan Publishing House, 1999), p. 457
3.  Thomas V. Brisco, *HOLMAN BIBLE ATLAS*, a Complete guide to the Expansive Geography of Biblical History (Nashville: Broadman & Holman Publishers, 1998), p.161

4. IBID p.162
5. Pat and David Alexander, Rapid Factfinder in *ZONDERVAN HANDBOOK TO THE BIBLE* (Grand Rapids: Zondervan Publishing House, 1999), p. 462
6. Thomas V. Brisco, *HOLMAN BIBLE ATLAS*, a Complete guide to the Expansive Geography of Biblical History (Nashville: Broadman & Holman Publishers, 1998), p. 160
7. James Strong, S.T.D., LL.D., A CONCISE DICTIONARY OF THE WORDS IN THE HEBREW BIBLE in *STRONG'S EXHAUSTIVE CONCORDANCE OF THE BIBLE* (Nashville: Royal Publishers, Inc.), p. 36, #2235
8. Pat and David Alexander, Rapid Factfinder in *ZONDERVAN HANDBOOK TO THE BIBLE* (Grand Rapids: Zondervan Publishing House, 1999), p. 474

## Chapter 9

1. James Strong, S.T.D., LL.D., A CONCISE DICTIONARY OF THE WORDS IN THE HEBREW BIBLE in *STRONG'S EXHAUSTIVE CONCORDANCE OF THE BIBLE* (Nashville: Royal Publishers, Inc.), p. 26, #1481
2. IBID p. 36, #2268
3. IBID p. 48, #3091
4. IBID p. 47, #3068
5. IBID p. 100, #6797
6. IBID p. 100, #6780

## Chapter 10

1. Thomas V. Brisco, *HOLMAN BIBLE ATLAS*, a Complete guide to the Expansive Geography of Biblical History (Nashville: Broadman & Holman Publishers, 1998), pp. 174-187, 198-201, 212-215
2. BETWEEN THE TESTAMENTS in the *HOLY BIBLE, KING JAMES VERSION, PTL COUNSELLORS EDITION*, (Nashville: Thomas Nelson, Inc., Publishers, 1975), pp. 856-863
3. Thomas V. Brisco, *HOLMAN BIBLE ATLAS*, a Complete guide to the Expansive Geography of Biblical History (Nashville: Broadman & Holman Publishers, 1998), p. 174
4. IBID p. 212
5. IBID p. 212

## Chapter 11

1.  James Strong, S.T.D., LL.D., A CONCISE DICTIONARY OF THE WORDS IN THE GREEK TESTAMENT in *STRONG'S EXHAUSTIVE CONCORDANCE OF THE BIBLE* (Nashville: Royal Publishers, Inc.), p. 37, #2434

2.  IBID p. 31, #1982

3.  James Strong, S.T.D., LL.D., A CONCISE DICTIONARY OF THE WORDS IN THE HEBREW BIBLE in *STRONG'S EXHAUSTIVE CONCORDANCE OF THE BIBLE* (Nashville: Royal Publishers, Inc.), p. 47, #3068

4.  James Strong, S.T.D., LL.D., A CONCISE DICTIONARY OF THE WORDS IN THE GREEK TESTAMENT in *STRONG'S EXHAUSTIVE CONCORDANCE OF THE BIBLE* (Nashville: Royal Publishers, Inc.), p. 44, #2962

5.  James Strong, S.T.D., LL.D., A CONCISE DICTIONARY OF THE WORDS IN THE HEBREW BIBLE in *STRONG'S EXHAUSTIVE CONCORDANCE OF THE BIBLE* (Nashville: Royal Publishers, Inc.), p. 74, #4899

6.  IBID p.11, #342

7.  James Strong, S.T.D., LL.D., A CONCISE DICTIONARY OF THE WORDS IN THE GREEK TESTAMENT in *STRONG'S EXHAUSTIVE CONCORDANCE OF THE BIBLE* (Nashville: Royal Publishers, Inc.), p. 78, #5547

8.  James Strong, S.T.D., LL.D., A CONCISE DICTIONARY OF THE WORDS IN THE HEBREW BIBLE in *STRONG'S EXHAUSTIVE CONCORDANCE OF THE BIBLE* (Nashville: Royal Publishers, Inc.), p. 118, #7886

9.  James Strong, S.T.D., LL.D., A CONCISE DICTIONARY OF THE WORDS IN THE GREEK TESTAMENT in *STRONG'S EXHAUSTIVE CONCORDANCE OF THE BIBLE* (Nashville: Royal Publishers, Inc.), p. 55, #3874

10. IBID p. 24, #1391

11. James Strong, S.T.D., LL.D., A CONCISE DICTIONARY OF THE WORDS IN THE HEBREW BIBLE in *STRONG'S EXHAUSTIVE CONCORDANCE OF THE BIBLE* (Nashville: Royal Publishers, Inc.), p. 26, #1471

12. IBID p. 15, #615

13. James Strong, S.T.D., LL.D., A CONCISE DICTIONARY OF THE WORDS IN THE GREEK TESTAMENT in *STRONG'S EXHAUSTIVE*

*CONCORDANCE OF THE BIBLE* (Nashville: Royal Publishers, Inc.), p. 20, #1096

## Chapter 12

1.  James Strong, S.T.D., LL.D., A CONCISE DICTIONARY OF THE WORDS IN THE HEBREW BIBLE in *STRONG'S EXHAUSTIVE CONCORDANCE OF THE BIBLE* (Nashville: Royal Publishers, Inc.), p. 32, #1961
2.  James Strong, S.T.D., LL.D., A CONCISE DICTIONARY OF THE WORDS IN THE GREEK TESTAMENT in *STRONG'S EXHAUSTIVE CONCORDANCE OF THE BIBLE* (Nashville: Royal Publishers, Inc.), p. 25, #1510
3.  An Expository Dictionary of New Testament Words in W.E. Vine, Merrill F. Unger, William White, Jr., in *VINE'S COMPLETE EXPOSITORY DICTIONARY OF OLD AND NEW TESTAMENT WORDS*, (Nashville: Thomas Nelson, Inc., 1996) p. 470
4.  Edward W. Goodrick and John R. Kohlenberger III, GREEK TO ENGLISH DICTIONARY AND INDEX TO THE NIV NEW TESTAMENT in *The STRONGEST NIV EXHAUSTIVE CONCORDANCE* (Grand Rapids: Zondervan Publishing House, 1999), p. 1583, #4377
5.  IBID p. 1583, #4376
6.  James Strong, S.T.D., LL.D., A CONCISE DICTIONARY OF THE WORDS IN THE GREEK TESTAMENT in *STRONG'S EXHAUSTIVE CONCORDANCE OF THE BIBLE* (Nashville: Royal Publishers, Inc.), p. 47, #3339
7.  IBID p. 37, #2440
8.  IBID p. 65, #4633

## Chapter 13

1.  James Strong, S.T.D., LL.D., A CONCISE DICTIONARY OF THE WORDS IN THE GREEK TESTAMENT in *STRONG'S EXHAUSTIVE CONCORDANCE OF THE BIBLE* (Nashville: Royal Publishers, Inc.), p. 79, #5614
2.  IBID p. 22, #1242
3.  IBID p. 17, #859
4.  IBID p. 77, #5485
5.  IBID p. 66, #4686

6. J.I. Packer and D.J. Wiseman, *NEW BIBLE DICTIONARY, THIRD* EDITION (Leicester, England and Downers Grove: Inter-varsity Press, Reprinted 2006) p. 1068
7. James Strong, S.T.D., LL.D., A CONCISE DICTIONARY OF THE WORDS IN THE HEBREW BIBLE in *STRONG'S EXHAUSTIVE CONCORDANCE OF THE BIBLE* (Nashville: Royal Publishers, Inc.), p. 39, #2483
8. IBID p. 66, #4341
9. IBID p. 116, #7965

## Chapter 14

1. J.I. Packer and D.J. Wiseman, *NEW BIBLE DICTIONARY, THIRD* EDITION (Leicester, England and Downers Grove: Inter-varsity Press, Reprinted 2006) p. 246
2. James Strong, S.T.D., LL.D., A CONCISE DICTIONARY OF THE WORDS IN THE GREEK TESTAMENT in *STRONG'S EXHAUSTIVE CONCORDANCE OF THE BIBLE* (Nashville: Royal Publishers, Inc.), p. 54, #3857

## Chapter 15

1. James Strong, S.T.D., LL.D., A CONCISE DICTIONARY OF THE WORDS IN THE GREEK TESTAMENT in *STRONG'S EXHAUSTIVE CONCORDANCE OF THE BIBLE* (Nashville: Royal Publishers, Inc.), p. 41, #2737
2. James Strong, S.T.D., LL.D., A CONCISE DICTIONARY OF THE WORDS IN THE HEBREW BIBLE in *STRONG'S EXHAUSTIVE CONCORDANCE OF THE BIBLE* (Nashville: Royal Publishers, Inc.), p. 111, #7585
3. James Strong, S.T.D., LL.D., A CONCISE DICTIONARY OF THE WORDS IN THE GREEK TESTAMENT in *STRONG'S EXHAUSTIVE CONCORDANCE OF THE BIBLE* (Nashville: Royal Publishers, Inc.), p. 58, #4151
4. IBID p. 76, #5438
5. IBID p. 49, #3498
6. IBID p. 71, #5020
7. James Strong, S.T.D., LL.D., A CONCISE DICTIONARY OF THE WORDS IN THE HEBREW BIBLE in *STRONG'S EXHAUSTIVE CONCORDANCE OF THE BIBLE* (Nashville: Royal Publishers, Inc.), p. 80, #5315

8. IBID p. 111, #7585
9. IBID p. 115, #7845
10. James Strong, S.T.D., LL.D., A CONCISE DICTIONARY OF THE WORDS IN THE GREEK TESTAMENT in *STRONG'S EXHAUSTIVE CONCORDANCE OF THE BIBLE* (Nashville: Royal Publishers, Inc.), p. 13, #536

## Chapter 16

1. An Expository Dictionary of New Testament Words in W.E. Vine, Merrill F. Unger, William White, Jr., An Expository Dictionary of New Testament Words in *VINE'S COMPLETE EXPOSITORY DICTIONARY OF OLD AND NEW TESTAMENT WORDS,* (Nashville: Thomas Nelson, Inc., 1996) p. 1
2. James Strong, S.T.D., LL.D., A CONCISE DICTIONARY OF THE WORDS IN THE GREEK TESTAMENT in *STRONG'S EXHAUSTIVE CONCORDANCE OF THE BIBLE* (Nashville: Royal Publishers, Inc.), p. 7, #26
3. IBID p. 27, #1651
4. IBID p. 37, #2434
5. IBID p. 16, #769
6. IBID p. 26, #5241
7. IBID p. 29, #1793
8. IBID p. 71, #5020

## Chapter 17

1. James Strong, S.T.D., LL.D., A CONCISE DICTIONARY OF THE WORDS IN THE HEBREW BIBLE in *STRONG'S EXHAUSTIVE CONCORDANCE OF THE BIBLE* (Nashville: Royal Publishers, Inc.), p. 57, #3722
2. James Strong, S.T.D., LL.D., A CONCISE DICTIONARY OF THE WORDS IN THE GREEK TESTAMENT in *STRONG'S EXHAUSTIVE CONCORDANCE OF THE BIBLE* (Nashville: Royal Publishers, Inc.), p. 58, #4137
3. IBID p. 20, #1096
4. IBID p. 77, #5485
5. James Strong, S.T.D., LL.D., A CONCISE DICTIONARY OF THE WORDS IN THE HEBREW BIBLE in *STRONG'S EXHAUSTIVE CONCORDANCE OF THE BIBLE* (Nashville: Royal Publishers, Inc.), p. 36, #2233
6. IBID p. 98, #6663

7.  IBID p. 93, #6293
8.  James Strong, S.T.D., LL.D., A CONCISE DICTIONARY OF THE WORDS IN THE GREEK TESTAMENT in *STRONG'S EXHAUSTIVE CONCORDANCE OF THE BIBLE* (Nashville: Royal Publishers, Inc.), p. 44, #2962
9.  IBID p. 47, #3340
10. IBID p. 19, #968
11. www.ministrymagazine.org, Ministry, International Journal For Pastors

# BIBLIOGRAPHY

1.  An Expository Dictionary of New Testament Words in W.E. Vine, Merrill F. Unger, William White, Jr., An Expository Dictionary of New Testament Words in VINE'S COMPLETE EXPOSITORY DICTIONARY OF OLD AND NEW TESTAMENT WORDS, (Nashville: Thomas Nelson, Inc., 1996)

2.  BETWEEN THE TESTAMENTS in the HOLY BIBLE, KING JAMES VERSION, PTL COUNSELLORS EDITION, (Nashville: Thomas Nelson, Inc., Publishers, 1975)

3.  BIBLICAL CYCLOPEDIC INDEX in the HOLY BIBLE, KING JAMES VERSION, PTL COUNSELLORS EDITION, (Nashville: Thomas Nelson, Inc., Publishers, 1975)

4.  Edward W. Goodrick and John R. Kohlenberger III, GREEK TO ENGLISH DICTIONARY AND INDEX TO THE NIV NEW TESTAMENT in The STRONGEST NIV EXHAUSTIVE CONCORDANCE (Grand Rapids: Zondervan Publishing House, 1999)

5.  James Strong, S.T.D., LL.D., A CONCISE DICTIONARY OF THE WORDS IN THE GREEK TESTAMENT in STRONG'S EXHAUSTIVE CONCORDANCE OF THE BIBLE (Nashville: Royal Publishers, Inc.)

6.  James Strong, S.T.D., LL.D., A CONCISE DICTIONARY OF THE WORDS IN THE HEBREW BIBLE in STRONG'S EXHAUSTIVE CONCORDANCE OF THE BIBLE (Nashville: Royal Publishers, IncJ.I. Packer and D.J. Wiseman, NEW BIBLE

DICTIONARY, THIRD EDITION (Leicester, England and Downers Grove: Inter-varsity Press, Reprinted 2006)

7. Pat and David Alexander, Rapid Factfinder in ZONDERVAN HANDBOOK TO THE BIBLE (Grand Rapids: Zondervan Publishing House, 1999)

8. Thomas V. Brisco, HOLMAN BIBLE ATLAS, a Complete guide to the Expansive Geography of Biblical History (Nashville: Broadman & Holman Publishers, 1998)

9. www.ministrymagazine.org, Ministry, International Journal For Pastors, Hans K. LaRondelle, The Fall of Babylon in type and antitype, Archives 1989, September

Printed in the United States
By Bookmasters